A REVOLUTION OF RULES

A Revolution of Rules

THE REGULATORY REFORM OF INDIA'S NONPROFIT SECTOR

ERICA BORNSTEIN

STANFORD UNIVERSITY PRESS
Stanford, California

Stanford University Press
Stanford, California

Library of Congress Cataloging-in-Publication Data
Names: Bornstein, Erica, 1963- author.
Title: A revolution of rules : the regulatory reform of India's nonprofit
    sector / Erica Bornstein.
Description: Stanford, California : Stanford University Press, 2025. |
    Includes bibliographical references and index.
Identifiers: LCCN 2025003436 (print) | LCCN 2025003437 (ebook)
    | ISBN 9781503642287 (cloth) | ISBN 9781503643192 (paperback) |
    ISBN 9781503643208 (epub)
Subjects: LCSH: Nonprofit organizations—India. | Nonprofit
    organizations—Law and legislation—India. | Nonprofit
    organizations—Government policy—India.
Classification: LCC HD2769.2.I4 B67 2025 (print) | LCC HD2769.2.I4
    (ebook) | DDC 361.7/630954—dc23/eng/20250417
LC record available at https://lccn.loc.gov/2025003436
LC ebook record available at https://lccn.loc.gov/2025003437

Cover design: annweinstock.com
Cover photograph: joephotostudio/Adobe Stock

The authorized representative in the EU for product safety and compliance
is: Mare Nostrum Group B.V. | Mauritskade 21D | 1091 GC Amsterdam
| The Netherlands | Email address: gpsr@mare-nostrum.co.uk | KVK
chamber of commerce number: 96249943

For Aneesh and Elijah

CONTENTS

ACKNOWLEDGMENTS

In the long journey of writing this book, I have incurred more debts than can be represented in the published text. Apologies in advance to those inadvertently omitted. Writing is not done in isolation, and many of my interlocutors, friends, family, and colleagues have inspired me from near and far. I hope you see our conversations in these pages. To all the academic audiences who listened to parts of this book over the years and gave constructive feedback, thank you.

My deep gratitude goes to the nonprofit workers, Activist Donors, Professional Critics, and Accountability Guides in New Delhi who welcomed me into their active lives and reminded me of the power of association: your optimism and dedication to public good continue to inspire. To all the change-makers from the sidelines, anonymized in this book, this book is for you. Thanks also to family and friends in India for being there along the way: Didi and Jijaji, Bhavna and Dunny, Veena and K. K. Kapur, Anku and Siddharth, Lalla and Lena, and so many others, whom I won't name to preserve anonymity. Ethnographic research over many years produces lasting friendships, and it is difficult not to honor these relationships with named gratitude, but you will know who you are, and may even see yourselves in these pages. And thanks to my family in the United States for their encouragement along the way, especially to my late mother, Gloria Bornstein, who always supported my creative endeavors.

Research was made possible by generous research fellowships, including a JNIAS Fellowship at the Jawaharlal Nehru Institute for Advanced

Study, Jawaharlal Nehru University (2012–13), and an American Institute
for Indian Studies (AIIS) Senior Research Fellowship (2016–17) that enabled fieldwork in New Delhi in summer 2017. A 2012–13 sabbatical leave,
along with writing fellowships from the Center for International Education (2011–12), and the Center for 21st Century Studies (2016–17) at the
University of Wisconsin–Milwaukee made this research possible. Early in
the process of putting my project together, in 2010, a collaborative Ober-
mann Center Interdisciplinary Research grant facilitated a summer of
reading together with Meena Khandelwal and Mark Sidel about diaspora
philanthropy.

To my Milwaukee friends and colleagues—Ivan Ascher, Laura Beldavs
and Jeff Sommers, Patrick Belgarde-Smith, Joel and Esther Berkowitz,
Paul Brodwin, Rachel Ida Buff, Kennan Ferguson and Carolyn Eichner,
Elena Gorfinkel, Richard Grusin, the late Ihab and Sally Hassan, Tracey
Heatherington, Jennifer Johung, Ingrid Jordt and Kal Applbaum, Nan
Kim, Richard Leson, Thomas Malaby, Anna Manson-McGinty, Mike
Newman and Elana Levine, Peter Paik, Bernie Perley, Patrice Petro,
Jason Puskar, Anne Pycha, Kumkum Sangari, Lisa Silverman, Jocelyn
Szczepaniak-Gillece, and Bill Wood—thanks for all the walks, meals,
coffee, and camaraderie.

To my writing collaborator and friend, Anu Sharma, thanks for seeing
the way around dark corners during the COVID-19 pandemic. I'll never
forget our writing group in 2021, with Jennifer Curtis, for providing a
writing rudder, reality check, and general inspiration to keep going when
the world shut down. To Ilana Gershon, who generously sponsored a 2022
book workshop for the manuscript in progress, and to Mark Sidel and
Meena Khandelwal for reading the whole thing. I'm grateful for your suggestions (though errors or omissions are mine alone). Ilana, your good
sense echoes in my creative imagination. Thanks to my editor at Stanford
University Press, Dylan Kyung-lim White, who helped see this project to
publication, my careful copy editors Elspeth MacHattie and Catherine
Mallon, my production editor Gigi Mark, and to the two anonymous re-
viewers for their critical and productive feedback. At the University of
Oregon, thanks to Lamia Karim, Lynn Stephen, and all the colleagues
who welcomed me into my new intellectual home. Thanks to Mike Mu-
rashige for his encouragement, keen intuitive take on writing patterns, and
developmental edits.

My total love and appreciation go to Aneesh—my favorite interlocutor and coffee conversationalist, partner, and love of my life, for bearing with me during the many years it took to research and write this book and putting up with my agonizing about the details—and to my creative, out-of-the-box-thinking son, Elijah; thank you both for making sure I never took myself too seriously. Never underestimate the power of joking.

Finally, I have previously published some parts (now substantially revised) of some chapters in this book: see Erica Bornstein and Aradhana Sharma, "The Righteous and the Rightful: The Technomoral Politics of NGOs, Social Movements, and the State in India," *American Ethnologist*, 43 (1): 76–90, 2016; and Erica Bornstein, "The Report: A Strategy and Nonprofit Public Good," *Humanity* 10 (1): 109–31, Spring 2019.

LAWS GOVERNING NONPROFITS IN INDIA

This brief orientation section outlines the laws and the regulatory time-lines that I focus on in discussing the history and current significance of nonprofit regulation in India.

MAJOR LAWS

1860   Societies Registration Act
1882   Indian Trusts Act
1920   Charitable and Religious Trusts Act
1956   The Companies Act
1961   The Income Tax Act
1976   The Foreign Contributions Regulation Act

REVISION AND AMENDMENT TIMELINES

The Companies Act, 1956

2012   The Companies Bill.
2013   The Companies Act, revised.
2015   Rules published.
2020   The Companies Act, amended.

The Income Tax Act, 1961

1962   Commenced.
2009   Direct Taxes Code (DTC) Bill.
2010   Discussion paper created; introduced in Parliament.

2012 Report submitted to Parliament.

2017 Expert committee set up by NDA government.

2019 Report of DTC task force submitted to Finance Minister.

2020 Pending budget processes to take steps to implement DTC.

The Foreign Contributions Regulation Act, 1976

2006 Foreign Contributions Regulation Bill, published by the Parliamentary Standing Committee on Home Affairs.

2010 Foreign Contributions Regulation Act, revised.

2011 Commenced.

2012 Rules published.

2015 Rules amended.

2020 Foreign Contributions Regulation Act, amended.

Additional Regulatory Legislation

2000 Foreign Exchange Management Act.

2007 National Policy on the Voluntary Sector.

2012 Multi-State Societies Registration Bill.

2023 Finance Bill (previous iterations in 2002 and 2017 Finance Acts).

ACRONYMS

CSO   Civil society organization, *or* community supported organization, *or* community service organization
CSR   Corporate social responsibility
DTC   Direct Taxes Code
FCRA   Foreign Contributions Regulation Act
FEMA   Foreign Exchange Management Act
GOI   Government of India
MSSR   Multi-State Societies Registration Bill
NGO   Nongovernmental organization
NPO   Nonprofit organization
PIL   Public interest litigation
SAG   Social action group
VO   Voluntary organization

A REVOLUTION OF RULES

INTRODUCTION

Nonprofits Make Worlds

What is it about nonprofits that inspires so many to passionately support their agendas and others to adamantly seek their control? In India between 2010 and 2020, laws regulating the nonprofit sector were dramatically reformed, reconfiguring relationships between corporations, nonprofits, and the government. Many assume that nonprofits are defined by the causes they champion, but I argue something else in this book: that the nonprofit form is shaped by its regulation, in a process of democratic and political negotiation. Without the associational space of debate over social norms, codified into nonprofit law, democracy is in peril. Nonprofits are strange institutions. They look like corporations, but they don't make profits. They are public, but not the government. The protagonists featured in my story include reformers: nonprofit workers, lawyers and accountants, philanthropists and civil servants. If lawyers file class action suits to make law, and lobbyists work to change law, then who makes the rules of law? This book is about the rules of nonprofit law, who makes them, who changes them, and how this takes place in India. My cases exist in a gray area, out of the limelight of activists and protesters, in a border zone of professionals and volunteers who toil at the fringes of law to influence laws regulating nonprofits and civil society.

These social reformers conduct their work on the sidelines—in workshops and consultations in unassuming offices and meeting halls, through report writing and petitions. These activities, while central to lawmaking processes, are often considered peripheral. I write to shift this lens, to acknowledge the unsung heroes of democracy—a cast of characters that will carry us through this book of nonprofit leaders (whom I call *Professional Critics*), Indian philanthropists (*Activist Donors*), and lawyers and nonprofit accountants (*Accountability Guides*). Reformers worked to shape law and nonprofit labor, but the regulatory reform of the sector also shaped their work. Thus, throughout this book, I ask readers to do something a bit unusual—to think of laws and institutions as nonhuman actors in dynamic relation to social worlds, much as we have come to understand climate change, or artificial intelligence, both of which have met with dramatic global calls for international collaboration regarding their regulation. Like the environment and technology, nonprofits and the philanthropy that fuels them travel across national borders and are regulated by national governments. These nonhuman actors—nonprofit institutions, laws, reports, and workshops—are socially created. They have neither minds nor voices as people do, yet they operate in ways that alter nonprofit social worlds, and in this way I consider them actors. When new laws are passed or older laws are amended and revised in periods of regulatory reform, nonprofits and the people who run them must respond and adapt, and through this practice nonprofit worlds are defined. Nonprofits also constitute a labor sector, and this book is an ethnography of that sector's regulation. Regulation can be protective, restrictive, and faciliatory. For example, governments regulate processes, products, and institutions to protect the public from harm. Automobile safety regulations protect against potential accidents and facilitate road safety. The taxation of substances such as cigarettes and alcohol also provides a protective regulatory framework for human behavior, and some regulations enable markets, goods, and services, allowing them to flow freely. Through regulation, the government can be enabling or controlling, and the regulation of the nonprofit sector, like other forms of regulation, takes place through law and public policy.

Nonprofit Worlds

In 2015, the Indian Government cancelled the ability of over 9,000 NGOs, including the Ford Foundation, to receive foreign funding, and put dozens more on a state-sponsored watch list. It froze Greenpeace's donation accounts and accused the nonprofit of interfering with national development. Greenpeace India was eventually barred from receiving foreign funds. The reaction by civil society groups was fierce. They accused the government of a crackdown and took to the media. They organized educational clinics and lobbied the government to reconsider the cancellations. One civil society organization filed a public interest litigation (PIL) case alleging that one law, the Foreign Contributions Regulation Act (hereafter FCRA), was being misused to target NGOs, and demanded an independent body conduct an inquiry. The government, meanwhile, defended its actions as an effort to weed out ghost NGOs, errant NGOs, and NGOs threatening national security. State-led bureaucratic housekeeping occurred annually, but this sweep of cancellations was dramatic. After the crackdown, some nonprofits registered as charitable companies, instead of as trusts or societies, altering their reporting relationships with the government. All of this took place in the wider, global context of nonprofit regulatory reform, which included increased efforts by NGOs to advocate for supportive laws, growing restrictions on global civil society, and greater dependence by governments on philanthropy to fund national social welfare programs. In this instance, the FCRA became an actor in nonprofit worlds when it was enacted and nonprofits were required to respond. But nonprofit institutions were actors in this scenario as well. They filed their forms and were considered legal entities by the government.

The nonprofit sector (also called the *social sector* in India) is, as already mentioned, a labor sector, and when nonprofit institutions are cancelled and must close, employees lose their jobs (Shetty and Seth 2023). The nonprofit sector is estimated to generate 2 percent of India's gross domestic product (GDP; ibid.). It supports work in small towns and villages, as well as in urban centers, and provides critical services to vulnerable populations. Cancellations have a domino effect on staff of nonprofit organizations (hereafter NPOs) and their beneficiaries. The nonprofit sector has been called the "invisible sector" with an "invisible workforce," even though it is a source of formal employment (Tandon 2017; Shetty and Seth 2023). However, nonprofit jobs are not like jobs in other sectors, such as business or government, because nonprofits aim to bring about social change.

A recent report, *India's Million Missions: 75 Years of Service Toward Nation-Building: India's Non-Profit Sector Report* (Sarin et al. 2023), written by individuals representing a collaborative group of Indian NPOs (CSO Coalition@75), argues for more recognition of the nonprofit sector in terms of its contributions to the nation since India's independence (also see Tandon 2000, 2002, 2003). The report is based on research by a group of civil society members, and it is mammoth—168 pages long, full of data, and funded by Indian and international civil society organizations and groups. It outlines the vast scale of NPO sector work in India, with 16 million employees, 21 million nonprofit honorary board volunteers, and millions more who support the work of and the causes served by Indian civil society organizations (hereafter CSOs). Its authors argue that civil society organizations are economic engines of growth and contribute 2.7 million jobs and the output of 3.4 million full-time volunteers to the economy, generating figures higher than those of the public sector. And, as mentioned, this substantial group of CSOs produces as much as 2 percent of the nation's GDP.

As with all CSO reports (including the ones about which I write in this book), the *Million Missions Report* makes recommendations: specifically, to improve collaboration with the government and to rationalize tax exemptions for the nonprofit sector. These recommendations emerged from a history of reform and negotiation (Tandon 1996, 2002; Sen 1992, 1999), and aimed to establish the credibility and legibility of the nonprofit sector in the face of the proposed 2023 Finance Bill. The report engaged with the Finance Bill's proposed provisions for civil society regulation, and it was part of a long-standing policy-making conversation that had been taking place between the nonprofit sector and the government since the colonial era. This proposed Bill, which was passed into law in 2023, included provisions that would greatly affect India's nonprofit sector regarding funding and governmental reporting processes. The Bill included provisions for increased monitoring and surveillance of NPOs, a universal ID for NPOs (administered through the Ministry of Home Affairs), and increased surveillance of domestic philanthropy to CSOs. It threatened to criminalize the social sector by allowing selective governmental targeting of NPOs. The media argued it was a systematic assault on charitable bodies, one that disabled instead of enabling charity work (Shukla 2023). The 2023 Finance Bill followed a decade of rapid regulatory reform that had included the 2002 Finance Act, which altered acceptable spending provisions for tax-exempt institutions, and the 2017 Finance Act, which restricted charitable organizations from giving donations to other charities (Dadrawala 2023). In the weeds of these regulatory changes were increased governmental surveillance of grant-making foundations, limitations on inter-charity donations, and increased regulation of domestic philanthropy. These regulatory provisions were presented to a sector that had previously been, for the most part, loosely regulated (Bornstein 2012b). The proposed 2023 Finance

Bill is a small part of a much longer story, which I tell in this book, of the centralization of nonprofit and philanthropic regulation, much of which has been achieved through the regulation of a category called "charitable purpose." This regulatory reform has centralized monitoring and stifled dissent (*New Indian Express* 2023).

Historically, and globally, nonprofits have been considered a third sector in relation to markets and states. Structurally ambiguous, they embody a bifurcated power to both bolster and challenge state legitimacy. They depend on philanthropy for their existence, whether via state contracts or private donations. They are considered public institutions, and they receive tax subsidies from governments and financial contributions from donors in support of their public-serving work. Yet, in contrast to public and private corporations, they are not profit making. The term *nonprofit* applies to a profound diversity of political and social approaches, types of institutions, and scales of operation. Their influence is internationally vast and locally specific. In India's nonprofit (social) sector alone, in 2020, there were estimated to be approximately three million nonprofit organizations at work (Jagtiani 2020). Despite the inherent diversity of this institutional category, all nonprofits share a common capacity to challenge and harness the state in the name of the public. This capacity is made visible and negotiated in regulatory struggles that take place though law making.

India is a nation with one of the most vibrant and diverse nonprofit sectors in the world. It is also where civil society autonomy, state legitimacy, and democracy have been fought for and shaped through battles over nonprofit sector regulation. The stories I tell feature Indian nonprofit reformers, leaders, accountants, lawyers, and auditors in their legal struggles over the political potential of civil society. Nonprofits are public institutions that receive tax dispensations from governments, provide state mandated-welfare services, and regularly, publicly, critique governments for social welfare failures. I also write of the decade of legal reform (2010–2020) during which nonprofit law was centralized and dissent was silenced. Because nonprofits are donor dependent, small tweaks to philanthropic regulation transformed not only the way nonprofits did their work but also what they were legally permitted to do. By the end of this book, I hope readers will see that to understand nonprofits and their relationship to democracy in the world, one must look to sites of struggle over the nonprofit form and its regulation.

The story I tell is situated primarily in New Delhi, where national policies are made, but it also features the work of nonprofits and corporations beyond the national capital. It is based on ethnographic research I conducted in India in 2012–13 and 2017 with NPOs, advocacy groups, and civil society leaders working to change nonprofit law in an increasingly restrictive political environment, as well as with corporate actors tasked with taking on state-mandated programs of corporate social responsibility. I concentrate upon the social life of legal reform surrounding the revision of two key laws: the Foreign Contributions Regulation Act (FCRA; originally enacted in 1976 and revised in 2010, 2015, and 2020) and the Companies Act (originally enacted in 1956 and revised in 2013 and 2020). I explore the activism and advocacy surrounding these laws in the making: that is, during each law's proposal, amendment, and implementation. These social processes occurred in dynamic conversation with legislative efforts to restrict the nonprofit sector's capacity for political critique. In India's nonprofit sector, policy—including rules, institutional norms, regulatory principles, and laws—has been created through a dialogic process that far exceeds the legislative realm. It is made by nonprofits assisting each other and lobbying the government to alter laws that regulate—facilitate and restrict—their work. Through workshops, conferences, and collaborative report writing in India's political capital, nonprofit lawyers, accountants, directors, and staff wrote what I will call nonprofit policy's *horizon line*. Regulatory reform involves rewriting the horizon line of policy and determining the direction in which institutions will evolve.

Voluntary organizations in India have, historically, lobbied the government for effective regulation of the sector. NGO leaders have collaborated with the government by participating in the former Planning Commission of India (reorganized as NITI Ayog in 2014) and writing the draft National Policy on the Voluntary Sector (Government of India 2007). Though this policy never became law, its creation speaks to the dynamic engagement that has existed between the voluntary sector and government civil servants. In this process, the voluntary sector did not request less regulation, it lobbied for better regulation and more comprehensive policy. Concurrently, NPOs have educated voluntary sector organizations to make sure they understand laws and do not violate them unwittingly. NPO advocacy organizations, such as those that welcomed me into their social worlds during my fieldwork, took it upon themselves to urge the Government of India (GOI) to pass progressive, enabling legislation.

Regulatory Policy and the Nonprofit Form

In India, and elsewhere, nonprofits are treated differently from other institutions by states, philanthropic donors, and public audiences. Their institutional form symbolically challenges the profit-seeking motives of capitalist economic action.[1] Whether politically Right or Left, nonprofits represent particular groups, public goals, and the good of communities, not the good of the one, at least in principle. Nonprofits are often defined by what they are not: in the case of nongovernmental organizations, for example, they are not government and not for profit (Kingma 1997; Lewis and Schuller 2017; Bernal and Grewal 2014). They are referred to by a library of terms, which I use interchangeably in this book as many nonprofit workers do in colloquial conversation. As much as the referential terms are fought over, defined, and redefined in local nomenclature, they are also used fluidly, and strategically, to emphasize the diversity inherent in the nonprofit institutional category. Terms such as CSO (civil society organization), VO (voluntary organization), NPO (nonprofit organization) and NGO (nongovernmental organization) all have specific etymological histories, contexts, and referents. But despite this taxonomic diversity, nonprofits all possess a unique symbolic and structural capacity to challenge other institutional forms. By analyzing what nonprofits do in the world, what they stand for, and why they are struggled over, we can see how the nonprofit form is a fertile site of institutional and political negotiation. Structurally, nonprofits engage in the work of democracy by representing specific publics in contested debates—whether politically Right or Left, they are at the center of political storms.

Nonprofits, no matter how they are structured or where they reside, resemble each other in that they are businesses that serve some form of public interest. Profit is not their operational motive. NGOs may make profits, but any profit gained must be reinvested in the organization, not distributed to stakeholders as with corporations. Though many nonprofits are run, and structured, like businesses, they rely on donations and possess tax-exempt status, a subsidy given by states to encourage their work in social welfare arenas. Some nonprofits do the welfare work of states, as service providers, and in this manner their existence can bolster and/or challenge state legitimacy.

In India, as in other places, large hospitals and schools fall into the same category as grassroots charities, and all trusts, societies, and charitable companies must register with the state in order to receive philanthropic donations, which support their work. In contrast to corporations—which may be either public firms, in which shareholders have rights and whose rights governments protect, or privately held firms—nonprofits do not have shareholders. They have *stakeholders*. Nonprofits act on behalf of publics, sometimes on behalf of a public welfare state, hence the tax subsidies given by governments in exchange for their public welfare work. Nonprofits receive benefits from states, but they do not have rights, and they are always governed: by boards, by donors, and by project covenants (Lewis 2001). Nonprofits rely on donations, and their tax-exempt status, determined by governments through law, encourages philanthropy. These qualities define the institutional structures of nonprofits and dictate the ways money, and power, travel through these organizations. This book attends to circuits of donation, focusing on how funding loyalties affect programmatic structures, and how regulation affects this field. As much as nonprofits speak of loyalty to members or communities, owing to their donor dependency their fiduciary loyalty lies with donors. Thus, governments can alter nonprofit engagement, in general, through the regulation of philanthropy.

STRUGGLES OVER LEGITIMACY

Nonprofits and governments vie for public legitimacy by providing public goods such as social welfare services. As much as governments cater to median voters in public goods provision, nonprofits cater to populations other than median voters (Kingma 1997). In his early writing on nonprofits and government relations, Bruce Kingma (1997) documents how in heterogeneous communities, such as India, where citizens overall desire a wider range of public goods than those sought by the median voters to whom governments tend to cater, there are likely to be more nonprofits producing public goods. Though the Government of India has historically supported welfare through numerous schemes and development plans, the issue of public goods provision has become increasingly politicized, and may even result in electoral gains (Thachil 2014). In this landscape of contested legitimacy regarding the capacity to provide social services, I explore what happens when the government takes control of public goods provision through regulation, and offers regulatory incentives for profit-making corporations. The Indian government, in over a decade of legal reform, tightly regulated the provision of public goods and "crowded out" advocacy and human rights–oriented NPOs from addressing issues of public welfare (see Kingma 1997 for the "crowd-out" thesis).

The shift occurred in nonprofit and corporate law, via the rules of legal implementation. The Indian government redefined public goods as private ones, allowing private sector firms to compete by selling similar goods in the market of social welfare provision, a market previously monopolized by the government, taken over by NPOs and their philanthropic supporters, and then reclaimed by the government through legal reform. Kingma (1997) refers to this as the "output model." Scholars of Indian civil society have called this process the "corporatization of the nonprofit sector" (Deo 2024; Srinath 2022). Much of this shift occurred in a hybrid space focused on charity-related subsidiary goods produced by NPOs, and the taxing of sales of these products as business income. Because NPOs are dependent on funding, they may create alternate funding streams, such as selling charity-related products (cards, t-shirts, etc.). When the government lays claim to these public goods by taxing and regulating these sales processes more strictly and allowing corporations to enter the stage of public goods provision through the regulation of arenas such as corporate social responsibility and business services, the government gains legitimacy from such public goods provision. Nonprofits have historically provided public goods that require public trust, such as education and health care, and by providing these public goods and essential public services, nonprofits in India had gained legitimacy that the government lacked.

In the revolution of rules, civil society became involved in legal struggles over the nonprofit form. Though nonprofits may be structured similarly to corporations, with directors, boards of directors, and hierarchically governed structures, we must not forget their orientation is not-for-profit, which affords them special freedoms in society and extra scrutiny by the government. When I refer to nonprofits, I signify organizations formally registered with the government, not ad hoc groups, a distinction to be kept in mind, though the boundary between formal institutions and informal civil society associations is unstable. Many ad hoc groups also inhabit the voluntary sector and do not make a profit. Yet, it is the not-for-profit nature of NPOs that binds what might be unrelated institutional forms together as a group for purposes of analysis.

Increasing Restrictions: National Regulation in Global Context

Regulatory policy for the nonprofit sector embodies a growing tension, between increased government regulation and the associational freedom upon which civil society groups have historically relied. Globally, international law protects the freedom of association and the right to resources, and the Universal Declaration of Human Rights (UDHR) asserts that access to resources is a self-standing right (UN Special Rapporteur, n.d.). Regional and bilateral commitments protect philanthropy across borders, and some of these commitments intersect with bilateral investment treaties, but there are also cases where restrictions are permitted under international law.[2] Yet, in this international context, NPOs must abide by national laws in the countries where they are registered and operate.

Historically, civil society groups and NGOs were promising global actors in post–Cold War democratic efforts, emerging as a sector of humanitarian intervention rivaling the power of states to address issues of global security. They constituted an associational revolution, which had a long history that included the civil rights movement in the United States, the anti-apartheid movement in South Africa, and the dissident movement in Central Europe, and which afforded nonprofits increased international power. The associational revolution fueled by civil society groups saw the close of the twentieth century, the fall of the Berlin Wall, and a renaissance that valued human rights, NGOs, and civil society engagement. Yet, the hopeful character of associational politics that traditionally characterized the work of the nonprofit sector always stood in contrast to a darker side: its political threat (Appadurai 2006). NPOs received substantial foreign funds as international policy actors. For example, in the early 1990s, foreign funding to NGOs was considered a "magic bullet" for development and democracy (M. Edwards and D. Hulme, cited in Dupuy et al. 2016). International donors supported NGOs to deliver public services, build civil society, and promote democracy (Dupuy et al. 2016, 299). Foreign funding facilitated NGO-driven human rights and development agendas.

The zeitgeist changed after 2001, with the U.S. War on Terror, and by 2004, the world found itself in the midst of a global "associational counterrevolution" (Rutzen 2015a). Not only were CSOs targets of suspicion in the War on Terror, they were also agents of U.S. President George Bush's "Freedom Agenda," which sought to advance democratic transitions in the Middle East. As a result, CSOs were suspected of being terrorists and agents of American intervention. Revolutions of the early 2000s—in Georgia, the Ukraine, and Zimbabwe—produced national laws restricting CSOs. In 2005, Russia adopted a high-profile law restricting civil society, and Eritrea and Uzbekistan followed suit. Between 2004 and 2010, as Rutzen (2015a, 7) notes, over fifty countries considered or enacted civil society restrictions, and since 2012, over ninety laws constraining freedom of association or assembly were proposed or enacted. The growing trend of laws restricting international philanthropy to civil society organizations followed patterns that Rutzen terms "philanthropic protectionism." Of these restricting initiatives, one-half constrained CSO incorporation or registration, one-third constrained international funding, and the remaining initiatives restricted freedom of assembly. In the chapters that follow, we will see this trend develop in the Indian context. In the global context, the third sector came to be viewed as a threat, a "source of human insecurity" (Sidel 2010). States have since tightened regulation, issued stricter governance procedures, and implemented new financial requirements. As Sidel points out, other factors also played a role, including an opposition to NGO advocacy, concerns about accountability, the growing role of political and religious giving, and the rapidly growing role of diasporas in programs of national development.

More recently, scholars (see Chimiak et al. 2024; Dupuy et al. 2016) have documented increased restrictions on civil society funding. For example, Dupuy et al. (2016, 300) found that between 1993 and 2012, one-fourth of the world's low- and middle-income countries restricted overseas funding to domestically operating NGOs, with the probability of restrictive law adoption exacerbated after nationally competitive elections. Governments in poor to middle-income countries waited until competitive elections to pass restrictive laws to govern civil society, as a means to secure future political victories. Restrictive laws implemented after elections limited NPOs' ability to receive foreign funds; specified amounts of money NPOs could legally receive; determined mechanisms through which NPOs could access aid; prescribed if and when NPOs could use foreign funds, including identifying issues upon which they could work; and specified reporting and tax requirements. All restrictions targeted foreign funding. In Ethiopia in 2009, for example, after competitive elections, the Charities and Societies Proclamation was passed to limit NPO work (Dupuy et al. 2015). After the law was enacted, two CSO types disappeared from Ethiopia: (1)

NGOs produced by increased foreign funding, and (2) foreign-aid dependent human rights NGOs. Remaining NGOs rebranded and restructured, with many cutting their human rights language and reframing activities to avoid governmental scrutiny and attack.

Governments have different regulatory styles toward nonprofits (Bloodgood et al. 2014),[3] and national regulation, whether permissive or restrictive, shapes NGO activities. For example, China's New Overseas NGO Management Law (2016) restricted NGO activity via a tactical governmental move, to gain benefit and minimize risk from the NGO sector (Hsu and Teets 2016).[4] The law stated that NGOs operating in China must not threaten China's security, or its national or ethnic unity, and an effect of this restrictive law was increased support of domestic NGOs. Hsu and Teets note that registered NGOs increased after the law, as it reinforced close relationships between some NGOs and the state and increased governmental control over their affairs. Small community-based organizations focused on what these authors call "issue areas," and those with "sensitive memberships" were forced to close. Many of these groups were not registered with the government and operated in a "legal gray area." Groups considered politically sensitive had difficulty receiving governmental approvals and faced approval processes stalling to the point that projects were no longer viable. China's new law shaped governmental regulatory control, increased state legitimacy via regulatory control over the social sector, and reduced "sensitive issue" social work.

The aim of these regulatory shifts has been not only to control money but also to control NGOs and political dissent (Weinstein and Christensen 2013).[5] Strategies of control include specific, regulatory techniques impeding philanthropy to NPOs, such as requiring government approval to receive foreign donations; stigmatizing international funding through "Foreign Agents" legislation; placing caps on international funding; mandating fund routing through government channels; adding burdensome reporting requirements; placing restrictions on internationally funded activities; and restricting funding from specific countries and donors. Globally, national laws have also restricted NPO formation and registration and discouraged associational activity through invasive oversight. Lester Salamon (2014, 2015) captured the shift in Russia, from state funding restrictions to developing "toolkits for collaboration." Through specific legal provisions, the government restructured state-NPO relations with a sector that had been previously left to its own devices.[6] The Russian case, as Salamon points out, is one instance where a government could maintain "dual realities": repressive regulatory processes governing NPOs and new nonprofit support programs.

National governments joining the associational counterrevolution support restrictions that bolster state sovereignty, enhance transparency and accountability, facilitate aid effectiveness and coordination, favor national security, and employ counterterrorism anti–money laundering methods (Sidel 2010, 2019a, 2019b; Moore and Rutzen 2011; Rutzen 2015a).[7] In addition to these global trends of philanthropic protectionism, NPOs must navigate an increased governmental "audit culture" (Strathern 1996/7, 2000; also see Power 1999). Nonprofits today must address challenges posed to their structures: challenges involving self-sufficiency, accountability, their bottom lines, and stakeholders. This is particularly arduous for nonprofits operating in arenas that cannot be easily quantified, calculated, and assessed, such as social change.

Institutional Ethnography and the Study of Bureaucracy

Indian laws regulating nonprofits comprise a mutable encyclopedia of categories and definitions, enforced by the state, demanded by nonprofits, negotiated and fought over, with details worked out in the rules of implementation. If I were to study nonprofits and their internal mechanics, I would situate myself inside a nonprofit. If I were to study the regulation of nonprofits, where would I locate myself as a researcher? Using an approach called *institutional ethnography*—developed by the feminist and Marxist Canadian sociologist Dorothy Smith (1987)—Marjorie L. DeVault (2006) argues that this particular form of investigation is useful for exploring "textually-mediated social organization." Building on Marx's broad definition of labor as a creative act, institutional ethnography studies how work processes are coordinated. Labor in this type of analysis is broadly defined: formal and informal, paid and unpaid. Mothering, for example, is work, and not all work occurs within the boundaries of institutions. Like categories of nonprofit institutions in the face of the law, challenges over categories—of what activities are, and are not, considered valid work— become legal battles, for wage equity and rights.

Institutional ethnography is a theoretical orientation and methodological technique that recognizes how institutions legitimate some types of work and delegitimate others. An institutional ethnographer explores all work in a setting and notes the activities that are recognized, institutionally accounted for, and those that are not, including which labors fall into the frame and which are ignored. Social relations in institutional ethnography represent connections among work processes. Institutional ethnographers focus on texts produced by institutions, and the means through which technologies of control are bureaucratized—for example, through institutional mechanisms such as charts, reports, strategic plans, and mechanisms for coordinating activity across different sites (coordinative apparatus)—analyzing textual coordination (not taking it for granted), policy documents, accounting records, and funding proposals. These bureaucratic techniques are entry points for understanding the institutional mechanics of organizations, and how power flows within them.

Institutional ethnography begins with embodied experience. Dorothy Smith's work explored single mothers and schools, asking why certain families were considered defective. She focused on institutions: teachers, school administrators, health care providers, and child protective services, and how school officials, as institutional representatives, marked and judged. Certain social forms fell into nameable and manageable categories, through relations she termed "ruling relations." For example, schools depended on mothers for auxiliary work. When mothers couldn't help less skilled children keep up with schoolwork, it became a problem of inequality, resulting in an institutional shift to "fixing single mothers," instead of changing the organization of schooling. Focusing on relations of ruling allows institutional ethnographers to document and analyze the gendered organization of work (DeVault 2013). Institutional ethnographers focus on categories created by institutions: what is included and what is left out? Another example is Timothy Diamond's ethnography of a nursing home (in DeVault 2013), which documented institutional processes in health care, exploring how care was structured around carefully documented bureaucratic tasks, such as leading and reporting on twice-daily exercises or turning bedridden patients and making notations on "Restraint & Position" forms. These "inscriptive processes" informed ethnographic analysis regarding how an institutional gaze was generated and put into place. The focus on "shift changes," is another example, as institutional moments were marked and noted. Institutional ethnographers analyze webs of texts that inscribe broader discourses, while locating the terrain of institutional capture in people's everyday activities. These ideas have been taken up more recently by organizational ethnographers focused on meetings (Pedersen and Humle 2016).

Dorothy Smith's work, along with her scholarship on standpoint theory, involves seeing power relations from everyday experience. As a feminist sociologist, Smith is interested in exploring relations of ruling from the perspective of women—asking what was left out of the concept of work from the standpoint of women's lived experiences. In *The Everyday World as Problematic* (1987), Smith asks, while walking down the street: Where does one see the state? In Canada and the United States, if one has a dog one must pick up its poop, and it must be on a leash. The state made these rules. Certain houses are more kept up (homeowners) versus rental properties (capital distinctions). What streets are policed and which are unkempt? This is where the state becomes evident. Which lawns are mowed, which sidewalks shoveled, at what time of day do certain people walk outside? Noticing these everyday patterns seen by walking on the street, one can observe and understand the norms structured and reinforced by the state, and those which become marked upon transgression. What happens if one does not pick up after one's dog? Does one receive a ticket? Is there peer pressure? Ruling relations are visible in the structures of everyday life, and through institutional ethnography, one analyzes what is protected and what is valued by institutions—in the above example, it is property owners and property. Institutional ethnography involves three procedures: (1) identifying ideological procedures used to make work accountable; (2) having a generous notion of "work"; and (3) using social relations to analyze how work shapes social courses of action. For nonprofits, and the cases I explore in this book, we ask where the rules reside. Who makes the rules that structure nonprofit institutional engagement, and how do these rules, written and unwritten, structure the everyday worlds of those who work in nonprofit worlds?

The legal reform of nonprofits involves bureaucracy, but it does not take place exclusively in the sites one might expect, such as courtrooms, Parliament, or government offices. Reform takes place in nonprofits themselves and in the gatherings they create to manifest their social worlds—in conferences, workshops, meetings, and in reports. Historically, nonprofits have been considered threatening to the state, and they have been invested in state transformation. They have also provided social services guaranteed as state entitlements. The nonprofits with which I conducted my ethnographic research in New Delhi held forums, organized conversations, lobbied civil servants, and wrote reports. They mediated with their grassroots constituencies and spoke on their behalf. They were located in India's capital, where governmental policy was made, but they also had representatives and kindred spirit organizations all over India. These organizations represented the hinterlands and invited members from far flung parts of the nation to the center to make their points, on paper, in person, and as people's representatives and institutional spokespersons for publics and constituencies. Nonprofit legal reform was a bureaucratic political process.

Studying bureaucracy ethnographically could not be drabber. People sat in offices, wrote reports, held meetings. This type of research may be considered "studying-up" (Nader 1972; Gusterson 1997), though within the parameters of those with I studied, there were power gradients. There was up and down within nonprofits, between nonprofits, between rural and urban organizations, and those with powerful resource-rich charismatic leaders, and those for whom getting anything actually done seemed an impossible struggle due to incompetent staff and few resources. The diversity of the sector at times made it difficult to consider it a sector at all. Many of the organizations that I studied wrote reports, which were produced though workshops, and which constituted a particular form of advocacy seeking to communicate with the state and reframe the terms of debate in the process. Through this bureaucratic activism, nonprofits engaged the state through bureaucracy in order to lobby the state for a space to negotiate laws governing NGOs. The state, which enacted and enforced law, was also bureaucratic. One may wonder, what aspect of processes of legal reform were not bureaucratic? As I write about the intersections of these bureaucracies, I am also writing about the relationships between bureaucratic processes. Report writing, and the social activities that created reports, such as workshops and assessments in nonprofit advocacy efforts, were bureaucratic social processes.[8] Bureaucratic documents were instruments of bureaucratic organizations. They helped to constitute organizations as institutional entities (Hull 2012a, 253) and were active agents capable of defining social worlds (cf. *actants*, Latour 2004; Latour and Woolgar 1986). Reports were artifacts of social processes and they framed and delimited social life. Report writing and the workshops that produced them were constitutive of advocacy.

Ethnographers face specific challenges when studying bureaucracy. One is to resist the deterministic nature of bureaucracies, because when bureaucracy is implemented by people it is inherently indeterminate (Hoag 2011). Ethnographers of the state have shown how bureaucracies create abstract templates, rules and laws that must be interpreted and applied on a case-by-case basis in social processes that involve negotiation (Gupta 1995, 2012; Gupta and Sharma 2006). To analyze reports without an understanding of the social lives that create and use them would ignore how actors defined, and inhabited, their institutional worlds. Bureaucracy tends to be opaque, and this empowers bureaucrats in their roles as gatekeepers. How does one study bureaucracy without foreclosing its indeterminacy (cf. Hoag 2011; Gupta 2012)? At times, bureaucracy becomes structurally violent toward those who are excluded, such as the poor or the illiterate (as in Gupta 2012), and as such it is dangerous, a "rule by nobody" (Hoag 2011, quoting Hannah Arendt). Bureaucracies enforce laws, rules and prescribe abstract behavior. Bureaucracy eschews authorship, whereby bureaucratic authority attains a gaze from nowhere (Matthew Hull, cited in Hoag 2011; cf. Donna Haraway 1988 on the "God trick"). Bureaucracies can be depoliticizing, turning political problems into technical ones (see Ferguson's 1994 analysis of development as an "anti-politics machine"); and they can be harnessed, re-politicized, and moralized as well (cf. the "technomoral politics" discussed by Bornstein and Sharma 2016, and Sharma 2024). Bureaucracy is strategically deployed, often for political aims—to limit certain types of institutions and social practices and encourage others.

A vulnerability of studying bureaucracy occurs when researchers believe bureaucracy's functional discourse (Hoag 2011). Documents, such as reports, are supposed to achieve goals, and the functionalist perspective makes ethnographic fieldwork with non-normative approaches to bureaucracies difficult. For example, while studying report writing, it was difficult for me not to interpret the reports through a persistent lens of achievement: in other words, did the reports meet their goals? Did they serve their purpose? The dominant narrative of bureaucracy is function, and analysts of bureaucracy may tend to measure bureaucratic discourse against bureaucratic rubrics, such as laws and regulations (Hoag 2011). Anthropologists studying bureaucratic advocacy must try not to let the idealizing frames of bureaucracy predetermine analysis, in order to avoid binaries of success or failure as analytical categories. Bureaucracy is very seductive. It pulls you in and threatens to colonize consciousness. Aware of this, and as a result of resisting more instrumental temptations of success narratives and functional analysis more broadly, in this book I am not concerned with whether or not nonprofit advocacy works. Instead, I want to explore how it works. In report writing, some reports have afterlives, effects, and consequences, while for other reports, the acuity of the intervention must be understood to be the process of report writing itself.

One approach to researching bureaucracy is to study bureaucrats as they embody and create bureaucratic structures.[9] Here we see where the promise of bureaucracy is not tidied into complete or single frames. Bureaucratic worlds are material worlds, producing graphic artifacts that mediate knowledge production (Riles 2001; Hull 2012a, 2012b; Latour and Woolgar 1986). To reify the solidity of bureaucratic positions in the process of researching them is to ignore the fluidity that bureaucracy seeks to control. In the instance of bureaucratic advocacy, NGOs and governments used reports to reify the "state" and the "NGO" as conceptual categories. Bureaucracy is filled with waiting, a form of bureaucratic power that ethnographies of bureaucracy have emphasized. For example, Gupta's ethnography of the Indian state, *Red Tape* (2012), analyzes how state bureaucracy wields structural violence upon the Indian poor, and how bureaucrats used periods of waiting to solicit bribes. Hoag (2011) calls bureaucracy a "hope-generating machine," as anything seems possible in the indeterminacy of bureaucratic process. Waiting involves hope that one's needs will be met and concerns will be addressed. He terms his research on South African immigration bureaucracy an "orbit of optimism." Bureaucratic knowledge is not total. It is contingent, partial and co-produced (cf. the study of a mining corporation in Welker 2014). Yet, bureaucracies function as "objectivity machines" and act as universalizing authorities (Hoag 2011, 87). Attempting to show "how bureaucracy really works," according to Hoag, is to risk "reinscribing bureaucracy with the same logics meant to be unsettled."

Report writing for NGO advocacy groups functions as prescriptive and descriptive, designs of and for reality. The self-referential nature of reports is a tactic that reifies and scripts activist networks (Riles 2001). In contemporary global NGO advocacy, social media and the internet have expanded communicative potential at a speed faster than light. Documents are transported without attendance at conferences, being sent instead via social media, email, and webpages, and they can be weaponized and politicized. Social media facilitate new forms of global activism and dissent, and philanthropic donations (Jakimow 2012). These may facilitate new forms of political control and violence, as advocacy networks are deployed both by the Right and the Left and can be mobilized strategically. Nonprofit advocacy brings nonprofit worlds into view; it produces institutionally legible social forms, and it reinforces and reifies itself in the process. The process of creating institutionally legible communities is part of nonprofit labor.

Scope of the Argument

Chapter 1, "Writing the Horizon Line," argues that regulation is a horizon line for nonprofits. As rules changed in India via regulatory reform, non-profit organizations (NPOs) came together to navigate regulatory change and alter the course of reform. This chapter engages with meeting ethnography in anthropology, and analyzes a pair of events that occurred four years apart: an annual NGO convention when nonprofit laws were being proposed and rules written, and an NGO conference after laws had been passed and rules implemented that became a collective reckoning. In both events, the nonprofit sector sought to navigate and reorient itself to the shifting horizon line of nonprofit policy in creation. Chapter 1 explores the role of agonistic and antagonistic politics in processes of negotiation between nonprofits and the state, over such issues as public good, taxes, and social welfare provision.

The legal category of charitable purpose is a particular type of nonprofit policy horizon line that has historically been used as an instrument of social reform and a space of political engagement. Chapter 2, "Charitable Purpose as a Political, Regulatory Frame," is a historical analysis of the legal instrument of charitable purpose. It traces its use in colonial reform movements, during struggles for India's independence, in the Emergency and its aftermath, and during globalization and subsequent economic liberalization. Charitable purpose is found in a cluster of laws governing nonprofits, including tax law, registration laws for societies, trusts, and charitable companies; laws regulating foreign philanthropy; and corporate law governing mandatory corporate social responsibility. The chapter considers the role of politics in the history of charitable purpose and social reform.

As India liberalized its economy and reached out to its global diaspora for investment, it clamped down on foreign funding to NPOs. With increasingly strict regulation of foreign philanthropy through the revised Foreign Contributions Regulation Act (FCRA), the stage for rights-based work shrank, and NPOs educated the sector on the rapid regulatory reform through advocacy clinics. Chapter 3, "Regulating Philanthropic

Corridors," is a portrait of FCRA reform as amendments were passed and rules written. Chapter 4, "Navigating the Rules," analyzes the work of public accountability and the demonization of nonprofits, as reformers helped each other to navigate the shifting regulatory terrain. In the growing climate of suspicion, it became increasingly necessary for NPOs to become legible to the state, and new dangers emerged around being political. The chapter is also a meditation on failure for nonprofits, which came to be determined by the rules of nonprofit law. Donors, NGO leaders, and accountants all worked together to reframe the sector in the court of public opinion, navigate rulemaking, and encourage reform that enabled nonprofit work.

Negotiations over the rules of philanthropic regulation took place in workshops, which were spaces of democratic debate, negotiation, and dialogue. Chapter 5, "The Power of Association," follows reformers as they attempted to write national policy on the nonprofit sector. Regulatory reform took place in a thicket of distinctions over the rules of law, and involved understanding charitable purpose, learning how to handle money appropriately, and heeding lists of unacceptable activities. This chapter explores tools such as manuals, liaison offices, credibility certificates, and norms brochures, as well as the shifting role of political activity as an acceptable category of nonprofit-sector work. Workshops often produced reports, which were a particular type of nonprofit public good. Chapter 6, "Reports as Mobilizing Technologies," explores report making as a form of collective engagement. It analyzes reports that spoke for the public, for the sector, and for the philanthropic ecosystem itself, and highlights two reports: one on challenges of voice and the other on challenges of representation.

As the government opened its arms to corporations for social sector work through revisions to the Companies Act (2013) with its 2 percent social responsibility tax, corporations scrambled to adjust their existing CSR practices and the nonprofit sector was reframed. Chapter 7, "The Responsibility to Act," explores the effects of revisions to the Companies Act. It takes us to the work of corporations revising their existing social welfare work in light of the new law and examines its effects on the nonprofit sector. It features the CSR work of a large IT company and a rural fertilizer company in north India, both of which experienced shifting loyalties, from the communities in which they worked to more centralized governmental oversight. The Conclusion, "Becoming Legible," asserts that to understand nonprofits we have to look to their regulation, specifically, the regulation of donations. Because nonprofits are donor dependent, shifts in the rules regarding their life source—philanthropy—alter the nature of these institutions themselves, and these shifts are tidal waves for democratic processes. The Conclusion suggests increased attention be afforded to the political stakes in this process, including those of nonprofits becoming legible to the state through the efforts of the unsung heroes of social reform: Accountability Guides, Activist Donors, and NPO leaders such as Professional Critics.

A fast overhaul of rules is a revolution. When rules are revised in rapid succession, especially in relation to laws pertaining to the nonprofit sector, the state has the upper hand and can institute political change through a revolution of rules. For nonprofits in the social sector, scrambling to understand and contend with new rules can be chaos. A revolution of rules instills confusion and fear. In response, and in this decade of reform, civil society groups—Activist Donors, Professional Critics, and Accountability Guides geared up to respond. They resolved—together and in association as an informal group, a gathering of an institutional sector—to take charge, to critique, to fund, and to guide those in the sector through the constant changes in the thicket of new rules. Rules are not laws, but policy. They constitute spaces of implementation where law is enacted, understood, interpreted, used, and enforced. In the midst of rapid legal reform, some NGOs may not have realized they were breaking the new rules. A revolution of rules can be used as a political strategy, but the associational response to rapid legal reform is also a strategy. Governments make changes to laws and rules in dialogue with those who must implement them and those who are governed by them, and this dynamic process sits at the heart of reform.

ONE

Writing the Horizon Line

A horizon line is an apparent distinction that perceptually separates earth from sky. A horizon line is a theoretical line, obscured by the aberrations of terrain, trees, buildings, mountains, lived environments, and natural formations. A true horizon line is a perfect circle that surrounds the viewer.[1]

The horizon line is often synonymous with "eye level." In art, a horizon line is connected to perspective. It allows artists to control the height of a viewer's eye and emphasizes distinctions, or boundaries, between sky and earth. Thus, a horizon line is an orienting frame that controls perspective. It gives a reference point to subjects in drawings and paintings. Regulation is a horizon line for nonprofits. As in drawing and painting, or any visual setting, it is an orienting frame that controls perspective—articulating what is, and what is not, part of the subject being regulated. For nonprofits, regulation defines them. It creates boundaries between nonprofits and other institutional forms—of politics, civil society, the public, welfare, and corporations. Imagine being in a car driving in the desert. The horizon line stays the same though it also changes—as you drive you are moving, but the earth and the sky are always ahead. This is the image of the horizon line that I ask readers to keep in mind: as an orienting frame, a structural constant, and a measure for perspective. Imagine you are a nonprofit (if a type of institution can be a subject). You look toward the horizon line of regulatory processes as an orienting frame, as an *ever-changing constant*. Regulation, as policy in formation, is a time and planning horizon of future orientation, as well as the anticipation of a future that will soon be past, codified through assessment. Policy, as a horizon line, distinguishes between types; it demarcates citizens from refugees, minors from adults, for-profit institutions from nonprofit ones. As policy becomes law, these social categories are institutionalized, implemented, managed, and sometimes policed.

Like a visual horizon line, policy surrounds a viewer. When we are thinking about policy, and policy making, what or who comes to mind? Bureaucrats in offices, lawmakers, and legislators, perhaps politicians. These are policy-making actors. But so are nonprofit workers, accountants, and legal advisors, all of whom strive to navigate the rules of policy and work to rewrite the horizon line for their constituencies. Civil servants in India also labor to write, and implement, the rules of policy, at times in conversation with nonprofits representing their constituencies. The horizon line of nonprofit policy is created through a social process of struggle over regulatory reform, which occurs between government actors and nonprofit reformers. This struggle—and the regulation it produces— constitutes the nonprofit form. Policy horizon lines are moving targets, always being done and undone relative to the perspective of observers. Policy struggles take place over, for example, the production of specific instruments in workshops and through report writing, producing documents that eventually become new horizon lines, orienting frames, stable forces for a moment, tributaries of regulatory dialogue. Consider corporate social responsibility as a policy initiative. It assumes corporations can be socially responsible institutions. As a policy horizon line, corporate social responsibility shifts relations between corporations and nonprofits, challenging their contrasting institutional forms. Historically, in India, nonprofits were considered prosocial. They led social activism, provided social welfare. In 2015, when the Indian government released its Intelligence Bureau (IB) report on nonprofits, and asked, "Who will watch the watchdogs?" it signaled a policy shift and a new horizon line.

A pair of events—a convention in 2013 and a conference roundtable in 2017—are featured in this chapter. Bookends of sorts, these two events taking place four years apart marked a unit of time during which the horizon line for India's nonprofits shifted. The convention was a call for solidarity and the conference was a collaborative reckoning, and the two events were attended by some of the same actors. Both events engaged those who worked in the Indian nonprofit sector while shaping it. Focusing their attention on laws and rules, these informal policy makers navigated a volatile, legal-political terrain, one that Randeria and Grunder (2011; also see Hirschl 2006) have termed the "juridification of politics," a concept that refers to the "creation and interpretation of rules, regulations and new soft law instruments by a range of actors—public and private, and international" (Randeria and Grunder 2011, 187; also see Comaroff and Comaroff 2006 for a related concept of "lawfare," and Bornstein and Sharma 2016 for the historical context in India). The juridification of politics produces an "ill-defined domain at the intersection of international private law, public international law, technical norms and soft law" (Randeria and Grunder 2011, writing about India). Policies, as they are formed in judicialized struggles, "acquire law-like qualities and produce effects similar to the workings of law in the everyday life of individuals and communities in the global South" (ibid., 187–88). The juridification of politics creates a space of governance in which the state "appears to disappear" and "constructs and dismantles itself in ways that render it unanswerable" (ibid.; also see Randeria 2007, regarding "the cunning state" that redistributes responsibility). Through the juridification of politics, political battles are fought through law (including indigenous law, Seider 2020). The juridification of politics is related to the judicialization of politics, which is the reliance on courts and judicial means to resolve political conflict (see Mustafa 2018 on juridification/judicialization of religion; also see Hirschl 2006). Randeria (2007, 2) has argued that far from globalization producing the decline of the nation state, it has produced a new landscape of legal negotiation, in a world of re-regulation rather than de-regulation. The heterogeneity of normative orders produces "legal uncertainty and unpredictability of rule-making."

When I first began this project, I set out to focus on law and law making in the periphery of policy process, but I did not focus on policy per se until I returned to work through my field material. It was then that I realized my interlocutors were developing, or seeking to develop, policy. In the workshops, report-writing sessions, and meetings I attended, the focus was on the amendment process for existing laws, writing the rules of law, and guiding the implementation of a law where possible. If, as many anthropologists acknowledge, policy is not a top-down process but instead a messy coming-to-be (Lea 2020), then we must consider regulation as a particular type of policy that strives to be complete—as in authoritative—but is always in the making. The anthropology of policy focuses on policy's interpretive community, broadly defined: including policy makers, critics, the media, and those affected by policy itself.

In order to be legible to the state, and to agitate for supportive regulation from the state via laws, legal amendments, rules, and policy creation, the Indian nonprofit sector strove to present a unified front: to the media, to the government, and to itself. As much as the government could render itself invisible and unanswerable through policy creation, nonprofits struggled to maintain communication with an increasingly opaque governmental apparatus. Nonprofit policy makers in New Delhi included social groups, or types—collections of people doing similar types of things. I've created three analytical categories to articulate social action in the policy-making arena. (1) *Activist Donors*: large and influential private philanthropists and directors of Indian foundations who historically had influence in the governmental arena. These leaders and innovators in the nonprofit sector became increasingly important as international philanthropy was restricted through revisions to the Foreign Contributions Regulation Act, and as NPOs turned to domestic philanthropy to support their programs and agendas. (2) *Professional Critics*: directors of large NGOs that engaged in policy making on behalf of smaller, regional, and disaggregated groups of Indian NPOs. They represented institutions in the rural periphery, speaking multiple languages, embracing varied religions, and inhabiting diverse cultural spaces. This group aimed to be inclusive and representative in its advocacy work conducted on behalf of member groups and affiliated NPOs. Some worked to write draft laws, others led workshops and managed report writing processes. They advocated for the nonprofit sector, and through their work constituted an entire discursive field of civil society advocacy for civil society itself. (3) *Accountability Guides*: those who helped the sector with reporting and advocacy processes. They included accountants, auditors, and NPOs working to educate the sector on changing regulatory frameworks. They considered themselves guides, protectors, and a productive disciplinary force in their efforts to engage with the shifting legal landscape. They worked with NGOs, foundations, and granting agencies, and focused on accountability mechanisms and on educating the nonprofit sector about regulatory reform. They are some of the heroes of my story.

Meeting Ethnography

The anthropology of policy has focused on how policy shapes the ways individuals construct themselves as subjects (Shore and Wright 1997). Policy is a language, a form of power, a cultural agent, and a political technology. Following the work of Michel Foucault, anthropologists have studied "discourses" of policy—the categories that shape human action, including the Foucauldian critiques of development discourse of the 1990s (Ferguson 1994; Escobar 1994). Policy is not a top-down control mechanism; it is a form of governance that structures how people organize themselves. It codifies norms and values and articulates organizing social principles that empower some and silence others. And policy, as a form of power, conceals its own operation through its normalization. It seems rational and self-evident as a core symbolic horizon and an analytical key.

Anthropologists of policy study "through" (Shore and Wright 1997), using multiple ethnographic sites to track webs of power, in relations between institutions and discursive formations. Policy can't be studied through traditional participant observation in a single setting. One must analyze interactions between multiple sites, tracing policy connections and the ways policy shapes ordinary worlds. Like law, policy is not located in one social arena. Like law, policy communities are contested political spaces (ibid., 14). Policies are "windows onto political processes in which actors, agents, concepts, and technologies interact in different sites, creating or consolidating new rationalities of governance and regimes of knowledge and power" (Shore and Wright 2011, 2). Policy is a classificatory, regulatory logic, made by people and by institutions.

A shift in anthropological thinking has occurred regarding ethnography in and of organizations. Schwartzman (1989, 1993) paved the ground for the ethnography of institutional settings such as organizations. Her work on what she termed *meeting ethnography* has influenced generations of anthropologists since, including those who study complex organizations. Complex organizations offer unique challenges of access, membership, and entry, and contemporary anthropologists challenge ethnographic assumptions of participation in such institutions. Doing ethnography in organizations may not be "new," but it does delimit the researcher's capacity for engagement in specific ways that lend a creative approach to thinking about ethnographic practice and institutional forms. For example, Pedersen and Hulme (2016) call attention to the intersections between organizational studies and anthropology. Organizational studies approach ethnography through field studies: shadowing, writing, interviewing, and producing thick descriptions of institutional life (as in institutional ethnography; Smith 1987). However, organizational ethnography also focuses on what "organizing" means in institutional, ethnographical work. Pedersen et al. (2016) urge us to understand that organizations are more than settings and places, and instead suggest attention to the act of organizing as a space of sociality. To conduct ethnographies of complex organizations is to study meaning making and interpretation. Organizations are not static and closed entities. Institutions are "fragmented networks or clusters of social interaction that occur in specific times and spaces" (ibid., 4), of which ethnography aims to make analytical sense. Key for my approach is the view, which I share with organizational ethnographers conducting meeting ethnographies, that institutions are dynamic and approaching them ethnographically must be dynamic as well. Organizational ethnographers approach institutions as active social spaces, querying "how people, together with artefacts, live their lives and make meanings through interaction, talk, and interpretation" (ibid.).

Organizational/institutional spaces create unique fieldwork dilemmas, where knowledge is often co-created while research is being done, with institutional ethnographers sometimes doing what is called "shadow work" and at other times being part of the institution itself. Pedersen et al. (2016) note that institutional ethnography is not just the study of institutions as actors or ethnography that takes place in institutions. It is a particular methodological and theoretical context for investigating social processes. Because institutions/organizations are fragmented, they also produce an environment where ethnographic engagement is fragmented as well, and ethnographers find themselves doing episodic ethnography, in meetings, for example, or following an institutional conversation, or following a process over time and with different actors in varied settings. This produces artifacts and organizational systems that include, in the case of my work, laws, reports, and workshops. With a focus on polyphony, ethnographers of institutions study action, the improvisation of collective engagement, where the power and associational nature of *organizing* becomes apparent. Mikkelsen (2016, 17–39), for example, writes of how conflict is handled in an NGO: it is the context for analysis and setting for research. She is concerned with processes of "sensemaking" that take place due to pre-existing knowledge from past experiences and that frame the ways people act. For

Mathiesen (2016), strategy in organizational settings is a way of thinking collectively about where the institution goes. Institutions, Mathiesen
argues, are collectivities that must be performed. She analyzes speech acts
in a "stakeholder engagement department" of a global biotech company to
argue that, like gender, strategy is performative—it must be done, and as
it is enacted it has the potential to reinforce existing structures and/or alter
them. Organizational strategy is a site of meaning making—through the
articulation of institutional mission, vision, dreams and hopes. Mathiesen
explores what strategy does, institutionally, as well as how it is created and
enacted. The episodic nature of institutional ethnography is analyzed by
Johansen (2016), who writes of an institutional process through points of
entry, with meetings as inflection points, and episodic research as a valuable way to understand institutional life.

   In line with organizational and meeting ethnographers, I did not aim
to write an ethnography of a single NPO, but instead studied institutional
fields, constituted by a community of organizations and individuals that
moved between institutional spaces, some of which identified as NPOs,
others that were found in governmental settings such as the civil service,
and yet others that operated in corporate settings. Members of this loosely
defined and fragmented community moved between institutional spaces,
some inhabited more than one space, and appeared in interstitial and in-
tersectional institutional sites where members (staff, boards, volunteers)
from different NPOs gathered to write reports collectively and conduct
workshops and conventions. This space of sociality manifested as the
power of association. My ethnography also included interlocutors such as
corporate actors running CSR programs and civil servants working for the
state, as their engagement also shaped what civil society advocacy work
was, and what it could be, through collaboration and contrast.

   My ethnographic research took place over a decade of episodic
fieldwork—via report writing, through workshops, and in meetings of
various kinds including those that planned reports and workshops. As for
other anthropologists conducting meeting ethnography (Schwartzman
1989, 1993; Thedvall 2013), and anthropologists focused on policy (Nyquist
2013), this is a common practice for studying institutions via ethnographic
methodologies and techniques. Thinking about institutional ethnography
as the study of episodic processes frees the research from impossible ideals,
such as studying an entire institution. Johansen (2016, 117–33) observed
meetings and took fieldnotes, and scheduled conversations as interviews.

I too followed this ethnographic path, though I also spent an extended amount of time with one particular organization over the course of a year, and I participated in its work processes: collaboratively writing reports, taking lunch breaks, chatting informally, planning and attending workshops, and having meetings to assess results and strategize next steps. Like other members of the institution, I was not privy to all meetings or all conversations. Institutional life is partial and fragmented by nature, though collectively organized through work processes, tasks, and shared goals. In complex organizations, like those studied by meeting ethnographers and by me, doing ethnography relies on partial perspective. One studies institutional phenomena rather than the everyday. One studies episodic processes, rather than the organization itself.

Thedvall (2013, 106–19) uses the concept of "punctuated entries" to analyze organizations ethnographically. In her study of policy making in the European Union, she finds her field site to be meetings, which occur over time and follow a punctuated rhythm, occurring in more than one space. Meetings are gatherings for policy makers, and they too experience policy making in a punctuated and episodic, institutional manner. Meetings, for Thedvall, are the ethnographic field. Nyqvist (2013) writes about the ethnographic study of policy and focuses on the "relativity of access" in institutional settings as a process of mutual navigation. Some parts of institutions are not available to ethnographers, just as employees don't have access to all parts of institutions. In my work as well, budgets and budgeting processes tended to be out of bounds (a black box of sorts, vulnerable and private for the NPO). Access was an issue to be problematized, negotiated, and accepted. Nyqvist (ibid., 91–105) offers an interesting thought experiment, in a context where there is legislated total access to policy making (a social insurance department in Sweden). She writes of how she and her informants navigated access, and restricted it. Her research occurred in bureaucratic settings of policy making, and she did not see it as a loss that she did not interact with her informants in their private lives. When she bumped into an informant and they both pretended not to recognize each other to preserve the backstage of their non-work lives, she interpreted it as the navigation of access in institutional ethnography: what is contained in institutional life versus what is not. Policy making is a performative stage—and what is done is meant to be front stage. Following the "suits," as she calls policy makers, is a process of polymorphous engagement, that involves meetings, listening to gossip (private matters in public settings), and closing the door as well. What the ethnographer "decides to ignore" is also part of the institutional ethnographic process, especially when the ethnographer is tasked with studying policy—and the making of official versions of things through presentations and performances. All of this access is mutually navigated by ethnographers and informants in institutional settings. One could argue this is the case for all contemporary ethnography, but in institutional settings of public policy, it tends to be normative, and formative, behavior.

A Gathering

In 2013, at an annual meeting, a gathering of sorts, members of India's large and diverse nonprofit sector came together to discuss common affairs and to strategize a way forward. The convention was run by a membership organization that had convened more than 200 organizations in Delhi to discuss the identity of nonprofit sector. The director spoke of how the identity of the sector was in question. "Anyone can register [as an NGO]," he said, but "What is our good work?" It was an "apex" organization, an NGO that represented other NGOs, and the director argued the identity of the sector was at stake. He urged its membership to emphasize their positions. That year the NPO was celebrating its twenty-fifth anniversary, and the annual meeting was festive, though urgent topics such as perceived threats from the state were also addressed. A new tension was emerging, between nonprofits that demanded rights and entitlements from the state and the economic and political elite that distributed governmental resources and regulated the sector. New actors were entering the sector through proposed revisions to the Companies Act (2013) that would mandate a 2 percent corporate social responsibility provision. How could NGOs in the room work together to solve growing mistrust? The government was controlling the sector rather than regulating it, which had adversely affected NGO work. Foreign funding had declined since the global economic recession of 2008, when foreign endowments shrank, and funders had dramatically scaled back their assistance. In this wider context, the Indian government restricted foreign funding through revisions to the Foreign Contributions Regulation Act (FCRA), and introduced incentives for corporate-sponsored social welfare. This double-pronged transformation of the regulatory landscape altered the balance of philanthropic power and redefined the types of projects that nonprofits could engage in with foreign funds.

During panels and in conversations, NPO leaders remarked that the sector was suffering a loss of identity. Voluntarism was being professionalized, which hurt smaller organizations and favored ones with larger managerial capacities. Groups at the meeting spoke of local competition between NPOs for scarce resources, which limited their ability to come together. As much as the government, which was the Congress Party at the time, sought to hold NPOs accountable, voluntary groups at the convention discussed holding the government accountable as well. The meeting was filled with activists and NPO workers who had lived their lives in the sector. They were adamant about their important social role. A prominent NPO leader, a Professional Critic, argued civil society should no longer be called the third sector: "We are the glue," she said boldly, "We are what holds the government and the people together." NPOs brought different players together, she said, their role was to enable, facilitate, and be a "constructive challenger." The organizing NPO's membership consisted primarily of small, rural NGOs, which enjoyed the midday meal alongside conference panelists (NGO leaders, donors, philanthropists, and civil servants). The convention was an opportunity for nonprofit actors from different backgrounds—service provision and activism, bureaucrats, donors, and NGOs, large and small—to come together to think and discuss what the "it" of the voluntary sector was, and what it could become. Given the eclectic nature of India's immense voluntary sector, it seemed like a mammoth task. The group was by no means unified. The philanthropists and corporate representatives inhabited a world different from the world of the representatives of the small, rural NGOs. One could see it in the fancy saris of the Activist Donors who urged the rural NPOs to take action; in the suited demeanor of the Accountability Guides who sat on panels to explain the laws; and in the rural NPO directors who came to Delhi in their colorful *kurtas* and *jholas*, speaking on behalf of marginalized populations—some of these directors may have also been members of these marginalized groups. Body language, style of dress, and verbal language used marked internal hierarchies within the sector mapped onto resource bases, and their relative distances from the policy-making gravitational pull of New Delhi.

India's voluntary sector was diverse, densely populated, and difficult to regulate. At that time, it spanned an estimated two million nonprofits (now an estimated three million; Jagtiani 2020) registered with the state, as well as copious uncounted, ad hoc self-help groups, people's organizations, and social movements. The sector was in fact so diverse that some of the institutions in the room may not have considered themselves part of the same group at all. Within this broad category, tensions of orientation that historically divided the sector—between social movement/activist types and NGOs working as service providers for the state—were paused (Bornstein and Sharma 2016; Kamat 2002; Kothari 1986; Sheth and Sethi 1991). One could broadly demarcate a particular division into those who attempted to make social change from without, working against established institutions, and those who strove to make change from within, using existing institutions to reform society. Even the category of what constituted an NPO or an NGO was up for grabs. Some NGOs subcontracted to other organizations; some were subcontracted by the state; others rallied against governmental policies. NGOs were hard to define and hard to count; they were a catchall category that included schools and hospitals as well as youth and farmer groups. "Creating a list of active NGOs is like aiming at a moving target" (Watkins, et. al. 2012, 291; Tandon 2017, for India). It was an "unwieldy non-system" that included even small-scale ad hoc groups (Watkins et al.). Though voluntary organizations and NGOs could be distinct in their aims and targeted audiences, as nonprofits they shared certain structural characteristics: uncertainties regarding donor dependency and short-term contracts (ibid.). Some of the ways in which NGOs coped with uncertain fiscal and political environments were bowing to the pressure to professionalize, altering their objectives and structures, and following institutional growth agendas. Bureaucracy played into this institutionalized trajectory in the form of donor reporting and assessment demands.

The ubiquity of NGOs in India has not been viewed entirely positively by activists, who have historically accused NGOs of pacifying civil society groups and eliminating political opposition (Kamat 2002). The professionalization of the nonprofit sector has been seen critically by activists as a form of co-optation by corporate and state forces and agendas (INCITE! 2007). Some have accused NGOs of humanizing capitalism, paving the way for dispossession and serving elite interests (Choudry 2013, 25). Activists have asserted that some environmental NGOs have been complicit with the state in its development interests, and that NGOs—as an institutional form—have proliferated in service to the state, while the state has dismissed NGO protest as anti-national (see Kapoor 2013, 45–74, regarding mining and anti-mining groups in Orissa). Thus, though NGOs may begin in support of social movements, they risk pressure to shapeshift in order to preserve government licenses or to receive foreign funds. If NGOs didn't comply with governmental rules such as the FCRA, they risked being de-registered, defunded, and eventually closed. The threat of a crackdown on and closure of thousands of NGOs pushed some activist NGOs previously resisting the state to conform to state expectations and agendas, alienating those NGOs from their original activist base. Only as state-compliant service providers could NGOs benefit from multilateral and bilateral aid, alongside state and donor funding. Some activists and scholars have claimed that NGOs were responsible for the "NGOization of democracy," the NGOization of grassroots politics, and the professionalization of dissent. Citing Arundhati Roy, Sangeeta Kamat (2013, viii), for example, argues NGOs are an "indicator species": "the greater the devastation caused by neoliberalism, the greater the outbreak of NGOs."

Perhaps the structure of NGOs was partly to blame for the ways they tended to professionalize dissent (Choudry and Kapoor 2013, 14). In larger NGOs, staff were not activists but trained managers. NGO staff may represent activist groups, but they were mostly brokers, intermediaries, and professional staffers advocating for others. Due to the compliance structures of donor funding, NGOs enforced managerialist governance practices. The critique of NGOs as bureaucratic institutions followed the lines of thinking developed by theorists of audit culture; especially, how bureaucratic structures are by nature formalistic (Strathern 2000). Not only reporting expectations burdened NGOs; their bureaucratic structures oriented what was possible, including defining aims and objectives. The types of institutions and groups of which I write—those involved in legal and regulatory advocacy—worked from within the system to promote legal reform and encourage sound managerial practices. They used the terms "good governance" and "accountability." They provided auditing services to other NGOs, while claiming that being verified enhanced legitimacy in the donor marketplace. These NGOs were not only complicit with auditing hegemonies; they reproduced them. Yet rather than assume these endeavors involved total co-optation, I propose we think about their work as another form of advocacy in a global context where civil society groups were increasingly under attack. These NGOs were formal institutions that privileged legal-organizational frameworks, and they were organizations that were registered with the state. Of course there were other avenues for social reform, and with increased regulatory oversight, some civil society groups opted to go under the radar completely instead of negotiating with the state for amenable regulation through bureaucratic means.

The groups featured in this book worked toward reform through what they called research and advocacy. One example of such an organization worked on behalf of its member institutions, some of which may have been on the more activist side of the spectrum. Early on in my research I read about its work on the web, and I reached out to its director, who kindly welcomed me as a researcher into the organization. I parked myself in the office and participated in and observed its work during my 2012–13 sabbatical in Delhi. It was one of many organizations I include in my research whose names I have anonymized due to the punitive attacks on NGOs occurring as I write. This organization aimed to speak for the nonprofit sector, to articulate issues that institutions on their own could not, due to fears of state retaliation. As we will see, the role of nonprofits as public institutions, and as voices speaking for communities, is a key component of their bifurcated political strengths and vulnerabilities, as well as their capacity to demand legibility from the state.

The nonprofit sector was so diverse that it took labor to make it recognizable to the government, a necessary effort for requesting legal accommodations from the state for the sector itself. With a sector so diverse, how and why should we persist in even conceiving it as a sector? In 2013, this was part of the political struggle at hand. Through nonprofit advocacy, groups democratically representing a diverse collection of institutions formed a coherent entity to negotiate strategically with the state for legal reform. These organizations were not an encompassing set of institutions, quite the contrary. Their work occupied a strategic political space in the global context of increasing scrutiny of nonprofits and civil society groups. NPO advocacy organizations did not exist in the margins, though they claimed to represent other, smaller groups that did. They oriented their work toward institutional reform through report writing and research-based education initiatives. Delhi, as the political capital of India, was a center for policy formation, and NPO report-writing advocacy followed a center-to-periphery model. Draft reports were written in Delhi and circulated to national networks of membership organizations. Member institutions were invited to Delhi to debate and comment upon the reports, and NPO staff traveled regionally within India in order to present draft reports in workshop form, and to hear from member institutions about their concerns regarding legal reforms in process. Workshops and reports, as we will see, focused on laws affecting the voluntary sector: those regarding the reform of taxes, philanthropy, governance, and registration. The endeavor encapsulated the micro- and macro-politics of regulatory forces and their bureaucratic implementation. Because NPO membership contained a diverse set of groups, NPOs and activists were not pitted against each other: they came together. In the shrinking space for civil society engagement and dissent, the disparate groups formed a solidarity-building, democratic system of negotiation.

At the convention, members and guests aligned their previously kaleidoscopic perspectives. The Activist Donors encouraged the sector to pay attention to the youth, who had different desires from the older generations of voluntary sector workers. They urged attendees to encourage youth to lead the nonprofit sector, and discussed the emergent leadership vacuum. A representative from NASSCOM (National Association of Software and Service Companies, the trade association for the Indian IT industry) and others in the corporate sector, as well as the Professional Critics, spoke of a wave of future funding heading to the sector through a new corporate social responsibility (CSR) provision in the Companies Act (2013), enacted in the same year as the convention. The audience expressed excitement regarding the potential future funding. At breaks and during lunch corporate representatives were swarmed by representatives of small NGOs seeking information on corporate resources for social development. Business cards were handed out like promissory dreams, and invited guests were flocked by NGOs after appearing on panels. The Activist Donors were the rock stars of the group, speaking from the stage with the authority of money amplifying their years of experience. They sat with the Professional Critics at lunch. The smaller NGOs sat with the Accountability Guides and NPO staff, sharing experiences from their work worlds, professional intersections, and shared knowledge. The room was filled with older NGO workers, and there were few young representatives aside from the organizing NGO's staff, who happened to be mostly young women.

The convention was organized as an annual meeting. A philanthropic vacuum had emerged regarding funding to civil society. An Activist Donor argued that given the decline in flexible resources to civil society from international sources, and given the challenges civil society actors faced at the governmental district level—where fund allocations created dependency on the local political and official decision makers who could grant the release of these funds—there was a need for new, flexible support from domestic sources for civil society groups. Distinguished speakers heralded from government, civil society, and the corporate sector. They populated panels where people spoke about their experiences and local concerns in the sector, and on how aid was replacing trade in the new global landscape. There was a panel on working with corporations, featuring government representatives from The Federation of Indian Chambers of Commerce and Industry (FICCI) and the Confederation of Indian Industry (CII) who were tasked with organizing corporate social responsibility, as well as representatives from NASSCOM, the trade association of the Indian information technology (IT) and business process management (BPM) industry, and a panel on change, with civil society leaders (Professional Critics) and Activist Donors discussing the new landscape of civil society engagement. A keynote address was delivered by the Minister of Rural Development, and a panel on strategies for navigating the new landscape attracted eager audiences.

The mostly small, rural-member NGOs, who had come to Delhi to network and to learn about current NPO laws, were different from the Delhi–based NGOs, who were urban, savvy, and in the know. I chatted with a woman who worked for an NGO focused on women's empowerment in northern India, advocating for women at the state level. She spoke of her experience with the FCRA and the role of the District Magistrate (DM). If a DM knew the NGO, then they would recommend that NGO for a FCRA certificate, which was needed to receive foreign funds. Only with the FCRA certificate could a donor receive an income tax deduction. Not only did it function as a license for foreign donations, but it linked the local NGO with the state and with the foreign donor. Her NGO had been in existence for more than four years, but it had just started its advocacy at the state level—focusing on making sure that existing laws were properly implemented. It wasn't focused on changing laws (as the larger member organizations were); rather it targeted its work on implementation, and worked with the local police on issues of domestic violence, livelihoods, and youth. This NGO had been a member of the organizing NPO for eight months and had attended some workshops in the region where it was based. Its concern was that if an organization missed one step of the FCRA license process, then it would be blacklisted. Laws were there, but what was the use of the laws if they were not implemented properly, she asked. Bureaucracy held both the threat of punishment and the hope of facilitation.

The annual convention was a ritual act that produced a sense of togetherness and collective effervescence. An NPO staff member introduced the conference with a degree of formality. Dressed in a formal sari, she talked about the "spirit of development and togetherness," acting as a community-building cheerleader for the nonprofit sector. Each of the voluntary organizations had come to Delhi with its own unique, regional concerns, while the organizing NPO paid for travel and lodging during the convention. If they arrived as separate entities, they left as members of a group, of the nonprofit sector. In one panel, a working NPO committee member spoke of voluntarism and how NGOs were misunderstood. As nongovernmental organizations, some had "earned bad names as an NGO," but the voluntary sector had done tremendous work from its inception, and he emphasized this focus. Reflecting on past performance, one could address shortcomings and praise areas done well. "We [the sector] may have failed in terms of tax and FCRA reforms. [But] we ourselves are to be blamed for that," he said; "It is an outrage." He urged the voluntary sector to synergize efforts and to move forward. Actions must be based on values, he argued. "We are the torchbearers. Voluntarily we have taken responsibility."

The distinguished guest, a Member of Parliament, arrived late. Lamps were lit; pictures were taken. A nonprofit leader spoke, observing that the task ahead was not easy. He lauded the size of the sector. He listed successes of the sector, including the Right to Information and Right to Food campaigns, both of which had resulted in the formation of bills that eventually became laws. Yet a noose was tightening around the sector. Nobody in the media was writing about the good work of the sector. But if money was lost, then the media documented it. "You people jointly need to communicate about this," he appealed.

The organizing NPO's chairperson spoke of a perceived threat: those demanding rights and entitlements from governmental structures and political parties were seen as threatening by those holding power. When NGOs demanded transparency from the government, the government pushed back with transparency requirements for the sector: "You are asking—how about you? . . . How to solve this mistrust?" he mused. Regulations were increasing, creating a new environment of control, moving from regulation to control: we "can't do anything without asking." When that was combined with declining resources, owing to the global recession of 2008, tensions increased over these diminished resources and increased regulations. A new understanding was developing between the government and corporations. The section of the voluntary sector that did not want to be co-opted was becoming isolated. It was in this context that accountability issues were becoming central to the relationship between nonprofits, the government, and corporations.

New leadership in the sector was not emerging. When the distinguished guest speaker, a Member of Parliament from Orissa spoke, he echoed these concerns. "You have to take leadership!" he yelled to the crowd. "There is no escape!" After a session on voices from the field, and a panel on global India, structural contradictions became starkly apparent: in India, NGOs were contained in a national frame, due to their regulation through tax laws and the FCRA. Regulation defined them as a group. Yet, they were also part of the larger international network of civil society and human rights organizations. The government, meanwhile, wooed foreign and diaspora capital through *foreign direct investment*, which was being liberalized, and which had entered the international landscape of aid provision. The regulatory strangulation of the voluntary sector resulted from a basic disconnect between the global aid framework on the one hand and, on the other, national laws and the potential ways in which local NGOs, and the government, could infiltrate the more isolated, largely undeveloped, rural hinterlands of India. The small, local dialect–speaking NGOs at the conference seemed far removed from the world discussed at a panel on India's global footprint.

Day two of the conference focused on the relationship between nonprofits and corporations. Panelists—the head of Corporate Social Responsibility for FICCI, the director of the NASSCOM Foundation, the head of a large NGO, and the executive director of CII—explained how the voluntary sector had knowledge and skills but not resources, while the government had links to international donors and corporations. The potential for matchmaking and partnership was offered to the audience as an inspiriting potential future, a new horizon line. The government head of CSR for FICCI spoke of non-negotiables in partnerships, of common value systems, and of problems—where corporations "just want to write cheques and give it to them, and the voluntary sector thinks this is the best thing." Instead, she promoted a meaningful relationship and argued that it was necessary for NPOs to actively write policy objectives: "You must make corporates think," she said, and "develop long term vision in partnership. Don't just go to get only the money." She spoke of the new clause in the Companies Act (Section 135) that mandated corporate social responsibility funds from companies, funds which were to be allocated toward social welfare. "What touchpoints in society are there?" she mused. "What is this CSR? Companies are trying to define that [space] between corporate sector and NGO sector where conversation can happen." It was an "evolving landscape" and a "new paradigm." The future was not just about resources being put in, but "about community ownership" and "value-based partnerships." It sounded inspiring. The horizon line was moving.

When the CEO for the NASSCOM Foundation took the floor, she spoke of "strategic philanthropy," of donations of software and services (and how one needed to have a FCRA certificate to get both). Her foundation ran a program called Big Bridge, which facilitated the donation of computers from the corporate sector. It also ran training programs in Mumbai for NGOs to learn about computing and social media, a program supported by Microsoft, LinkedIn, and Facebook. She spoke of ways corporations could help NGOs develop their HR, management, finance, and communication activities. Yet, one of the largest challenges for the corporate sector, she argued, was to be able to trust and assess the capabilities of NGOs, and NGOs had to do certain things to demonstrate their trustworthiness: being transparent, submitting annual reports, and supporting impact assessments. She urged NGOs to create "value-added" offerings in this new partnership with corporations: to think beyond direct financial contributions and synchronize not just values but actual work. Corporations had skills too, which NGOs could use. As she spoke, it became apparent that NGOs were an entry point for corporations into communities, and a way to infiltrate—if not create—new markets. How could the NPOs drive this tidal wave of change?

The audience was largely rural, grassroots NGO workers. One could see from their body language that they were not city people. They spoke many languages, including rural dialects, and differed from the panelists and presenters who were government officials, businesspeople, academics, MPs, and senior members of the nonprofit sector. There was a clear gap and disconnect between the audience of those working directly with NPO clients (fieldworkers) and the Delhi-based, politicized planners. The new India under construction was being imposed, not from afar or from

outside India, but from within India itself. From the other India, not the
rural India with the problems, but the city India, with its shopping malls,
and development, and internet. This gap was the real one, and the one in
which political fissures could occur. The gap between the panel and the audience was voiced in question-and-answer periods, where some members
of the audience stood up and said, "We have no idea what you are talking
about." And, "Come to our village and see what we do." It was difficult
for me to ascertain if there was hostility in these statements or simply
an expression of the difficulty or even impossibility of communication on
some issues. The audience did not address the panelist presentations—they
had their own concerns. They wanted to reach the corporate sector to avail
themselves of corporate funds but didn't know how. Audience members
expressed stress and anxiety at corporations taking over their sector, and
they talked over the panelists as they tried to respond.

   One panel populated by the Professional Critics and Activist Donors
focused on big NGOs and philanthropists. They spoke of the role and
expansion of the voluntary sector, and emphasized that they were "not
elected representatives" (not government). Nonetheless, NGOs had taken
it upon themselves to occupy a watchdog role on behalf of those whom
they cared for, those with whom they wanted to work, and those whose
lives they wanted to improve. These were chosen roles. There were people
who had taken on the role of affecting and changing policies as well, but
policies had to grow from practice. "When we meet," one panelist admit-
ted, "we cry about indifference from the government and persecution."
Some had come to accept that in its relationship with NGOs, the government "like[s] to treat us like vermin, like rats." They send in smoke and
heat till the rats can no longer stay. They "try to smoke us out." Things
were difficult, he said, and the voluntary sector had to be tough. There was
a power in numbers—though NGOs did things on a small scale, the government thought in terms of thousands of villages. He argued that NGOs
should give the government credit in the development partnership: "The
moment you capture center stage from bureaucrats you are no longer there.
But if you give them credit they can say, 'We can work with the voluntary
sector.'" The government had taken over the language of rights, but in villages there was still no water or education. "What is use of having a lot of
rights?" He advocated that NGOs hold the government accountable for its
development promises. This was the role of Professional Critics.

   An Activist Donor spoke of leadership in the sector, that youth had to be involved. Senior NGO leaders discussed society at a crossroads, and how the identity of the voluntary sector was uncertain. These were motivational speeches, geared toward inspiring the audience of NGO fieldworkers from all over India. The tone of the final panels was hopeful, idealistic, positive, and encouraging, as they rallied the sector. "Autonomy and freedom are earned, not handed down. Earned from our own actions," one panelist remarked. Yet the questions from the audience circled back to CSR, and corporate monies. There was confusion, and the audience sought information, not motivational speeches. Those coming to Delhi for the annual member convention were senior sector workers, the old guard, wearing earth tones: men in suits, sweaters, vests, fleece. Women in saris and sweaters, salwar kurtas. In this crowd, there were many more men than women. Perhaps these were the ones who could make it to Delhi. The NPO hosting the conference had paid for members' accommodations at the conference site, along with meals and train fares. A list of funders for the conference and the NPO hung on the wall. It too was a nonprofit supported by donations. Because nothing was outside the need for philanthropy in the nonprofit sector, shifts to the philanthropic regulatory framework redefined the very existence of NPOs. Everything was at stake.

New Horizons of Political Contestation

The struggles of Indian NPOs exist in the global context of increased legal pressure on nonprofits to regulate their affairs. Lester Salamon (2015) has documented a global shift whereby states outsourced their welfare responsibilities to nonprofits, in a trend he termed the "nonprofitization of the welfare state." Once state functions were outsourced to nonprofits, NGOs were pressured, through laws, to behave, function, and regulate themselves in a way that was considered legitimate by the government. This phenomenon has had consequences for nonprofit institutions and the public services they provide, such as education, health care, social welfare, and poverty and humanitarian relief. Some have called the increased privatization pressure on nonprofits in this outsourcing model the "corporatization of the nonprofit sector" (see Srinath 2022 and Deo 2024 for this outsourcing shift in India; see Sidel 2019a and 2019b for global context). In addition to the relationship between governments and nonprofits, the relationship between corporations and NPOs is relevant to legal reform. Institutionally, corporations manifest a certain type of rationality: of profit seeking. Nonprofit organizations were increasingly being compared to corporations in this regard and were required to conform by showing measurable results. As governments ceded welfare work first to nonprofits and then to corporations, nonprofits were threatened, their institutional form challenged by profit-seeking models, regulatory systems, and structures. This structural shift, like climate change, is not visible in its totality; it can only be rendered through component parts and interlinked processes.

Nonprofit regulation is intimately linked with state sovereignty. Across the world governments have selectively and strategically cracked down on nonprofit sectors while collaborating with them. Strong states such as Russia, Turkey, Hungary, China, and Hong Kong once controlled nonprofits with a heavy hand. They also turned to them and integrated them into sponsored social welfare provision. Extreme cases are Russia's 2012 Foreign Agents Law,[2] which restricted foreign funding to nonprofits, and Hong Kong's National Security Law, which restricted freedoms of association and assembly.[3] Increased regulation followed two earlier periods: the global associational revolution of the 1990s, during which global development bodies supported NPOs instead of states, and the global associational counterrevolution in which states cracked down on civil society groups protesting the state (see Rutzen and Shea 2006; Rutzen 2015b). If the nonprofitization of the welfare state incorporated NPOs into governmental welfare schemes, the programs were then corporatized and privatized in the corporatization of the welfare state: the hyper-rationalization and formalization of the nonprofit sector that uses corporations as a model and incorporates for-profit entities into welfare provision (Sidel 2019a). Eventually, states used the corporatization of the welfare state to co-opt nonprofits and control dissent. Once incorporated, NPOs were no longer capable of governmental critique. They became an arm of the state, a hegemonic force unto themselves. In the co-optation model, states created strict laws that restricted NPOs, then created toolkits for collaboration, and finally funded the nonprofit sector. When the donor base of NPOs was the state itself, NPOs lost their critical capacity. Nonprofits receiving state funds were reluctant to bite the hand that fed them.

Nonprofits are hydra-headed bellwethers of democratic action. They may engender antagonistic forces critical of the state, or act as hegemonic forces that enable state agendas. Rather than assuming nonprofits stand for radical opposition to hegemonic projects of rule, or as governmental agents, the space of the nonprofit allows us to think politically about certain institutional possibilities of social action that are not possible through other institutional frames, such as the corporation or the state. If institutional structures generate certain possibilities, what are the possibilities generated by nonprofit-ness? Because of the unique structure of nonprofits, certain things are foreclosed: profit, for example, and in many cases financial independence.

Political philosopher Chantal Mouffe (2013), in her book *Agonistics*, offers a way out of the conceptual binary of radical politics versus hegemony. Mouffe argues that conflict is built into democracy and that debates involved in radical politics always produce conflict. Agonism, as opposed to antagonism, is a pressure valve that releases tensions and protects against violence. Given that conflict is constitutive of hegemony and cannot be overcome, it must be accepted. Mouffe argues for a pluralism that does not reconcile all views: not everything can be resolved. This itself has become a political stance. Arturo Escobar (2018) argues in favor of a quest for political autonomy in relation to global capitalism's hegemonic domination, a quest to be undertaken particularly by indigenous groups, marginalized communities, and those living in the Global South. If democratic politics is a process of hegemonic influence and inherent counter-hegemonic challenge, the "democratic paradox," for Mouffe (129–46), is the fact that antagonism is the political and it cannot be removed. Democratic politics involves conflict.

Hegemony is a basic function of political order, and it contains an always implicit challenge to its existence. Antonio Gramsci (1971) writes about counter-hegemonic struggles as "wars of positions" that wedge a crack in structures of power and suggest avenues for change. There is hope in this theoretical orientation—that political orders can be transformed. For example, nonprofits may be counter-hegemonic to capitalism, standing in as a possible threat to the prevailing order, of another way of doing business. Yet, counter-hegemonic forces always contain the potential to become new hegemonic forces themselves: nonprofits may become an arm of the state. Each counter-hegemonic struggle builds upon previous struggles, building solidarity for mobilization (cf. Mouffe's "chain of equivalences," 2013, 133). The Left does not have a monopoly on these tactics, and the Right has also skillfully utilized these mechanisms to gain support for their political agendas. This basic model of entrenched contest, Gramsci's "war of positions," which references the trench warfare of World War I with its tunnels and strategic practices of digging in in order to gain ground, is a contentious political terrain. In contemporary politics as well, nonprofits and NGOs have been weaponized by both the Right and the Left to fight their strategic political battles and to achieve their political aims. Mouffe's work analyzes the project of democracy as it is fought through the critique of existing institutions. In the case of Indian NPOs, they fight for legal reform of the nonprofit sector by working from within. Their efforts contrast with the radical art of refusal that rejects institutional forms as inherently hegemonic.[4] An agonistic approach involves adversaries who recognize the legitimacy and demands of their opponents, and accept rules according to which conflict can be regulated. Indian advocacy NGOs worked with existing governmental institutions in order to engage with, and change policies.[5] Agonistic politics are not antagonistic politics, though they do involve conflict. The agonistic model is "conflictual consensus," an alternative to deliberative models that require resolution and aggressive models that demand radical opposition.[6]

Let's start with the proposition that nonprofits are agonistic. They may have been brought into the state as social welfare providers. They may challenge the state to try to better it or to change it. Threatened by this counter-hegemonic force, the state may crack down via regulation and law. The Indian state, has controlled the nonprofit form through regulation, reducing threats that civil society groups can pose to governmental legitimacy. Nonprofits challenge the state through the language of representation; they seek entitlements for marginalized groups, and in the process, call attention to the failures of the state, highlighting inadequacies and foregrounding deficiencies. In turn, the state retaliates with its own representational arsenal, by calling out nonprofits as corrupt, bad, or failures, and implementing regulatory mechanisms to control them and/or facilitate their work in relation to the state. When threatened, the state shuts down NGOs, requires extra bureaucratic procedures, provides them with hoops to jump through, papers to file, regulations to abide by. This agonistic struggle always threatens to become antagonistic. If the aim of hegemonic change is to transform state institutions, and as nonprofits try to do this it requires agonistic engagement. When I asked the director of an Indian NPO what they did, he said: "we agitate." In India, NGOs also represented their own hegemony, described by Choudry and Kapoor (2013) as "NGOization." They did not operate outside the system; they worked from within for reform.

A Reckoning

Four years after the 2013 convention discussed here, I met with a foundation director who reflected on the changes he had seen in recent years. Prime Minister Narendra Modi and the Bharatiya Janata Party (BJP) had come to power, and the laws that had just been passed in 2013 had since found their rhythms of implementation. What was on the horizon in 2013 had come to be a new reality in 2017. As an NGO activist, the foundation director was involved with the Planning Commission, writing reports and framing sustainable development goals, and was instrumental in writing the Civil Society Report. Civil society organizations were part of all of the governmental ministries; they were everywhere, so at that time the input from civil society groups was integral to governmental policy making and planning processes regarding development. The change was not about all civil society groups being kept out of planning processes. He said, reflectively, "It's our kind of civil society which has come down. There's another civil society which has gone up." He referred to the Hindu majoritarian Right, which had gained ground as a grassroots, Right-leaning, civil society political movement. Earlier, when he had worked to challenge the Twelfth Five Year Plan, people like him were considered sellouts by hardcore activists, because they worked from within the state. He reflected on the changing nature of the relationship between civil society and the state and expressed an urgency regarding identifying what was taking place. The comfort that many NGO leaders experienced regarding their input on governmental processes was changing, and some NGOs were being frozen out of the dialogue. "We need to figure that out," he said.

> We are the ones who created those spaces and a model where we were very comfortable. We thought that we would be able to formalize spaces, or say, the national advisory council, which you know, which had all our friends. We were all very happy that we had direct access to [Sonia Gandhi], the Prime Minister. We could get any legislation, not necessarily passed, but onto the highest table. [. . .] That's something that we've created.

However, since that time, the political Right had taken on the tactics of the Left and deployed them better, on a bigger scale, with a larger purview. In 2017, civil society groups were no longer being consulted. For people like him, who had successfully entered the state in order to work

with it, the government seemed to be pulling back from civil society collaboration. Before, he was critical of the government, but there was a space
for dialogue.

By 2017, the agonistic politics had become antagonistic. What does it
mean for NGOs and nonprofits to be co-opted by the state? Beyond their
service functions and access to specific, sometimes remote or marginalized, populations, which are critical spaces of government-supported welfare, we may consider the process of co-optation itself a particular type
of legal engagement, and as Laura Nader has written, "harmony ideology."[7] The harmony model—of alternative dispute resolution—was institutionalized into a "soft post-confrontational mode," a type of "controlling
process." Legal consensus-building is an ideological process that becomes
the status quo and supports ruling elites.[8] As harmony becomes a virtue,
consensus is sought in a move toward conflict avoidance, and the valoriz-
ing of negotiation domesticates the unruly language of rights and their
concomitant demands.

In 2017, at a conference roundtable, some of the same NPO leaders that
had attended the 2013 annual convention gathered together to discuss ways
forward, after the implementation of the Companies Act and revisions
to the FCRA, both which had changed the horizon line of their work.
The arena for civil society had shrunk between 2013 and 2017, and the
tone had changed; a new sentiment, one of fear, pervaded the discussion.
The civil society roundtable was an emergency meeting and a collective
reckoning, where strategies for moving forward were discussed. It was a
flashpoint, not an end but a moment of legal reform frozen in time. Some
of this reform was due to civil society engagement through law. Some was
due to implementation initiatives, birthed by civil society's dialogue with
the government, which were then extracted by the government and used
to control the nonprofit sector and to silence critique and dissent. Civil
society had entered the governmental terrain and had been kicked out. In
2017, it was standing outside closed doors, fearful of reprisal through laws
such as the FCRA and the Companies Act, which civil society groups had
agitated to reform.

So much had changed in the intervening years between the gathering
of the convention and the reckoning of the conference. In my conversations
with leaders of the sector, many paused to reflect on these shifts. Those involved with leading civil society as grant-makers and philanthropic influ-
encers had earlier enjoyed a collaborative framework with the government.

Some were involved in the Planning Commission, served on special committees, and engaged in conversations and consultations surrounding the development of five year plans. There was respect and dialogue between civil society organizations and the government. A CSO leader described their efforts in the Five Year Plan consultations as "anchoring that entire process." They said: "I could walk into their office. That was the level. I would go and say, 'What are you doing?' They would listen to me with respect." NGOs gave critiques to the government, and the government not only listened, but acted upon details of the critiques, using them to govern better. At one point, the government even distributed a critical report that an NGO had written. By 2017, however, the relationship between civil society and the government had become a "confrontational framework." NGOs were being frozen out of the dialogue and they were no longer being consulted.

One thing that had changed was the political leadership of the nation. The BJP was elected in 2104. Governmental schemes upon which Narendra Modi's party had campaigned were posted on billboards. They were also sticking points in conversations with Activist Donors. Some saw the toilet building and public sanitation campaign efforts as interfering with "people's rights to access public funds" for water and sanitation. Toilets were constructed and not used. Public service announcements appeared in the form of movies—*Toilet: A Love Story* (2017)[9] and *Pad Man* (2018)[10]—in which male villagers came to see the values of building toilets for women and providing menstrual products for their female kin. These arenas, of social terrain, had been the work of the NGO sector, especially in villages. Now, in urban centers like Delhi, the blockbuster films appeared in major cinema halls, touting the progressive nature of change. Yet, this populism had a darker side. Activist Donors spoke of the context in which they worked as hurting minority groups, of the army perpetrating human rights violations, of increased mob violence, and of "fascism" (a word that was used). Secular India was being challenged by a majoritarian Hindu India, politically promoted by the government, if not by action then by its silences. Civil servants were not part of this change, and many of them experienced fear alongside NGO-sector workers stemming from increased surveillance and reprisals for critique and dissent.

The Activist Donors were vocal and strong in their critique, denouncing the CSR provision in the Companies Act as it was not political, did not support rights-based work, and did nothing to challenge corporations.

CSR could not be involved in political conversations. Because CSR was mandated by the government, it changed with the new government and the business lobby. It effectively squeezed civil society out from governmental social service programs, at least those working in policy instead of service provision. Corporations were building their own foundations, headed by HR personnel guiding "run of the mill projects." The law was only aspirational, some said. "Responsibility should mean justice," one Activist Donor remarked, and corporations did not do justice work. Some Activist Donors articulated the need to unhinge philanthropy from the corporate sector in order to do their justice work.

There were also serious issues of legislative implementation, gaps between the progressive laws advocated for by civil society groups and society itself. Laws had changed, but society had not. That CSR was aspirational—a new horizon line to contend with—made this gap painfully obvious to those who strove to make change. Some Activist Donors argued CSR was out of civil society. "We don't speak the same language," they said; civil society and corporations worked with different time horizons and objectives. NGOs used a long-term strategy focused on social change, with ten-year models, and goals of protecting democracy. Corporations, in contrast, focused on "outputs and outcomes," with different success metrics, lists of acceptable activities (which did not include the protection of democracy), and projects that ran in the short term of a fiscal year. They also supported the status quo. The battle lines had been drawn, not only between civil society and corporations through the government's implementation of the CSR provision in the Companies Act, but also in the distinction between civil and political society.[11] Civil society had become a fringe player in politics, though it was still engaged in the political battle to "protect the republic." Political society, meanwhile, had sought access to state power.

What were Activist Donors to do? They did not sit quietly and complain. They realized that philanthropy was political, that philanthropists were free—they did not depend on donations, didn't need to raise funds, and in this sense, they had no constraints. Their fiscal flows, and giving practices, were regulated by registration laws governing trusts, societies, and charitable companies. Because these were Indian donors, their funds were not governed by the FCRA, though this situation would later be proposed for reform in the 2023 Finance Bill, which included provisions for regulating inter-charity domestic donations with increased scrutiny and a heavy hand. At the time, regulation could structure the funding flows of trusts, societies, and charitable companies, but not the content of their work. It did not determine where their money went or the types of projects upon which their money was spent. Some found a solution by going "under the radar" and by working on new forms of "collaborative philanthropy" and "activist philanthropy." "Don't be loud," one Activist Donor said. How does one make change when social advocacy is dangerous? Others used different terms—"strategic philanthropy" instead of "social justice." They sought to inspire new ways to tackle Dalit discrimination by investing in school uniforms or making classrooms inclusive. Some tried to approach the CSR trend as a grant-maker, by encouraging investment in certain areas, by not accepting CSR because it did not address development or social choice, and by taking an advocacy role in the grant-making landscape: one could "get $200,000 or influence $20 million" one Activist Donor explained, "We don't need resources. If we can influence where the money is going, we would be delighted."

Activist Donors dealt with governmental pushback to their efforts partly from their privileged structural positions. Indian foundations were difficult to hate. When their outspoken participation was questioned in governmental circles, they were careful to follow the law, and did not attack specific people. Class privilege helped, as did their social networks and connections, though nobody was immune. Many recounted the story of Public Health Foundation India (PHFI), which had become a parable in the nonprofit sector, repeated to me as a warning: the foundation had worked with the government, and its FCRA license was cancelled (Singh 2022). Civil servants were also afraid, whispering in hushed tones with me over lunch, in case someone who was not open to critique overheard their concerns. It was a question of strategy. Some asked, "Were we wrong" for "sleeping with the enemy" and "working so closely with the government on development and change?" They argued that one couldn't see the state as the enemy and that the primary job of the civil sector was "to make power accountable." There was a problem with being exclusive, they said, as they existed in the same social and political space. New lessons had been learned: that they should not be in such a close relationship with the state and that their job was "to remain outside the state."

Professional Critics, the directors of large and powerful Indian NGOs, had become spokespeople for the sector. They organized forums, funded smaller NGOs, worked with the government on policy for the sector, and were prominent in conversations surrounding reform of legislation that touched the sector. Because of their stature in India and the historical role of their organizations in providing services, implementing national policies, and leading the sector, they were not targeted themselves—yet—though they were vocal, and critical about the legislative reform reorienting India's nonprofit sector. A few Professional Critics argued that the government blamed NGOs for its national economic woes: for example, in the Intelligence Bureau report of 2015, and the crackdown on nonprofits. A product of the new government–voluntary sector relationship was increased surveillance, emergent in the relationship between legal reform and implementation, specifically regarding the FCRA and the Companies Act. In the FCRA, the answer to "What defines political activity?" had still not been clearly determined. The BJP had become a watchdog in certain areas, especially in regions where mining and other extractive industries took place. The CSR provision in the Companies Act came to be intimately tied to surveillance of "troublemakers."

One Professional Critic experienced increased auditing of their NGO. Nonprofits, even large well-established ones, were increasingly under scrutiny. They considered this tactic an aspect of the drive to crush dissent in the country. They regularly received scrutiny letters; one received them annually. What did such letters entail?

> Under scrutiny means they will call you to the income tax office. You have to take all your records. It is an audit. And they'll ask you for all kinds of details. So, they'll ask you why did you hire a venue for a conference. You know? You have to show all your records. You'll be asked the most inane questions by somebody who doesn't understand your work. "Show me your salary structure." Questions we'll get, "What does the CEO get?" "Why are you being paid x amount?" Yeah, "Why are you being paid? Why are you not voluntary?"

Whether this scrutiny was due to their financial threshold, being larger NGOs, or due to the type of work they did was debated. "Why do NGOs need to exist in this country?" was a key question about which Professional Critics had much to say. They provided jobs, raised their own funds, didn't pollute the environment, and stepped in where government had failed society. In fact, many asserted, social welfare began with civil society groups, which had taken nothing from the public and would not destroy the planet. Accountability itself, one Professional Critic emphasized, was tied to not-for-profit work and voluntarism in the sector. "I think for accountability you need to have some kind of non-paid work so that the sector is seen as voluntary," they explained.

Regulatory reform had had a "chilling effect" on the sector, and in this environment, space was shrinking for NGOs. The government was encouraging CSR funds to be channeled to the government, and not to the nonprofit sector. If civil society in India had been the conscience of the nation, "now the government is its own conscience." Professional Critics lamented it had been a mistake to assume the FCRA was simply governmental bureaucracy and that the law would not be used against the sector. "We slept through it," one remarked. Professional Critics argued that giving funds for CSR couldn't wash away corporate sins: "If you've made a profit while harming the environment, people's rights, and all of that, and the top spenders are, of course, the biggest violators." Moreover, mandatory CSR was "bad for corporate responsibility." The landscape had bifurcated, between government and corporations on one side and NGOs and activists who were increasingly afraid on the other. They considered CSR a form of co-optation, "shut up money" so that NGOs didn't raise their voices against the government, and a "hype and smokescreen for corporate misdeeds." A preferable approach, they argued, was for corporations to be scrutinized, and indeed, some NGOs were working on this. An even better approach, a Professional Critic explained, would be to encourage corporations to be legitimate corporate citizens:

> We're saying you have to be a legitimate corporate citizen. That's the first threshold. That we establish you do no harm. And then, we can talk to you about maybe whether [you are] equipped to do some good, but should you pass the test, if your products and services and being in existence has degraded the environment and has caused all kinds of problems and has led to your oil workers adding to deeper poverty and they're ruining your land with their lobbying for land, for your lower tariffs, for your tax holidays, all of this. And then, what good is this ill-gotten profit that you've raised as a result of such work.[. . .] When you talk to corporate house you must pass them on the same lens that you pass an NGO, and they want to work in partnership with me, as a nonprofit. They want to know my governance structure. They want to know my finances. Similarly, I would like to know where you're registered: in Canterbury Islands, Cayman Islands, Mauritius, you know? I'd like to know what the tax cases you have piled up against. I'd like to know your financials. I'd like to know what's your governance. So, I want to only

work with you on a level playing field as equal partners where we look at each other's facts and figures and then we decide to collaborate or not. You're not my benefactor, if anything, I bring you my years of work and experience on the ground.

NGOs were being left behind in CSR efforts. The problem with corporate philanthropy was that money came from industry, which was dependent on governmental permissions. "If you piss off the government, you really can't survive in this country," one Professional Critic said. Another exclaimed that CSR had become a form of service delivery, as CSR funds were increasingly directed to the government (Sundar 2018). Professional Critics argued it would be better to fund the social sector through taxes.

The devil was in the details regarding the new landscape of regulation, including CSR implementation. The law was formed at the center, but implementation was the state's responsibility, and it depended on NGOs to do the implementing. The reformed Companies Act made corporations more self-interested and enhanced existing inequalities. Banking and IT sectors were the largest industries, but they were located in urban areas. Since the CSR provision directed funds to be spent locally, this left rural villages out of the calculus: as one Professional Critic remarked, "Corporates do not exist at village level. It is only the NGOs who are existing and resisting." CSR redirected funds and created new funding tributaries.

International corporations working in India started local Indian offices incorporated as Indian institutional bodies. When these Indian subsidiaries would give CSR funds, those funds were Indian, not foreign. "It's all Indian money now," one Professional Critic exclaimed. Local companies gave to NGOs through CSR (or to the government), bypassing the restrictive FCRA. In this context, political scandals also became a contextual backdrop (as, for example, in the Vedanta mining case described by Joseph Kirschke, 2013). What were NGOs to do? They had no choice but to change their strategy and fundraise locally. One prominent NGO shifted such that 95 percent of its funds were supported by Indian donors. The utopia envisioned during the early CSR anticipation had passed. The Accountability Guides reminisced about how, in the early days, there was hope the CSR provision would bring NGOs and corporations to the same table, but that utopia was a dream. Instead, a brain drain redirected social sector labor from voluntary-sector to corporate-sector CSR programs.

The Supreme Court demanded the government create a system to evaluate and monitor voluntary-sector organizations (Rautray 2017). Some

Accountability Guides, as well as some of the Professional Critics had been invited to serve on the special committees to develop these evaluative models. At first, it seemed hopeful that civil society leaders were at the table, though expectations at that point were minimal. One recounted that he had been part of the committee but that he considered his role to consist of moderating opinions, "otherwise you will have five bureaucrats telling 'hang the voluntary sector.'" For the Accountability Guides, concerns stemmed from the fact that the FCRA had gone online, and there was nobody to appeal to. The new, and constantly revised, requirements created confusion if not panic. One could interpret the crackdown on the sector as a bureaucratic response to growing dissent and critique, or as a governmental response that turned political issues into technical ones (cf. "technomoral politics" as described in Bornstein and Sharma 2016). There was more at stake than rules and regulations and whether or not they were being followed. One Accountability Guide remarked in an interview that civil society was part of the "ideas brigade," representing the intellectuals who were ahead of society. Society, they emphasized, was slow to adapt, and this caused conflict. They assured me that conflict will always be there. It was just that the leaders of social change, in the ideas brigade, were vulnerable to their reliance on foreign funding. This was agonistic politics.

The Accountability Guides were concerned with what happened to the NPOs that struggled with the rules. Punitive responses were increasingly meted against rule-breakers and/or those that ignored governmental requirements. Moreover, certain groups, such as Christian NGOs, were being targeted (Bhalla 2017; Barry and Raj 2017). With the Hindu Right in the seat of power, governmental bureaucracy was not neutral. The effect of this, according to the Accountability Guides was species decline. The voluntary sector was being professionalized. "Now it's a job" one remarked, "These new managers had proper degrees. They would say, 'We want a good job. It's a good job.' It has become from that spirit to the job orientation, and then they come as the job for them." Due to the politics of the FCRA and the CSR provision in the Companies Act, the FCRA had become seemingly apolitical and CSR "completely safe." And "not only that, they need to stay on the right side of the customers. And they can't be seen on, going gung-ho on issues which will challenge existing social norms." The extinction of the smaller NGOs was a new loss, occurring due to the emphasis on institutional literacy and the fact that the increased infrastructure required for legitimacy cost more. As NGOs tended to protest in areas where large corporations worked, such as extractive industries, they were bound to conflict with corporate agendas and the state. In response to this new landscape, the Accountability Guides worked on processes of certification and "norms enforcement," educating NGOs on "how to prove you're a good NGO." Certification in donor circles was a form of symbolic capital—if an institution was deemed reliable,[12] funding streams could be encouraged. One NGO worked to develop a norms brochure, formalizing governance standards for the voluntary sector, though it was also aware that the process eliminated certain types of organizations from its certification programs. Another group worked on trainings, with accountants and legal advocates, to educate the sector on how to report correctly.

Conclusion

In the civil society roundtable of 2017, leaders came together to strategize a way forward. One leader remarked that civic space was expanding, but for whom? The government was giving support to their own civil society organizations as there was an ideological sync between the right wing and the government. The BJP was building the grassroots, delegitimizing NGOs from the professional classes, and in the process, stigmatizing NGOs. Civil society groups were losing freedom, owing to fear. Witch hunting was going on, student protests were targeted, and international NGOs could no longer criticize the government (see Baviskar 2023 for a broader critique; also see Human Rights Watch 2023). Right to Information activists were being threatened (Sharma 2024). Leaders spoke of how CSR had become machinery to destroy dissent. The government was controlling the money and competing with NGOs for CSR funds, and Indian funds were difficult to raise for democracy and justice programs. The group discussed the possible role of an ombudsman, to deal with conflict and fear. Then a very senior NGO visionary, a well-respected Professional Critic, stood up to speak. He argued that we "need to speak a different language." What do young people want? They wanted clothes, mobiles, sex, love. By focusing on deficits, he proposed, voluntary groups may have stopped the conversation with the youth of the next generation and lost touch with their aspirations. He lamented that NGOs had not done enough to instill a rights discourse into India. Perhaps, he suggested, our effort is "to find a new song and start writing the music for it now."

Through reform, the Indian government's regulatory shifts altered the work that NPOs were able to do within the frame of state legitimacy. This was neither without consequence nor struggle, and many nonprofits worked to reform the state through engagement in the regulatory process. These local struggles had historical precedents and prior patterns of engagement. In India, one must understand regulatory reform in its historical context. Between 2010 and 2020, India's nonprofit sector experienced a rapid regulatory reform of laws structuring NPO registration, foreign donations, and corporate social responsibility. The registration laws, many of which dated to the colonial era and included laws for societies and trusts, were part of a cluster of mechanisms that the state used to regulate the sector, and their revision altered policy for nonprofits. Previously, NPO registration laws were state based, with some states instituting extra regulatory previsions. The revisions to the FCRA in 2010 and the Companies Act in 2013 added a new, central, national frame for nonprofit -sector regulation. This, along with discussions regarding revisions to the Income Tax Act (proposed as a new Direct Taxes Code),[13] shaped policy dialogues between nonprofits, civil servants, and lawmaking bodies. The actors represented in this book wrangled with these laws in the making and aimed to affect their revision, rule-writing, and implementation.

This chapter started with a hopeful convention in 2013, when NGOs and NPOs came together as a group, and a sector, to engage in their own survival. The regulatory shifts that were to become solidified into laws were then on the horizon. Policy making for NPOs included rewriting the horizon line. By 2017, the shifts had taken place, with the entry of new corporate actors inhabiting a space of potential welfare provision. The governmental directives that centralized regulatory control of nonprofits through philanthropic regulation of foreign funding and a mandatory corporate social welfare tax were state instruments. In this context, NPOs used the tools at their disposal—workshops, conventions, conferences, meetings, and writing reports—to speak to the state and to write the horizon line of nonprofit policy.

TWO

Charitable Purpose as a Political, Regulatory Frame

In 2023, the Government of India proposed a Finance Bill to regulate charitable and religious purpose, tax exemption and liability. It contained stipulations for regulating inter-charity donations, including those by NPOs and corporations to other NPOs, with new rules for reporting (FMSF 2023; Centre for Advancement of Philanthropy [CAP India] 2023). The Bill proposed increased scrutiny and regulatory provisions for surveilling donations in the domestic sphere, adding onto existing FCRA regulations for foreign donations, and it brought punitive tactics and regulation provisions to domestic NPOs, much as the revised FCRA of 2010 had done for foreign funding. Many of these new restrictions would be carried out through the legal instrument and regulatory frame of *charitable purpose*. The detailed initiatives in the 2023 Finance Bill included removing a "retrospective exemptions benefit" (FMSF 2023), through which NPOs could apply for a tax exemption for charitable purpose via registration under Section 12AB of the Income Tax Act, 1961. The benefit had earlier allowed NPOs that were identified by the government as genuine charitable organizations a tax exemption for past years. The prospect of removing this provision presented potential hardships for NPOs with registrations already granted. In terms of inter-charity donations, the new rules and regulations in the 2023 Finance Bill identified a new threshold for allowable tax deductions for charitable donations, and specified where NPOs could apply donations. The Finance Bill of 2023 would affect NGOs sub-granting to smaller organizations.

From the colonial era to the post-pandemic present, across political parties and regimes of rule, charitable purpose has become a regulatory horizon line for social and political reform. Charitable purpose is a legal category, a conceptual frame, and a regulatory tool that has been used to define nonprofit practice, historically and in the present. It is also a category through which philanthropic donations to charitable groups are regulated. It is through charitable purpose that nonprofits become legible and governable. Thus, to explore charitable purpose is to understand the regulatory power of a legal category that resides at the heart of civil-society state relations in India. This chapter sketches a history of reform through the lens of charitable purpose. It lays the groundwork for understanding contemporary reform initiatives in the Indian nonprofit sector taking place through debates over charitable purpose. The chapter is divided into five historical sections, each of which explores the regulation of charitable organizations, philanthropy, and charitable purpose in a specific era. Laws are called Acts in India and I explore them as active spaces of political negotiation. Though the chapter periodizes patterns, I do not intend the eras outlined to represent a rigid chronology of events. I hope readers will see the iterative flow, the back-and-forth nature of struggles over legitimacy and public good fought through the regulation of nonprofits, via what can legally, and legitimately, be deemed of "charitable purpose."

The story of charitable purpose is one of philanthropic regulation, of tax exemption, and of service to the public good. Laws governing charitable purpose include tax laws, registration laws for nonprofits, and laws restricting charitable donations. The laws passed and revised to regulate philanthropy to NPOs in India address different aspects of charitable purpose and create rules for governing particular types of donations. They include, in addition to the Finance Bill mentioned earlier, the Societies and Trusts Acts of the 1800s, which segregated public and private, and religious and secular charitable purpose; the Income Tax Act, which defined tax-exempt donations; the FCRA (1976; 2010; 2020), which restricted political and foreign donations; and the Companies Act (1956; 2013), which defined charitable companies and mandated a corporate social responsibility tax on large companies. I mention the 2023 Finance Bill to signal that the historical debates I analyze represent historical patterns continuing today. Debates over the 2023 Finance Bill took place in a moment in time, but they represent a starting point for analyzing the history of legal reform. I start here in order to understand a historical pattern of socio-legal processes.

In the colonial era, categories of incorporation for societies and trusts were used to govern civil society associations. These institutional forms created a taxonomy of philanthropic intent, mapped onto distinctions of whether a group was religious or secular, and benefited an abstract public or private group. Distinctions, which mapped onto categories of colonial administrative governance, are still part of contemporary registration laws governing the nonprofit sector today. During the Independence struggle and in the early period of nation building, charitable groups were considered political but not punished for their nation-building work. During this era, the Income Tax Act (1961) outlined tax-exempt status, and the Companies Act (1956), created the category of charitable companies. Both of these laws have since become arenas of voluntary-sector advocacy. During post-Independence nation building, the idea of trusteeship, which was crucial to the legal form of the trust, was taken up by national reformers to promote social stewardship. Reform movements collaborated with the state and sought to reform it. During the Emergency, in the mid-1970s, the government sought to control political influence by restricting foreign philanthropy to political groups via the FCRA (1976). After the Emergency, civil society groups entered the state once again to reform it, becoming "watchdogs" of the state, and initiating legal mechanisms to hold the state accountable, such as Public Interest Litigation (Deo and McDuie-Ra 2011; De 2018), which institutionalized the capacity for individuals and civil society groups to challenge the state and demand legal reform.

As India globalized and liberalized its economy, charitable purpose was re-politicized through rights-based discourses of reform. International NGOs and local civil society actors sought to reform the state through law (Merry 2006; Keck and Sikkink 1998 for global context; Deo and McDuie-Ra 2011 for India). NGOs in India worked to pass a slate of social-reform legislation focused on issues such as women's rights, education, and anti-poverty in the heyday of global nonprofits and the period of associational reform. During this time, international organizations shied away from funding state welfare programs globally because governments were considered clientelist, illegitimate, inefficient, and possibly corrupt. Charitable institutions such as NGOs "mushroomed" and were hailed as a space for "good governance" and democratic change.

In late liberalized India, charitable purpose was revisited and reformed once again, recalibrating trusts, societies, and charitable companies in relation to charitable purpose, and redefining charitable purpose in tax law. In the early 2000s, the voluntary sector tried, and failed, to pass a national policy on the voluntary sector.[1] Corporations entered as new actors in national programs of social welfare through revisions to the Companies Act, and foreign donations were restricted through revisions to the FCRA. Reforms to the category of charitable purpose through the regulatory revisions increased nonprofit dependence on domestic donations for their survival, limited philanthropic support for political engagement, and altered what nonprofits could do in the name of public good. Between 2010 and 2020, the FCRA, the Companies Act, and the Income Tax Act were all revised to become more stringent. The shift began with the Congress Party and continued with more force when the BJP was elected to govern in 2014.

The broad historical context I sketch here is taken for granted by those working in the nonprofit sector, a type of collective institutional memory and shared knowledge for nonprofit workers who lived through more than one of the historical periods and engaged with one or more of the legal turning points. Each era brought new concerns, trends, preferred orientations and regulatory initiatives. During my research, as I spoke with those trying to reform the sector, the history was a reference point mentioned in passing as "the way things have been," demanding an always urgent "need for change" by nonprofit workers. At times it was recounted as an exercise in collective memory and solidarity building. Leaders of charitable organizations have been on the frontlines of advocating for change, and as social reformers their efforts to define and redefine the category of charitable purpose represented efforts to delimit state responsibility. In their dance with the state, NPOs worked out the boundaries and authorities of the state through shifting taxonomies of charitable action in a process of articulation that defined the non-state sphere as much as it defined the state. Thus, this chapter is a story of reformers and the state, through shifting historical periods and historically distinct understandings of charitable purpose governing philanthropic regulation. What belonged in the category and what did not, was evident in processes of drafting, negotiating over, and implementing law governing nonprofit, "charitable" organizations, and their funding flows.

The term *civil society*, used today to discuss reform movements, is an umbrella term that refers to varied forms of collective advocacy, in the world and in India, that occur in a sphere of political and social activity separate from the state and market (Deo and McDuie-Ra 2011; also Gramsci 1971). Civic actors involved in social reform constitute a broad range of agents and institutional configurations, including social movements, advocacy networks, community organizations, grassroots collectives, political parties, trade unions, and institutions that many would term nonprofit. Not all actors in civil society share a normative vision, and not all use progressive methods. The categories used, however, often have moral tones.[2] When civil society actors become institutions and not simply movements, incorporating as trusts, societies, or charitable companies, they are legally allowed to receive donations on behalf of a group and work toward public good—via charitable purpose. These institutional categories provide pathways for philanthropic support that initiate state oversight and governance. Nonprofits, and charitable organizations, register with the state (unlike social movements). Thus, they are in unique positions to negotiate with the state regarding laws defining charitable purpose.[3] In India today, nonprofits are required to register with the government as either societies, trusts, or charitable companies.

Colonial Reform: Charitable Gifts to Abstract Publics

New institutional forms for social groups—including incorporation for trusts and societies—were used by the British colonial administration in India to govern civil society, and in this process, charitable purpose was codified into law. Registration and incorporation laws for trusts and societies birthed the legal instrument of charitable purpose, that articulated a taxonomy based on donor intent: whether public or private, religious or secular. These new legal forms, governing charitable trusts and mortmain,[4] emerged simultaneously in Britain and in its Indian colony. The legal form of the trust in Britain was a precursor to the corporation and was based on F. W. Maitland's "tripartite contract" among (1) donors, (2) beneficiaries of the donor's gift, and (3) trustees that administer the gift.[5] In Victorian England, the trust concept encompassed both private trusts designed for the benefit of dependents such as widows and children, and public charitable trusts. The distinction between private and public charitable trusts was imported to India in the 1880s, during the same time the distinction was being codified in England (Birla 2009). A shift had taken place in

British case law regarding the concept of charity, from something benefiting a specific community to something benefiting an abstract notion of the public. This distinction existed concurrently with other legal fields and judicialized arenas such as civil law, which was territorial and secular (cf. also the concept of Personal Law; and see Kassam et al. 2016; Williams 2010).

The Indian Trusts Act of 1882 clarified procedures for public charitable trusts. In England, a charitable gift was one that was given with the clear intention of public benefit, to an abstract public: "If the intention of the donor was to benefit specific individuals, the gift was not considered charitable" (Birla 2009, 70; also see MacFarlane 2002; Maitland 2003). If the donor aimed to accomplish the abstract purpose of relieving poverty or advancing education or religion without giving any particular individuals the right to claim the funds, the gift was considered charitable. Charitable gifts were defined as benefiting only abstract others, such as causes, not specific persons, in a distinction that became critical to the emergence of the trust as a legal concept. By the turn of the century, the trustee had become the model figure of an ethical subject, a financial steward of corporations and charitable institutions (Maitland 2003). Charitable purpose included relief for the poor, education, medical relief, or "advancement for any other object of general public utility but does not include a purpose which relates exclusively to religious teaching or worship" (Birla 2009, 100).

Religion in British trust law was segregated from charitable purpose regarding abstract, general publics (also see Mansfield 2001). In practice, however, religious philanthropy in India did not fit the distinction between public and private social welfare. Hindu conceptions of *daan* conceptualized gifts as given through *dharma*, which relied upon an ethic of duty, and specified times to give and specific persons to receive gifts (such as a priests, or *sadhus*/renunciants). Righteous conduct could not be contained by the category of religion or limited to the realm of belief, as in England. The question of intent that British trust law imposed on philanthropic donation did not fit the living practices of giving and donation in either colonial or pre-colonial India, which straddled boundaries of public and private benefits from gifts as well as religious and secular concerns (Bornstein 2012a). Thus the colonial legal mode of a trust contract was imposed upon relational webs of affiliation that had historically supported social welfare through extended family networks, family temples, family deities, and merchant castes for Hindu communities, and waqf and zakat practices for Muslim ones (Birla 2009, 68; Benthall 2011 regarding zakat in

Islam and debates over cultural proximity). Colonial legislation regarding charitable purpose via the Trusts and Societies Acts was part of a colonial effort to control financial capital considered to be out of circulation; for example, in kinship and mercantile networks structured through kin, such as those circulating capital within the "Hindu Undivided Family (or, HUF)" (Birla 2009). This private domain of circulation hindered the movement of colonial capital, particularly within the extensive kinship networks and clan associations that facilitated merchant business by groups such as the Marwaris in northern and eastern India (Birla 2009; see Vevaina 2023 for a contemporary analysis). Mortmain law, which referred to the perpetual holding of land by a company or a charitable trust, was used in British colonial India to establish a rule against perpetual holdings except in the case of charitable gifts. The distinction between public and private charitable trusts "recoded customary social welfare" as belonging to a separate domain of religion and culture in relation to taxation. It was a pattern also visible in colonial responses to famine relief that privileged institutional forms of charity instead of those that were affinal, associational, and more informal (see Sharma 2001, 135–92, and Greenough 1982 for examples, and Powers 1989 for a parallel process regarding Muslim family endowments).

The trust contract in British law mirrored the model of the rights-based joint-stock shareholder, responsible for the company. Public discourse in Britain and India began to associate trust beneficiaries' rights with procedures used to protect shareholders and linked to public accounts and audits. Religious gifts, as well, fell into this legislation and were divided into those that were public (charitable religious trusts) and those that were private (religious endowments). The language of rights and beneficiaries, the distinction between public and private welfare, and the notion of trust, became contractual in relation to the charitable gift governed through colonial capitalism. The discursive shift from charity to known others or informal religious giving to institutionally regulated philanthropy that protected fiscal rights and responsibilities fit into the modernist conception of scientific philanthropy, which was distinguished from charity and was being advocated in Britain and the United States (see Gross 2003 and Friedman 2003). British colonial laws governing charitable donations (philanthropy), which included the Societies Registration Act, the Charitable Trusts Acts, and the Tax Acts instituted in the 1800s, although amended, are still part of the Indian legal landscape today, and nonprofits engage with this legal legacy on a daily basis (Rajaratnam et al. 2009; Agarwal and Dadrawala 2004; Dadrawala 2003).[6]

Legislation of the 1800s, including the governance of societies, trusts, and religious endowments, codified colonial distinctions between the social welfare of abstract publics and the social welfare of members of an organization that reaped benefits, such as religious groups. After independence, the Indian Tax and Companies Acts, passed in the 1950s and 1960s, reinforced notions of charity as gifts to an abstract public and provided tax exemption incentives for organizations with the category charitable institutional status. Collectively, the British laws for charitable trusts, societies, and endowments focused on the intention of the gift by the donor, which fit the British trust law paradigm. However, the segregation of religious and secular reform did not make sense in colonial India, as many nationalist social reform movements were religious (Deo and McDuie-Ra 2011). For example, Rammohun Roy, who established Brahmo Samaj as a response to British missionary activists in Bengal and supported the abolition of sati (1829), focused on education and property rights of women. Dayananda Saraswati established the Arya Samaj in 1875, which promoted women's education, opposed dowry and child marriage, and focused on the Vedas (an ancient Hindu text) to purify the religion. The Rashtriya Swayamsevak Sangh (RSS) was also formed during this time. These vibrant civil society organizations were religious reform groups that worked closely with the state, forging a connection that enhanced their public legitimacy alongside that of the state. Funded by the Indian elite and small local donations, these reform movements were linked to political parties. At Independence, their political connections would become beneficial as reformers became the leaders of newly independent India (Deo and McDuie-Ra 2011).

Charitable Purpose in National Reform: From Gifts to Rights

During struggles for independence, and in the early years of nation building, social reformers questioned colonial legitimacy and championed their initiatives in the name of public good. Nehruvian ideas of social development and Gandhian ideas of trusteeship built state institutions that worked for the public. The British legal concept of a trust was appropriated for nationalist purposes through the Gandhian concept of trusteeship, and the Charitable Religious Trusts Act (1920) identified religious trusts for public good and classified them as charitable trusts and tax exempt. The law elaborated the governance of finances and accounts of charitable religious trusts, enforced an ethics of public accountability, and was concerned with the mismanagement of large temples and mosques. It marked a shift in legislation dealing with gifts toward protection of rights, codification of rights-based benevolence, and reinforcement of the notion of the trustee as someone in service to an abstract public (Birla 2009, 128).[7]

Gandhi, as a lawyer turned activist, extended the legal and moral nationalist engagements with the state in the early twentieth century by building a political project of attaining *swaraj*, or self-rule based on moral principles (Bornstein and Sharma 2016). For Gandhi, swaraj was achieved by nonviolently challenging unjust colonial laws and institutions, and by uplifting Indian society by following the path of truth and performing selfless social service, especially in villages. After independence, some Gandhians continued voluntary grassroots work, while others collaborated with the Nehruvian state as welfare policy advisors and implementers. Today, state and nonstate groups continue to selectively claim the Gandhian legacy as a hallmark of their virtuous legitimacy (Bornstein and Sharma 2016; Hardiman 2003; Sharma 2014, 2024). Post-Independence, laws continued to reproduce the divide between religious and secular purposes initiated in the colonial era for institutions of social welfare. Laws governing charitable purpose segregated types of activities as belonging to either religious or secular charitable organizations, thus determining which types of institutions were to be highly regulated and which were to be left to their own devices. Donations to religious institutions fell outside the boundaries of fiscal regulation, while secular donations were intensely scrutinized, following divisions codified by Personal Law and contested (see Bornstein 2012a and 2012b on the regulation of religious giving; see Williams 2010 on Personal Law). In addition, the ability of secular charitable organizations to engage in political action became a negotiation between these organizations and the state, moving between control and reform.

The period of nation building after independence codified these critical relationships between social reformers, many of whom operated within the institutional category of charitable societies and used the category of charitable purpose to reform society and the state. In early independent India, charitable purpose was political, and after Independence new modes of legal engagement by social groups were created. Nationalist state leaders used respect for the rule of law to distinguish themselves from colonial rulers (De 2014), foregrounding law as a key instrument for constructing a free and just society. Law and constitutionalism consolidated and centralized the authority of the Indian state and were also seen as forces of socioeconomic transformation, through which a decolonized society could be democratized and developed (Chatterjee 2014). As the Indian Constitution came into effect (1950), people increasingly used the judicial mechanisms made available to them to protect their fundamental rights and limit government authority (De 2014). This spread of legalism further harnessed voluntary organizations and activists as defenders of public interest, welfare, and justice in relation to state institutions.

For social reformers, the category of charitable purpose was central to their dance-like negotiation with the state. At this point the reform was not yet antagonistic, though it may have been at times agonistic (as in Mouffe 2013). When dancers move seamlessly one cannot discern the leader—move by move, who is leading whom is a dynamic interchange, a tension, and a collaboration. There is a momentum to the dance, which takes on a life of its own. Reformers initiated laws, including the Hindu Code Bill of 1948 that sought to secularize civil law (and which was unsuccessful; see, Williams 2010). A spate of legislation was passed to address social concerns, representing efforts by reformers to engage the state, through law, to reform society. Just as the Hindu reformers of the 1920s "forced open the doors of temples to Harijans" (untouchables), and outlawed child marriage and sati (widow immolation), by legislating the social reform of religion, the state continued to assert control over Hindu religious institutions.[8] The late nineteenth- and early twentieth-century modernizing efforts of the Indian social reformers, which solicited legal intervention by the state, resulted in a series of legislative actions on Hindu religious and social matters, which included the Madras Devadasis (Prevention of Dedication) Act (1947), outlawing dedicating young girls to temple deities (as temple prostitutes); the Madras Temple Entry Authorization Act (1947), which made it a punishable offence to prevent any person on the ground of untouchability from entering or worshipping in a Hindu Temple (later, temple-entry provisions were added to the Constitution of India); and the Madras Animal and Bird Sacrifices Abolition Act (1950), which addressed animal sacrifice as an undesirable and "primitive form of worship." Through these reform acts, the legislative arm of the state became the instrument for "purifying" religion (Chaterjee 1998). In this manner, reform created new social norms that were codified in law.

National reform in this era was fought for through legal reform, and at times through the governance of religion. Between 1865 and 1939, over twenty legislative acts reforming Hindu social and religion were passed (Williams 2010). In early Independence, for example, debates over the Hindu Code Bill in the 1950s were taken up by reformers to modernize India. Via the reform of rules governing the laws of marriage, property and succession, gender became another dominant category of national reform. Williams (2010) has analyzed how debates over the Hindu Code Bill became sites of governmental authority, through which women's national progress was sought through the promotion of women's rights. Williams (2010, 117) discusses how nationalist conceptions expressed through these debates, sought to abolish distinctions within the category of "Hindu" and to enhance distinctions between Hindus and other communities, laying the ground for Hindu nationalist politics of the future. Through the development of Hindu Personal Law, and the regulation of gendered subjects in the Hindu Code Bill, state power increased.[9]

During this time, the Indian nationalist movement increased its involvement in the state administration and management of Hindu temples, some of which took place through the governance of charitable purpose, bifurcating it into religious and secular arenas. In the Madras Hindu Religious and Charitable Endowments Act (1951), a department of government was set up to administer and oversee Hindu endowments whereby a religious denomination still managed its own affairs, while the management of property was considered secular and became the realm of the state. The government sought to intervene in the realm of custom through its regulation, and the religious and secular legislative divide was reinforced through the distinction between Personal Law, which governed religious custom including religious law, and territorial law, which was secular. The radically secular Indian constitution further codified this religious and secular divide. Article 25 addressed freedom of religion by referring to state interference regarding exclusions of caste, marriage practices, and Personal Laws; Article 27 articulated that "no person shall be compelled to pay taxes for the support of any particular religion." While the state advocated freedom of religion, it historically interfered with religion for social reform, from colonial times onward (Khilnani 2007) The Indian secular state in its constitutional design does not infer a separation of state and religion; it presents a version of secularism that includes religion.

Like the public/private and religious/secular designations in the original taxonomic category of charitable purpose, some groups inhabited a new hybrid political/charitable form in early Independence, introducing a new divide that would become important for the regulation of charitable purpose in the future: that is, political activity, and whether or not charitable organizations could participate in politics. The RSS, which was formed as a nationalist movement in the 1920s, then evolved into a hybrid entity, part political party, part charity. Its hybrid character has, over time, become powerful: alternately challenging the state and inhabiting it as a political party. The RSS was formed in Maharashtra as the main organization for Sangh Parivar (the Family). The RSS is the "National Volunteer Corps," or the "National Volunteers Self Service Society," that boasts of being "the largest voluntary organization in the world." It is one of the largest organizations in Northern Indian civil society, with approximately 2.6 to 6 million followers. RSS uses charity and social welfare to cultivate Hindu nationalism through education, poverty reduction, health, sports, and development projects (Bhatt 2001; Hansen and Jaffrelot et al. 1998; Jaffrelot 2007; Simpson 2014; Bhattacharjee 2016; Sundar 2004; Anderson and Damle 2019; Thachil 2014). In 1964, the RSS set up the Vishva Hindu Parishad (VHP), or World Council of Hindus, and in 1979, it founded Seva Bharati (Indian Service) "to penetrate India's slums through social activities—free schools, low-cost medicines, etc." (Jaffrelot 2007, 19). The move from social reform to social welfare was not a big leap for the RSS, but it was one that produced new institutions constituting the Sangh Parivar (Family of the Sangh), which has since had political and electoral effects (see Thachil 2014).

The welfare programs of the RSS have since been used to build the legitimacy of the RSS as both a state-like entity and a non-state entity, which, when not integrated into state politics, could potentially compete with the state. Through this unique institution, we see how social welfare became intimately tied to politics, in an institutional case spanning colonial and post-colonial India. A social service organization, the RSS is not registered with the state; it is not an NGO. It is a social movement, a political movement, and a shadow governmental organization. It is a hegemonic institution, difficult to categorize, unregistered, and part po-

litical party. Its religious nationalism challenges notions of secular nationalist development. In the 1960s, Hindu nationalism gained momentum
through charitable groups. This mobilization strategy continues to this day
and is part of why, and how, charitable groups are regulated by the state
and seen as potentially threatening, and also why the specter of religious
nationalism hovers in debates in India regarding charitable purpose. It
shaped state power though the BJP's election in 2014 and is evident in how
the BJP has villainized and sought to control rights-based social welfare-
oriented NGOs.

Analyzing the BJP's rise with the 2014 election, Thachil (2014) argues
the BJP won electoral votes by using private volunteers to provide social
services (not governmental resources). He attributes the rise of BJP in 2014
with its alliance with the RSS and Sangh Parivar (the largest nongovernmental organization in the world), which worked with poor, Dalit and
Adivasi populations and built electoral support. The expansion of "private
welfare" explains the BJP's unique capacity to engage the poor (and win
votes) while maintaining the power of elites in the political party. The role
of nongovernmental organizations (like RSS) can effectively work to support the political reach and enhance the legitimacy of a political party like
the BJP. In the case of the 2014 election, this was achieved through social
services provided by "grassroots affiliates" working in areas of public goods
provision, such as education and health, and through grassroots volunteers who worked as "service activists" via *seva* (service). As Thachil argues,
while this may not have directly influenced votes, it may have had an effect
on voter loyalty. In this case, we can see the political growth of the BJP,
through RSS and Sangh Parivar, and the outsourcing of social services.
Understanding the political, as well as global reach of Hindutva,[10] assists
our understanding of how charity laws can be used as tools of statecraft,
through the regulation of charitable purpose.

The Emergency and Its Aftermath: Regulating the Political

The 1970s were pivotal for postcolonial politics in India (Kaviraj 2011), sig-
nifying a new phase in the judicialization of activism as well as a period
when the state tried to control the nonprofit sector: depoliticizing donations to voluntary groups from foreign entities and controlling the potential political influence of social reformers regarding the workings of
the state. As Indira Gandhi declared the Emergency, there was on the

one hand an explicit articulation of the developmentalist state's populist responsibility for social reform by securing people's basic needs and livelihoods, and there was on the other hand the exertion of the state's governmental power as it curtailed people's civil liberties and democratic rights. The Congress Party passed the Foreign Contributions Regulation Act (FCRA) in 1976 to scrutinize NGOs receiving foreign funds, invoking potential imperialist intervention by an ill-defined "foreign hand" to quash dissent. During the Emergency, charitable groups were considered a potential threat to the state, and through the FCRA international donations were tightly regulated, constraining financial support to nonprofits, nongovernmental organizations, and a new category of nonparty political formations (NPPFs). Through this regulatory reform, the state sought to control political influence. International charitable groups could no longer do work deemed by the state to be political.

The Emergency was also a turning point for civil society groups (Deo and McDuie-Ra 2011). Opposition was silenced through the Maintenance of Security Act, as over 36,000 activists and members of the press were jailed (ibid., 13). During the Emergency, collective advocacy outside the state was the only way to keep the state responsive, and after the Emergency, social movements emerged again as political forces. Also during this time, Hindu nationalists entered mainstream politics (ibid.), and as Deo and McDuie-Ra document, civil society in this era included a diverse group: press media associations, caste- and religious-based associations, peasant and farmer groups, labor unions, communist groups, social service organizations, and development organizations, as well as professional NGOs, local branches of transnational NGOs, ethno-nationalist groups, separatist groups, and militant communist groups.

When Indira Gandhi lost elections in 1977, the newly elected Janata government actively promoted rural voluntary organizations and set up semi-governmental bodies, such as the Council for the Advancement of People's Action and Rural Technology (CAPART), to support NGO activity (Kamat 2002; Sen 1993). In the post-Emergency period, civil society watchdog and social action groups, deeply suspicious of state institutions, sought to hold those institutions accountable. A new institutional category emerged in the social reform dance with the state. Non-Party Political Formations (NPPFs) were lauded as new types of civil society actors set to challenge government repression (Jenkins 2010; Kothari 1984; Sheth 1983; Sheth and Sethi 1991). NPPFs expanded the categorical capacity of political ideas, which came to include gender, environmental, and human rights concerns (Menon 2013).

Reformers began to use a new judicial tool of resistance during this time: Public Interest Litigation (also known as PIL). In the late 1970s, the Indian Supreme Court introduced PIL to reverse the judiciary's surrender to the executive during the Emergency and to influence legislation in the name of redistributive justice and compassion (Bhuwania 2014; Baxi 1980). The sphere of activism became judicialized, and its practice expanded into the 1980s as NPPFs filed PIL to question state acts, make policy interventions, and do grassroots political work (Fortun 2001). Voluntary sector groups began to systematically use the courts to challenge the state and demand redistributive justice.[11] The use of legal tactics by nonstate groups to expand the sphere of rights and hold state institutions accountable went hand in hand with closer governmental scrutiny over their activities. Subsequently, Indira Gandhi's re-election in 1980 led to a fresh round of repression of the voluntary sector as a result of the Kudal Commission inquiry into the workings of several NGOs for their alleged role in the fall of the Congress government in 1977 (Jenkins 2010). Rajiv Gandhi, who stepped into his mother's shoes in 1984, increased funding to NGOs doing nonpolitical work (Kamat 2002; Sen 1993), and encouraged state-NGO partnerships, but simultaneously proposed greater disciplining of the voluntary sector through a code of ethics (Kothari 1986).

Liberalization: For-Profit and Non-Profit Distinctions Reformed

As India began to liberalize its economy in the early 1990s, during the era of globalization, nonprofits and nonprofit leaders entered the state in order to reform it (Deo and McDuie-Ra 2011; Kassam et al. 2016; cf. Salamon's the "nonprofitization of the welfare state," 2015). Post–Cold War, the language of human rights dominated global governance initiatives, and states were considered clientelist and inefficient. Global institutions such as the World Bank turned to nongovernmental organizations in their programs for rebuilding societies. India's socialist legacy also began to shift during this period, as the state opened the economy and liberalized state-run institutions. Global institutions participated by venerating NGOs as ideal and efficient development partners, and the NGO sector grew exponentially: 12,000 Indian NGOs were registered with the Ministry of Home Affairs in 1988; they then grew to an estimated two million (Kamat 2002;

Mahapatra 2014); in 2020, they reached roughly three million (Jagtiani 2020). Public scrutiny of the voluntary sector increased alongside its size. The political Left critiqued NGOs in India, and elsewhere, for being bureaucratized and professionalized pawns in the hands of imperialist forces, including capital and donors, which were used to demobilize rather than promote "revolutionary" activism and change (INCITE! 2007; Jad 2010; Karat 1984; Petras 1999). The reworking of the frameworks through which the moral legitimacy and political potential of nonstate groups was assessed (Jakimow 2010) resulted in a widened chasm between nonstate actors— such as people's campaigns and movements lauded for their transformative and radical work—and NGOs deemed depoliticizing, conformist, even statist agents (Fisher 1997; Jenkins 2020; Kamat 2004; Kothari 1986). It was during this era that nonprofits entered the state once again in order to change it. A new spate of laws was passed, once again with the theme of social reform, this time in the name of rights, and charitable purpose once again became political. Some social movements became autonomous from the state during globalization. While previously NGOs had been funded by governments, international foundations funded developmentalist agendas. This funding strategy had an effect on the sector as large donors tended to control reform agendas.[12]

Late liberalization (2000 to the 2020s), was an era in which a global economic recession occurred alongside the growth of new social movements, including global anti-globalization movements and anti-corruption movements in India. The Right to Information Act, which was passed in 2005, put the Indian government under a microscope, and the Congress Party subsequently initiated its own regulatory reforms of nonprofit and corporate law. A key initiative in this reform was to invite corporations to participate in social welfare through revisions to the Companies Act (2013), which mandated a 2 percent social responsibility tax on large companies. Concurrently, the Income Tax Act (1961) was proposed for revision through the Direct Taxes Code Bill, which redefined the category of charitable purpose for tax deduction purposes, and the Foreign Contributions Regulation Act (FCRA 1976) was revised in 2010 to restrict donations from foreign sources potentially threatening "national interest." The Finance Bills of 2002, 2017, and 2023 added regulatory provisions for NPOs. This rapid regulatory reform occurred through efforts to articulate and codify charitable purpose through laws focused on institutional registration, tax exemption, and philanthropic control. When the BJP came to power in 2014, the pace of change accelerated. Though the new party inherited the regulatory reform process, it amplified its results. Laws, we must remember, are relevant only when they are implemented, and the BJP took it upon itself to implement these new laws in a restrictive and punitive manner.

Cases

I now turn to the years 2012 to 2013, when the political heat was high, and an election year was around the corner. Civil society leaders complained that it was difficult to get things done because it was an election year. In the political moment, questions of state legitimacy were central topics in public and media conversations. In an about-face, while the government was being accused of corruption through the IAC movement and new political parties were being formed through this movement (Sharma 2024), nonprofit work began to be framed as illegitimate. Charitable purpose became a symbolic legislative category, highly scrutinized for evidence of political activity through which the state sought to legitimize its efforts with the public. Deemed "anti-national," foreign funding was no longer allowed for political activities, and protests were curtailed, often violently. As the state reoriented nonprofits away from political critique and toward service provision, it formed new alliances with corporate agencies, squeezing out the potential for nonprofits to operate as they had in the past (Deo 2024). Being political as a nonprofit became a dangerous liability, and political activity was expunged from charitable purpose. The dance between nonprofits and the state shifted such that the political nature of charitable purpose became a risk, one to be tightly controlled by the state. The nonprofitization of the welfare state, through which the state ceded its developmental strategies to nongovernmental organizations, then shifted to the "corporatization of nonprofits," whereby corporations were mandated to support state-oriented social welfare. As new dance partners with the state, corporate actors were welcomed into the social development arena.

COMPARISON: TRUST, SOCIETY, CHARITABLE COMPANY

In 2014, what was the difference for a nonprofit between registering as a trust, a society, or a charitable company?[13] Trusts were the easiest and cheapest to form and run, but were unwieldy when it came to resolving disputes. It was a good form for bequeathing property to the public good (as in an inheritance), but it was not very transparent, as it did not have public reporting requirements. Trusts were the least regulated and controlled of the three categories of incorporation, and they were able to operate in most of India. Societies were the most democratically structured. Unruly and difficult to manage; they were good for collaborative activities involving participation by a large number of people and groups (as in rights-based work). They were moderately expensive to form and had moderate state-imposed reporting requirements. However, the area within which each society could act was limited to a single Indian state. If a society were to operate in multiple states, it would have to register in each state with the Registrar of Societies, presenting limitations for nationally oriented NGOs but a fine category for smaller, local groups. Section 8 companies were the most difficult and expensive to form and operate and had many reporting requirements. They were the most regulated and incurred the most penalties under governing law. Their boon was that Section 8 companies could operate in all of India. They were also controlled by the central government (NPO circular 2014; also see Bharat 2009). Organizations that wished to operate India-wide and that had a strong financial base would benefit from registering as Section 8 charitable companies.

Like the Constitution of India, which does not define religion, the Income Tax Act (1961) did not define *religious purpose*. Yet, having a religious purpose excluded an organization from garnering tax benefits. The Act defined charitable purpose as: "Relief of the Poor, Formal Education, Medical Relief, and Any other object of general public utility (including social welfare and humanitarianism, advocacy, social justice and empowerment organizations)." While many NGOs combined charitable and religious purpose in their activities in terms of tax benefits for donors, charitable purpose excluded anything related exclusively to religious teaching or worship. Religious trusts were treated like public charitable trusts in that they were tax exempt and thus not required to pay taxes to the Government of India. However, they differed from charitable trusts in that donations to religious trusts offered no tax benefits to donors. This was partly due to the history of colonial law, which segregated the regulation of religion and custom from territorial law, and the subsequent structure of the Indian Constitution post-Independence, which integrated religious law into the secular constitution via Personal Law.

In addition to trusts and societies, government-sponsored public welfare programs also existed, such as the program for earthquake relief and the Prime Minister's National Relief Fund. Gifts to these categories offered a 100 percent tax deduction for donors. When I began researching this project in 2010, governmental charities included the Prime Minister's National Relief Fund, the Prime Minister's Armenia Earthquake Relief Fund, the Africa (Public Contributions - India) Fund, and the National Foundation for Communal Harmony. Donations to secular charities listed in Section 80(g) of the Income Tax Code provided a 50 percent tax deduction for donors, with these provisos:

> The institution was created for "charitable purposes in India;" the institution or fund was tax exempt; the institutions' governing documents did not permit the use of income or assets for any purpose other than a charitable purpose; the institution or fund was not expressed to be for the benefit of any particular religious community or caste; and the institution or fund maintained regular accounts of its receipts and expenditure.

As in earlier eras, a distinction was made regarding the regulation of charitable purpose based on the intent of the donor's gift, whether it was for public or private benefit, and whether it had a charitable or religious purpose. Section 80(g) status under the Income Tax Code was sought after by NGOs because it provided incentives for donors via larger tax deductions. At the time of my research, religious NGOs did not qualify for 80(g) status if their activities served specific populations.[14]

Religion was still a governance domain in charitable purpose, and the GOI tried to address issues of unregulated religious donations. According to a 2009 NPO circular, in 2006, the GOI imposed a 30 percent tax on anonymous donations, which it later revoked. A new set of tax laws, the Direct Taxes Code Bill, was introduced and debated in Parliament, and NGOs organized to try to stop the legislation. The Bill, which was scheduled to take effect in 2012, replaced "charitable purpose" with "permitted welfare activities" and proposed to regulate that category more narrowly than charitable purpose. NGOs with any business-like activities would be taxed.[15] Although religious organizations were excluded from the proposed tax code Bill, secular organizations were increasingly being regulated.

A 2010 NPO circular on the Direct Taxes Code Bill called the Direct Taxes Code "charity as usual," while it alerted the NPO's membership to a new provision to heed regarding unspent income; it stated: "The revised

Direct Taxes Code Bill, tabled in Lok Sabha on 30th August, is fortunately like old wine, mellowed and rich, though with a new smart label. A quick glance shows that it generally retains the existing structure, though some critical changes are still there, including compulsory accounting on cash basis and a tax of 15 percent on unspent income." After describing detailed measures in the government proposal to amend the tax code, the circular concluded: "Tax on anonymous donations is back on the books. The bureaucratic phrase 'permitted welfare activity,' which saw furious reactions from the sector, has been replaced with the more acceptable 'charitable activity.'"[16] The back-and-forth of the rules and responses was a regular cadence of reform.

One NPO held a workshop for its membership on taxation policies and VOs, focusing on the Direct Taxes Code Bill. I attended the workshop alongside forty to fifty representatives of the NPO sector and a few civil servant guests. The room was filled with dialogue; it was an information-sharing session, a brainstorming retreat, and an airing of complaints. The group discussed how the government was making it increasingly difficult for NPOs to operate. A cash versus accrual change in the proposed law privileged corporations. The proposed tax code reform was discussed in relation to amendments to the Companies Act and the FCRA, in a constellation of reforms transforming the universe of NPOs. Their horizon line was being rewritten, but not by them. The NPOs attending the meeting debated what was taking place and what could be done. Some suggested discussing the law-in-process with government ministers, and others recommended lobbying the government for revisions to the proposed Bill. As the government was increasing restrictions on NPOs, it was also creating an enabling environment for corporations. The logic of this, according to the government representatives attending the workshop, was that by being tax exempt the NPOs were being given a government subsidy. The corporate subsidy was also considered a state investment.

Governmental control of the tax-exempt institutions the government saw itself as subsidizing fit the service-provision model, where the state outsourced social welfare to NPOs but maintained control through the fine print, the tiny rules, of the proposed Direct Taxes Code Bill. The issue of a "service tax" on charities received pushback from workshop attendees, as did the government's approach to NPOs as businesses and subcontractors. Organizations working with a rights-based instead of service delivery model experienced problems with the revised FCRA, and NPOs were alarmed by the suggestion that any NPO budgetary "surplus" could be understood as a profit by the government. Issues of profit motive and intent dominated the workshop conversation. Small NGOs were being hurt the most, some said. The workshop was an airing of grievances and collective worry about the new rules. How to cope and how to communicate with the government? Some attendees voiced concern regarding corporations creating nonprofits to avoid taxes. In 2012, the boundary between the government and civil society seemed porous and representatives seemed committed to problem solving in dialogue; the room was filled with alarm and hope.

A newsletter follow-up from another CSO workshop (held in 2013) analyzed proposed changes to the income tax code in relation to charitable organizations. The newsletter sought to educate its membership on tax history: how in the Income Tax Act of 1961, charities were designated as a separate sector and given tax exemptions because they worked for charitable purpose. The proposed revision to the category of charitable purpose had taken place through a long process, the newsletter explained. In the 2005–06 Union Budget, the government had announced its intention to introduce a revised and simplified Income Tax Bill. In 2009, the GOI released a draft of the Direct Taxes Code (DTC) Bill, and in 2010 the final draft of the Bill was prepared. The newsletter informed its members of this detailed history, and how a Parliamentary standing committee was constituted and eventually submitted a report in 2012 (seven years after the idea was first publicly announced). In the DTC Bill, which was intended to replace the Income Tax Act (1961) and the Wealth Tax Act (1957), the category of charitable purpose was replaced with "charitable activities."

A subtle shift in approach had taken place alongside a quiet revolution of the rules, and the sector faced new terms of implementation. An e-newsletter alerted its constituency of nonprofit member organizations that the GOI would emphasize the activities performed by an organization, not the purpose. This code shift moved from treating NPOs as tax-exempt entities to seeing them as "tax-paying entities." It proposed streamlining registration under the code to a single registration category for all NPOs. In the 1961 Income Tax Act, the tax benefit to donors was 100 percent of the value of the donation, while in the new code it was 50 percent of the value. Religious trusts were kept out of the new Bill. In the 1961 Income Tax Act, NPOs could spend 85 percent of funds received during the year and could carry over the remaining 15 percent. However, in the proposed

DTC code, NPOs were required to spend 100 percent of their funds in the fiscal year they were received. The 100 percent spending provision would make NPOs financially precarious, as they would have no budgetary cushion and long-term planning would become difficult. In the 1961 Act, NPOs could use unspent funds in the next five years, but in the proposed DTC code, the entire unspent amount was taxable. Through a small set of rules, NPOs were beginning to be treated as taxable, like corporations. The sector division between NPOs and corporations was being broken. Another issue of concern for the NPO sector in the proposed DTC Bill was the issue of cash versus accrual accounting. The intricacies and implications of the proposed DTC were hotly debated through a dialogic process of writing law that took place between NPOs and government civil servants,[17] but surrounding these proposed changes was an inherent suspicion of NPOs. The verity of charitable purpose was analyzed via the assessment of their activities, and new fiscal requirements limited the scope and potential of their annual expenditures. The proposed DTC Bill contained punitive provisions that put the NPO sector on the defensive.

Conclusion

Charitable purpose is a regulatory frame through which civil society and state actors have historically sought social reform. In early colonialism, the British imperial government created institutions, some of which still exist as regulatory mechanisms today. Trusts, societies, and charitable companies function as contemporary birth certificates for nonprofits. They are also governance rubrics that determine, through law, how institutions operate, accept donations, and run themselves. They orient types of institutions in relation to the state, which awards nonprofits tax-exempt status in exchange for their public duties and the provision of public goods. By governing charitable purpose, the state gains public legitimacy in the arenas where nonprofits work, such as social welfare and development. Yet, as NPOs do their welfare work, they also carry an inherent threat of critique of the state; their work on behalf of publics always already contains the potential message that the state is not doing a good enough job of public goods provision.

Laws that bear upon the activities of NPOs include those mandating registration, such as the Societies and Trusts Acts and the Companies Act, and also laws governing income tax exemptions (the Income Tax Act), and mandatory CSR provisions in the Companies Act, as well as restrictions on foreign donations in the FCRA, all of which, in some manner, redefine and regulate aspects of charitable purpose. The three tributaries I mentioned at the onset of the chapter—historical currents, religious and political distinctions, and the control of philanthropic pathways—braid together in the implementation of charitable purpose as a regulatory mechanism. The cluster of laws governing charitable purpose function as a living regulatory landscape that NPOs must navigate. It is a landscape where laws are amended, rules re-rewritten, and the discourse of unique aspects of charitable purpose contested. As much as the government has used taxonomies of charitable purpose to control civil society in the colonial era, civil society actors have since used the same categories in attempts to reform the state. The government has cracked down on nonprofits, and nonprofits have served as watchdogs of the government in a dance over legitimacy in service to public good. In this historical process, debating what can, and cannot, fit into the discursive frame of charitable purpose is a mechanism for nonprofit regulation and political engagement.

THREE

Regulating Philanthropic Corridors

"**T**raffic light," "window," "bridge," and "aqueduct" are spatial metaphors used by those in the nonprofit sector to conceptualize philanthropic governance. Because nonprofits are dependent on philanthropy for their survival, restrictions to philanthropic funding alter their very being, including what they can do and whether they can survive. In this part of my story, one particular law becomes a philanthropic corridor and takes center stage: the Foreign Contributions Regulation Act (FCRA). The FCRA altered the funding architecture for nonprofits, and became an instrument of statecraft. The law was introduced in the mid-1970s, amended in the 1980s during the Emergency, and made more stringent in the early 2000s during globalization. In 2010, it was revised to address philanthropy from the Indian diaspora. In 2015, it was amended again, increasing licensing requirements and restricting political activity with threats of institutional closure. Through the reform of the FCRA, our unsung heroes, accountants and lawyers of the nonprofit sector (Accountability Guides), responded to the shifting regulatory landscape and aided the NPO sector in navigating regulatory reform.

The FCRA was first passed in 1976, a time during the Emergency when international NGOs arrived to provide humanitarian relief after floods in Bangladesh. Fear of political interference was the incentive to regulate foreign NGOs, in order to prevent foreign funding to political parties after a controversy had erupted over funding for Parliamentary elections (Agarwal 2012).[1] The FCRA was amended in 1984 to include funding regulations for charitable organizations thought to be supporting political parties, and as the FCRA was revised so were efforts to increase governmental control. Under the 1976 FCRA, NGOs could receive contributions without restriction, but in the ordinance of 1984, NGOs required prior permission from the government to receive foreign funds, and a new restriction was put in place to limit transferring funds from one NGO to another.[2]

In the 1990s, as India liberalized its economy and the global economy blossomed, global restrictions on illegal funds transfers across borders became an international problem. As India reached out to its global diaspora for knowledge transfer, it sought funds via foreign direct investment, and citizen return. In 2001, the FCRA became a governmental concern in relation to global anti-terrorism legislation, a concern culminating in a draft revision of the FCRA in 2005, which was subsequently released and debated. In 2006, the Bill was revised and tabled in the Rajya Sabha (upper house of Parliament). The same year, it was referred to a standing committee of the Ministry of Home Affairs, and comments were invited from stakeholders. The revised FCRA (as a Bill) was cleared by the committee in October 2008, with recommendations for changes. Two years later, in August 2010, the Bill was discussed again in the Rajya Sabha, as well as in the Lok Sabha (lower house of Parliament), where it passed by a voice vote. Almost every MP agreed with the purpose and provisions of the Bill. It was signed into law in September 2010.

Ten years after the process of FCRA revision began, in March 2011, the rules and forms for the 2010 FCRA were drafted by the Ministry and put on a website for public scrutiny, and comments and suggestions were invited from the public. Many NGOs organized and gave feedback to the government about the pending rules. The final version of the 2010 FCRA rules was determined in April 2011, published in May, and implemented in 2012 (Agarwal 2012 and Sundar 2010 offer an extensive chronological history). This was the ebb and flow, the rhythm of drafting and passing of laws, occurring over multiple years. At each turn, a law's passage and revision involved the Houses of Parliament debating it as a Bill and passing it as an Act, and then ministries and civil servants writing the rules to be implemented. The government periodically published draft rules for public opinion, and civil society groups were invited to respond. The quest for collective responses galvanized the nonprofit sector, which organized by writing petitions, lobbying civil servants, and at times even aided the process by drafting legislation.

Between 2012 and 2015, rights-based work became a target of the FCRA and of the government. This compounded with the struggles nonprofits faced after the 2008 global economic crash, which had diminished charitable endowments and reduced international monetary flows to Indian nonprofits. PM Modi was elected in 2014, along with the BJP, in a transfer of power from the Congress Party. In 2015, five years after the 2010 FCRA had been passed, the new requirements of the 2010 FCRA came into effect, mandating renewal of FCRA licenses with the government, which created apprehension in the NPO sector. Professional Critics and Accountability Guides worked to educate NPOs about impending legislative change. Some worked to reinstate licenses cancelled due to bureaucratic errors. From its inception in 1976, during the Emergency, the FCRA has been a tool of statecraft, and the newly elected BJP administration knew how use the FCRA as a legal instrument. The stage was shrinking for internationally funded rights-based work, and in 2015, the government released an Intelligence Bureau report accusing nonprofits of being anti-national. Meanwhile, corporate philanthropy sat in the greenroom waiting to enter the stage. As the government restricted international funding in order to control dissent, it supported corporate funding for development.

This chapter focuses on a particular temporal snapshot of governmental revisions between 2010 and 2015, and civil society responses to the FCRA through amendments, rule-writing, and advocacy efforts. I write of reformers in the nonprofit sector as they sought to weather rapid regulatory changes through FCRA clinics, and of the nonprofit auditors and accountants who worked to school the sector on the new rules and regulations. The FCRA 2010 and its rules of 2012 were long in the making, and the ethnographic snapshots I provide emerge from the early dialogic history between NGOs and state bodies over regulatory reform. The process I outline—structural, historical, and social—may be useful for analyzing current proposed revisions to the FCRA, focused on domestic philanthropy (Shukla 2023; Dadrawala 2023; Shetty and Seth 2023; FMSF 2023).

A research report by the Centre for Social Impact and Philanthropy (n.d.; an organization also known as CSIP)[3] offers a succinct overview of the structural changes to the FCRA and their effect on funding flows. (1) In the original law, passed in 1976, permission to receive foreign funds was granted by the government to an NGO for life. In the 2010 revision to the FCRA law, NGOs were required to apply for renewal of their FCRA license every five years. This increased both bureaucracy, which put smaller organizations outside India's capital at a disadvantage, and the potential for governmental oversight and surveillance. (2) The 2010 Act put a cap of 50 percent on funds being used for administrative purposes, and an emphasis on project expenses. This put rights-based advocacy organizations at a disadvantage, as their work relied upon neither services nor infrastructure/equipment. The social capital of social change was embedded in personnel, which were categorized as an administrative expense instead of an output or product. (3) The 2010 FCRA did not allow any funds to be used for anything of "political nature." It restricted funding for "*bandhs* (strikes), *hartals, raasta roko* and *jail bharo* thus limiting the kinds of activities funded"[4] The restricted activities were quintessential forms of Indian social activism. Political activities, defined broadly, were not fundable through FCRA, but exactly what constituted "political activity" was left for interpretation by government officials, through processes of bureaucratic, often extra, surveillance. (4) Finally, the central government was given the upper hand. The Act mentioned the central government could prohibit the acceptance of foreign funding that was likely to "affect public interest." In this revision, the central government gained regulatory and curatorial power to determine what was legitimate (legal) and illegitimate (illegal) social sector activity, including the role of political engagement.

As the 2010 FCRA rules were passed and the law began to be implemented in 2012, cancellations of FCRA licenses increased. The government did not specify its reasons for denying FCRA permissions, creating an environment of fear and anxiety in the nonprofit sector. Most Indian NPOs at that point, especially rights-based advocacy groups, were dependent on foreign funds, and they felt targeted and criminalized for their work. This would later increase with subsequent FCRA amendments. Prominent NGOs such as the Ford Foundation and Greenpeace lost their ability to receive foreign funds as they became focal points of the new FCRA law. Several became exemplars—case studies on punitive legislation, described as a bureaucratic "clean up" of the sector. There were also NGOs whose FCRA licenses were cancelled owing to completely bureaucratic reasons, but this was a separate issue. The former Deputy Secretary for the Ministry of Home Affairs, J. K. Chattopadhyay, was quoted in 2014 as stating: "As per the law of the country, you cannot accept foreign funding, while opposing the policies of the government. Agitation is a democratic right. However, FCRA does not permit NPAs to agitate against government policies or criticize the government using foreign contribution. Object all you want but find an alternative source of revenue" (Centre for Social Impact and Philanthropy n.d., 16).

Many cancelled organizations had been involved in political reform work. The Centre for Social Impact and Philanthropy report (n.d.) noted three NPOs that had their FCRA licenses revoked after being involved in protests against the Kudankulam Nuclear Power Plant in Tamil Nadu in 2012. Several organizations, including Indian Social Action Forum (hereafter INSAF), had their bank accounts frozen via the FCRA. The government argued their work was against public interest. Other organizations claimed differential and punitive scrutiny, such as Navsarjan Trust, Gujarat's largest Dalit-rights organization in 2015, and a public health organization doing research and advocacy to reduce tobacco consumption which had its FCRA account frozen, supposedly due to pressures from the tobacco lobby in 2016. These closures occurred directly after the 2012 and 2015 FCRA amendments, and similar closures continued to occur after FCRA's 2020 revisions as well.

The punitive legislative trend toward foreign philanthropy and political engagement was interpreted by those in the nonprofit sector as direct action against foreign funders. The government leaked an Intelligence Bureau report in 2015 stating that "social organisations funded by foreign donors were trying to undermine India's growth story and should be curbed." The GOI maintained a "prior permission" list of foreign donors in India, and all transactions by these donors necessitated approval by the Union Ministry of Home Affairs (MHA). The reporting responsibility was on grantees to write to the MHA and obtain permission before accessing donor funds, and the cumbersome process led donors to either stop or scale back their work in India. NPOs spoke critically of the opacity of the process on the government side, especially when accounts were frozen without any communication. The Ford Foundation was put on the prior permission list, later to be taken off and required to change its regulatory identity and register under the Foreign Exchange Management Act (FEMA). Compassion International, one of the largest faith-based donors operating in India, was put on the list and then decided to end its India operations (Bhalla 2017; Barry and Raj 2017).

Loss of funding for NGOs meant program reduction, scaling back, shutting down. Some rights-based advocacy organizations had licenses but no donors, because donors did want to deal with the volatile political and environment. This created, according to nonprofit workers, a "trust deficit

with government officials" and had a "chilling effect" on the sector. Another casualty was relationships with banks, which did not want the risk of
having social organizations as customers/clients if their funds were likely
to be frozen. Frozen funds were difficult to deal with and required extra
bureaucracy for banks, as foreign funded NGOs were becoming high-risk
customers.[5] The Centre for Social Impact and Philanthropy report (n.d.)
quoted a foreign funder who remarked upon how even NGOs that had
legitimate FCRA permissions and received funds from donors not on the
watchlist had difficulty accessing those funds. Banks held onto funds and
didn't release them to local branches unless they had seen the grant agreement and the paperwork. What did this mean in practice? What were
the programmatic effects of such tectonic funding shifts? Foreign funders
had to reframe their funding agendas and strategies. Some dropped funding for "social justice, advocacy, human rights, and governance from their
Indian portfolio." Others reframed the way they described their work, re-
fraining from using the term "rights," or from working in governmentally
determined sensitive geographic areas such as Jammu and Kashmir or the
Northeast. The changes to the FCRA law affected the type of work that
nonprofits could do.

Nonprofit organizations are either resilient or they are no more. There
is little legal recourse, aside from filing a Supreme Court case, after having
one's bank accounts frozen or FCRA licenses cancelled. Some NPOs successfully used the courts to challenge the new philanthropic restrictions.
INSAF used the Delhi High Court to unfreeze its bank accounts, although
it was not able to receive foreign funding. NGOs could challenge FCRA
cancellations in court, but the lack of new funding posed a different kind
of threat to NGOs dependent on foreign resources. They were forced to
seek domestic avenues of support and shift to funding streams from local
sources. An effect of this shift was that nonprofits challenging governmental interference in court were branded with the stigma of being high
risk for funders, which further restricted philanthropic resources. Another
alternative to sourcing funds locally was to change organizational structure and emulate a for-profit model by registering as a charitable company
through the Companies Act, instead of as a trust or a society.

A Traffic Light for Politics and a Shrinking Stage for Rights–Based Work

In India, many laws existed but many were also not enforced, or they were selectively enforced, and much of this book focuses on the implementation of the rules of law. The rules established under the FCRA were passed and implemented at the same time as the Companies Act (2013) was passed, and we must consider this pair of laws in tandem—one regulating foreign contributions and the other corporate social responsibility (CSR). Between the original FCRA of 1976 and the 2010 revised version, much had changed to alter the actions of NPOs and those that worked in the sector. The 1976 FCRA and the 2010 FCRA created two different regulatory frames, and this chapter analyzes the scope of the changes between them.

One expert on nonprofit legal shifts was an auditor and accountant, an Accountability Guide who worked in an advisory and advocacy capacity for NGOs. He didn't accept fees from NGOs directly, but instead worked with funders supporting civil society organizations. There were very few like him in his particular profession. Many NGOs didn't have access to resources to pay an accountant's or lawyer's fees, so he created an e-newsletter to educate the NGO community about legislative shifts affecting their status and operations. The Accountability Guide emphasized that people didn't worry too much about the laws most of the time. He compared the Indian situation to "America where every law gets enforced very seriously," whereas in India "we have so many laws which never get anywhere." However, when laws were enforced selectively, certain organizations (or groups) could be targeted selectively as well, and the uncertainty of implementation produced a culture of fear in the nonprofit sector.

The nonprofit sector was becoming highly regulated while the corporate sector was being encouraged to enter the country through deregulation of foreign direct investment. It became easier to donate to Indian development through a government bank that directed funds toward government-sponsored NGOs, whereas receiving foreign funds for anything political was becoming nearly impossible for Indian NGOs, and NGOs perceived their regulation as increasing, more so than for other types of groups. The GOI regulated everything from cooking gas to banking. It wasn't only the amount of regulation that was of concern to the NGOs, it was the public perception about the sector that had changed. The Accountability Guide explained that "people have had a soft spot for the sector." It had been lightly regulated because the social sector was "low cost" and laws regulating the sector were simple. There was not much "compliance cost." Reflecting on the simpler time, before 2001, when less paperwork was required by NPOs compared to corporate accounting and reporting, he said, "If you were an NGO or a trust you could just walk into a registrar's office, get a deed signed, and go open a bank account. You didn't even need to be registered to open a bank account."

He saw the regulatory shift take place after 2001, in relation to restrictions on fiscal regulation occurring globally. The Financial Action Task Force (FATF) was originally created in 1989 to regulate illegally laundered funds, and it eventually covered other issues as well. Two interlocked legal instruments aiming to control "illegal" funds transfer and political interference intersected in India: the FATF and the FCRA. The FATF altered India's engagement with philanthropic regulation globally, while the FCRA also regulated global fund transfers in India. The Accountability Guide considered the 2010 FCRA revision an effect of international pressures. Governments did not want to be considered as lagging in tracking corruption, as such behavior led to their being tagged as a "weak jurisdiction," and international pressure to prevent money laundering tightened NPO regulation. Another issue he identified was that NGOs had been focused on commonly understood activities, such as providing disaster and humanitarian relief, but when NGOs shifted their orientation toward rights-based economic and political empowerment, including good governance, the regulatory tone changed. The government depended on civil society groups to do welfare work in a partnership that generated governmental legitimacy. But then NGOs challenged governance itself. He spoke of working with an NGO in Dhaka, presenting information on Indian laws. He made a comment that the Indian government had a "comfortable relationship with Indian NGOs." There was critique but it was not adversarial. It was agonistic, not antagonistic. He attended a government conference where NGOs raised issues of Dalit atrocities, and the government received bad press on the issue. He saw this as another moment of transition, where rights-based approaches threatened GOI–NPO relationships.

Due to economic liberalization, the corporate sector grew with new initiatives opening foreign direct investment to international businesses such as Walmart, which vied for the Indian market. Corporations were "in the greenroom," but had not yet come on the stage. This was a transitional regulatory space. The Accountability Guide recalled attending a conference between the corporate sector and NGOs in the early 2000s. The conference was attended by corporate CSR representatives, with fewer foundation representatives attending, and the Accountability Guide described his memory of the room: "all these people wearing their suits and they have their ties, and wearing business suits, and the NGO sector was in, as you know, this riot of color in the ethnic and cotton and stuff like that. So, they were looking very out of place." The corporate people desperately tried to connect with the NGOs, but they didn't know how. They too were evolving into the newly formed social sector landscape, where they were being tasked with a more prominent role. The Indian government harnessed the corporate sector to institutionalize CSR, via corporate initiatives enabling their engagement in social welfare provision through the Companies Act (2013). Simultaneously, regulatory mandates in the 2010 FCRA constricted the rights-based work of NGOs. This dual regulatory move was critical to the regulatory reform of the nonprofit sector more broadly. CSR was focused on accountability and product delivery. The Accountability Guide recalled a corporate manager speaking to the NGO members present at a conference: "This fellow was saying, you know, if you want money from us, you have to study us carefully. You have to make a presentation. You have to tell us why we should fund this, what is in it for us. He was very frank." Meanwhile, foundation workers were moving into corporate CSR positions, bringing their knowledge to the corporate-led social sector. The Accountability Guide believed eventually a synthesis would occur between the nonprofit and corporate sectors in social welfare provision.

To facilitate these new CSR programs, some corporations started their own NGOs, while others donated their required CSR allocations directly to the government. Rights-based approaches to development and social welfare made the government go on both the "defensive and offensive." NGOs had become a powerful societal force, which was why the Accountability Guide thought they were being regulated. Only the powerful and influential were regulated: "So, if you are insignificant and you don't make a difference to the society, then no one is going to bother about regulating you. [. . .] I feel NGOs should recognize that they have made a difference. They are no longer just a cry in the wilderness. And that's why the government has become serious about them." He compared the FCRA to a traffic light that controlled rights-based work and opened avenues for corporate philanthropy toward government-directed development initiatives. Finance Minister Chidambaram had declared in the Lok Sabha (lower house of Parliament) that India did not want social and political discourse to be dominated by foreign money. The Accountability Guide drew a picture for me of a traffic light, explaining how the government restricted FCRA while opening "a major highway for corporate money." The 2 percent CSR provision in the Companies Act would "solve several problems for the government in one stroke." Business funding was not social-movement oriented, and it was easy to manage. Corporate money was conservative, serving industry interests. He didn't think the FCRA was well designed, though it was very powerful. It gave the government enormous amounts of power to regulate the sector and changed the direction of the sector. Because rights-based work was not easily available in India, nonprofits sought funding from foreign sources.

At first, NGO leaders were intoxicated by the anticipatory perfume of new corporate money swamping the nonprofit sector. The Companies Act was in bill form, and the shift toward corporate funding for development, away from rights-based funds flowing through the FCRA, was beginning to be the "master stroke" for controlling dissent, specifically in relation to corporate work in development zones. The Accountability Guide anticipated resistance to corporate expansion in places that were less developed—like Orissa or Jharkhand, which had active Indigenous/Tribal resistance movements toward development—would dissipate. Meanwhile, corporations and the government would benefit. "Because if you are taking my money, you are sitting with me, frequently talking with me, then you know you will start seeing my way of seeing. So, we become friends and then we don't quarrel with each other." It was not coercion, per se, rather redirection through regulatory processes: "because no corporate is going to do anything which will seriously annoy the government." NGOs would change their programming, the Accountability Guide predicted. This was in 2013, just as the new legislation had been passed and was just being implemented. Change was on the horizon.

The rollout of the 2010 revised FCRA was not smooth. "And that's where the government is having a lot of problems," said the Accountability Guide. "For the simple reason that NGOs find it very difficult sometimes to comply with the kind of relationships that governments demand." From the governmental side, the demands of legal reform were a bureaucratic effort to weed out ill-functioning or nonexistent NPOs. Illegitimate NGOs were an issue, and the bureaucratic solution was to increase reporting requirements, which hit NPOs, especially those for whom governance processes were not part of the culture of their work. Increased bureaucratic requirements presented another problem, where government funds could potentially be siphoned off by illegitimate "paper NGOs" that did not deliver the work. This suspicious category reflected poorly on the government as an NGO funder, and justified extra measures to control how government funds were allocated, and the GOI moved toward a mechanism for NGO accreditation that certified NPO legitimacy. Getting money from the government was "very complicated," he said, with paperwork. Due to the bureaucracy, some genuine NPOs stayed back and wouldn't engage with the government.

The problem of illegitimate NPOs was also one of governmental legitimacy, for even if NPOs failed to submit their reports, the government was still accountable. He explained:

> The government officers are afraid that if we [the government] give them money and these people run out then we will be left holding the bag. So, what they want is a mechanism by which someone will say that, "look, it's safe to give this NGO money." And later on, if that NGO runs off with the money, we can always say, "Look this fellow told me that it was safe to give to them therefore I gave it. If you have a problem, go and talk to this fellow." So, they want an accreditation mechanism.

The Accountability Guide was not against regulation, quite the contrary. He championed better regulation. Although political activities were prohibited in the 2010 FCRA, these activities were not defined. The Accountability Guide, whose professional responsibility was to help NGOs abide by the law, searched law dictionaries and case studies for definitions of the word *political*, but could not find legal definitions. An industry of FCRA brokers emerged to assist NGOs to navigate the stricter enforcement procedures of the FCRA, and nonprofit workers joked about the illegitimacy of these brokers. As the stage for NGOs doing rights-based work shrank, and as bureaucratic tracking increased, less institutionally literate NGOs struggled. They didn't have the staff to manage the complex legal issues on the horizon. The Accountability Guide articulated the experience of the sector as dancing on a shrinking stage:

> It's like they are dancing on a stage which is constantly being made smaller like one of those—some kind of weird movie, a Joker kind of movie where Spiderman is dancing on a stage and the stage keeps shrinking and he gets squeezed. So, this is what is happening [asks for

chai]. So, two things. One is that the space is shrinking, and the second thing is that it is also becoming very complex. And, NGOs do not internally have the necessary staff to really manage these complex issues.

SCOPE OF REFORM

Let us step back and examine the regulatory change between 1976 and 2010 in the FCRA, to see the detailed scope of the reform underway. Some of this may be tedious to read, but I offer it as an ethnographic environment that NPOs waded through daily. The 1976 FCRA regulated foreign contributions to associations and institutions. The 2010 FCRA required a certificate by an accountant for in-kind donations. The new FCRA regulated foreign funds from individuals, Hindu Undivided Families, associations, and Section 25 (now Section 8) companies. It did not apply to businesses that were not charitable companies. It applied to NGOs, and to philanthropists giving foreign contributions to those who were not kin. Remittances to kin were not part of FCRA if the amount was under 1 lakh (approximately US$2000). An NGO newsletter called this change: "FCRA Goes Nuclear." The old FCRA prevented organizations from working against public interest with foreign funds. The new FCRA stipulated registration could be denied if an NGO's work affected the "security, strategic or economic interests of the state." The new FCRA also regulated foreign hospitality support for travel, donations, and in-kind gifts to civil servants traveling abroad. The FCRA was global in its purview and oriented toward state security. It governed foreign contributions to India and civil servants traveling abroad. Politics was a key arena of legislative control, and with the FCRA's revision, *panchayats* (rural assemblies) became legislatures and could not receive foreign funds.

The 2010 FCRA was a radically secular law that regulated foreign donations to NGOs in a religious landscape where belief could potentially threaten national security. Inciting religious disharmony was considered grounds for revoking FCRA certification under the 2010 legislation. NGOs could have their FCRA certification revoked under the new law: if their activities were: (A) "Found to be aimed at conversion through inducement or force, either directly or indirectly, from one religious' faith to another;"[6] (B) "If the association is found to propagate sedition or to advocate violent methods to achieve its ends, and if the association is found to be creating communal tensions or disharmony;" or (C) "If the acceptance of foreign contribution by the association is likely to be prejudicial to the sovereignty and integrity of India; free and fair elections to any Legislature or House of Parliament; public interest; friendly relations with a foreign state; or harmony between any religious, social, linguistic, regional groups, caste or community."

The revised FCRA prevented "activities detrimental to national interest." One civil society worker stated, "The FCRA 2010 wags a finger at social activists, telling them to lay off or else!" A change in the 2010 FCRA had occurred in the definition of a *foreign source*, which included Indians abroad. Though NRIs (non-resident Indians) were Indian citizens and not considered foreign sources, PIOs (Persons of Indian Origin) and OCIs (Overseas Citizens of India) became foreign sources. Some had considered the Overseas Citizen of India card a form of conditional and partial citizenship, and the new distinction encapsulated much of what was at stake in the FCRA revision: an articulation of what belonged in the nation and what did not. The FCRA was a form of philanthropic protectionism. In a legal clause that an NGO director described to me as "a sword of Damocles hanging over one's head," NPOs were required to renew their FCRA licenses every five years. He feared no NGO dependent on foreign funds would be able to focus on its programming if they knew that in five years they would have to have their FCRA certification scrutinized for renewal. He said, "If you have been misbehaving in those five years. If you have done naughty things in those five years, well obviously your renewal may not occur." He believed this was how the voluntary sector was being controlled.

Within a few months of the 2012 implementation of the 2010 FCRA, 4138 NGOs had their registration cancelled, which increased anxiety, fear, and anger in the NGO sector. Of particular concern was how the new FCRA legislation restricted funds to NGOs that were overtly political in nature, including, farmers' groups, workers, students, or youth whose activities were overtly political, and organizations which engaged in strikes to support public causes. The clause may have been an assertion of the Congress government's attempt to maintain national security, and its attempt to clean up the NGO sector of undesired elements. However, the law interfered with India's rich associational traditions in the voluntary sector. Organizations that received funds through the FCRA could be religious, social, cultural, educational, and/or economic, but they could not be political in nature. An Indian foundation director asserted the government was tightening legislation because it was scared of NGOs. The anxiety about public protest and foreign funding was evident in the state's heavy-handed reaction to protests at a nuclear power plant in Kudankulam in Tamil Nadu. Reacting to the protests, the Home Minister said: "Foreign NGOs are supporting the Kudankulam protests. Nuclear energy is clean energy" (Bhatt 2012). Prime Minister Manmohan Singh, blamed foreign NGOs for inciting and funding the Kudankulam protests. Though the cancellation of FCRA permits caused an uproar in the NGO sector, a relatively small proportion of the more than two million NGOs in India received funds through FCRA.[7] The FCRA law stated a particular form (FC-6) must be filled out yearly, even when no foreign contribution is received in a year, but because many NGOs did not understand this component of the law, some of the mass cancellations were due to bureaucratic confusion over forms. This was also not the first time that such a purge was instituted by the government. The crackdown of July and August 2012, in which 4,138 organizations had their registrations cancelled, was for violations of FC-3/6 forms not being filed. In October 2005, 8,675 organizations had their FCRA licenses cancelled for not filing the out form FC-3, and 378 organizations had their registrations revoked. When they did not file such forms, organizations were illegible, and untraceable; it was through the FCRA that NGOs became legible to, and governable by, the state.[8] The 2010 FCRA had serious implications for NGOs doing rights-based work. Only a few people in India understood the new requirements, and most civil society workers were scrambling to keep up. The details may seem confusing; that is also how they were experienced by many nonprofit workers. The taxonomy had shifted in the thirty-four years between the law's 1976 inception and the 2010 revision, and the process of restrictive regulation continued.[9]

Global Diaspora Connect: Window/Bridge/Aqueduct

As much as the FCRA functioned as a traffic light for foreign philanthropy to NPOs, other mechanisms were simultaneously being built to facilitate diaspora philanthropy to India. Tens of millions of global Indians donate for poverty alleviation and economic development in India. Philanthropy from U.S.-based Indian communities increased so rapidly in the twenty-first century that some worried about its being accepted as a substitute for the Indian state (Sidel 2004b; Niumai 2011; Jakimow 2012). Philanthropy from the Indian diaspora is facilitated through social networks and NGOs that may be Indian-American, Indian, or international. It is also an area of research (e.g., Geithner, Johnson, and Chen 2004; Dusenbery et al., 2009; Shiveshwarkar 2004; Sidel 2004b; Viswanath 2003; Viswanath and Dadrawala 2004; Kapur et al. 2004). These networks and NGOs existed in a larger framework of national laws governing philanthropic fund transfers, economic development, and charitable work in receiving and sending countries. When I started this research, the three aforementioned categories of diaspora Indians donated to projects in India through NGOs: Non-Resident Indians (NRIs), Overseas Citizens of India (OCIs), and Persons of Indian Origin (PIOs). The population of overseas Indians in the United States in 2011 was estimated to be roughly three million, and remittances for India's development from its global diaspora were estimated at US$53 billion dollars; they increased to $100 billion by 2022 (Madhok 2022). Recipients of diaspora philanthropy were not only individuals; they were also nonprofit organizations that worked directly with those in need and at times with the state. NGOs played a crucial role in both the distribution and implementation of diaspora philanthropy and in the interaction with its state-based regulation. When individuals gave to projects in India, they could donate their funds either to a nonprofit registered in the United States as a 501(c)(3) organization, or to an Indian NGO registered as a society or a charitable trust, and due to this, NGOs faced different legitimizing parameters in the United States and in India. Yet, all of these organizations and individuals donating to India were vetted through the FCRA.

As India liberalized its economy, it reached out to its global diaspora for resources and skill-based investment in India's shining future. The Congress Party sought to maximize its highly skilled, tech-savvy diaspora for India's development, which had lagged behind expectations. Despite all the government's schemes, poverty and underdevelopment persisted in the nation at the tail end of the global associational revolution. Technology and the information sector had brought great wealth to many diaspora Indians, some of whom ran the top technology companies. How could the government bring some of that back to India, to write India's shining story? The government, specifically the Ministry of Overseas Indian Affairs (MOIA), made efforts to woo philanthropic resources from the global diaspora toward India's social development, via a government-sponsored trust called the India Development Foundation for Overseas Indians

(IDF-OI). Projects supported by IDF-OI were aligned with governmental development agendas, and its funds flowed through government banks.

I met with a representative of the ministry who discussed how it attended to the members of the diaspora, many of whom were considered to be India's philanthropic future. The MOIA facilitated "giving back" to India, as well as diasporic education and social welfare. Programs such as an Indian Community Welfare Fund for distressed Indians overseas partnered with nonprofits to help diaspora Indians living abroad. The ministry attended to gender issues such as assisting Indian women deserted by their NRI husbands, which was apparently a common phenomenon. The ministry offered country-specific cultural advice for Indian students abroad (in the United States, for example, it said students should "avoid fights, live on campus"; in Singapore, it recommended "don't point"). The Indian state, through this ministry, operated as a benefactor and social welfare provider for its overseas citizens. This wasn't too surprising or novel—national embassies did this all over the world. However, through this new ministry, diaspora Indians could send their children to India for cultural education and donate to India's development through the government, bypassing some of the government's most restrictive bureaucracy.

To facilitate philanthropic return, the IDF-OI functioned as a portal for donations to development. It defined itself as a "window" for overseas Indian philanthropy toward India's social development. The state in this metaphor was a frame, a guarantor, invisible, not troublesome. It protected inhabitants (citizens) from the outside. But it was not opaque; it was transparent. It was not a barrier. Its discursive self-representation repeated the word "credible" multiple times as a defining adjective. Due to critiques of corruption by the anti-corruption movement active at the time of our interview, I wondered why an overseas Indian would donate to a trust run by the Government of India. The director emphasized how the model itself was different.

> If I were to draw it for you, I would draw your attention to this window and say that above the window is the universe of the overseas Indians who, let's say for generic purposes, are social entrepreneurs or donors. And below the window are the recipients or the causes, which are dear to them. And the window is IDF-OI. It's only a pipe, a bridge that connects the two.

The foundation was a transfer mechanism and a bank. Overseas Indians could choose the organization, the geographic region, and the target of their donation. The foundation would guarantee receipt by the intended NGO within twenty-four hours; the donation would be exempt from FCRA legislation, and it would not incur an administrative fee. This differed from other NGOs required to abide by FCRA rules, and which allocated a percentage of donations toward administrative costs. As a government-run nonprofit, IDF-OI was oriented toward the Indian diaspora; it sought to develop India through its citizen-members outside the nation, and it structured a philanthropic transfer mechanism bypassing the FCRA. Due to its governmental authority, it indirectly served to legitimate the role of the state as having vetted the NGO and implicitly guaranteed funds would be delivered according to donor intent. The IDF program was directed toward government areas of need. In this way, it was in service to governmental agendas. But it also became a window and a bridge between India's global diaspora and the state's developmental agendas. It was, in effect, a mechanism for controlling diaspora critique and legitimizing the state.

IDF-OI was created after civil servants analyzed conditions in India to understand why its diaspora wasn't giving philanthropically through formal channels. They felt the volume of philanthropic capital fell short of its potential; something was wrong with its philanthropic corridor. The ministry had identified four problems and sought to invent an institutional structure to address them. The first was the regulatory regime itself: it was difficult for small investors to comply with the FCRA due to the rigor of the act, its bureaucracy, and red tape. To target the small investor living overseas the Indian cabinet gave IDF-OI special dispensation exempting it from FCRA. Those who donated through IDF-OI didn't have to go through the hassles of FCRA compliance. The model was more innovative than mere legislative exception. The foundation was registered as a nonprofit trust in India and was also attempting to register as a nonprofit charity in other countries. In an interview in 2012, it was described to me as a new form, whereby in the United States it would be a 501c3. The foundation in India would be the mother-hub, with satellite nonprofits registered also in the United Kingdom, Germany, the Gulf states, Australia, and New Zealand—each with an independent board of governors. On the Indo-American board, in addition to people of Indian origin, there would be people with other backgrounds as well, because, as the director explained, "it has to be truly global." Satellite offices would be exempt from tax in India as well as from tax in their respective countries. In other words, an overseas Indian (NRI, OCI, or PIO) could donate to the Government of India's foundation through a U.S.-based nonprofit and get a tax break. The structure was creative: the Government of India had become a trust that generated nonprofit charitable organizations in other countries. The government no longer harnessed solely the work of India's NGO sector; it was institutionally modeling itself as a transnational NGO.

The Congress Party had identified the problem with diaspora philanthropy: small investors had had bad experiences with Indian NGOs. Overseas Indians had invested money because their hearts were in a cause, and then they discovered that their funds didn't go toward the intended purpose. IDF-OI called this barrier the problem with "credibility at the back end." To address this, the government guaranteed that all funds sent for a cause would reach the cause, and this was accomplished without a charge; all administrative costs were borne by the government. Unlike donors using other portals that incurred small fees for transfer, donors that sent $100 to a girl-child through IDF-OI could be sure their entire $100 would go to the girl. This was possible because the trust's funds went through the government bank. Another problem the government faced was that most of the existing philanthropic pathways were faith-based or private/family channels. The IDF-OI director considered this form of giving undemocratic, and he sought to encourage philanthropy that was pluralistic and secular.[10] He emphasized the importance of diaspora capital flowing through secular pathways to ensure there was "democratization of engagement." IDF-OI dealt only with secular organizations. Since most philanthropy in India flowed through religious institutions or was religiously motivated, whether through daan, zakat, waqf; gifts to temples, gurdwaras, and mosques; or through the hawala transfers that channeled remittances from the Gulf states, this exclusion was significant. In the language of IDF-OI: "access to opportunity must be a secular ethic." The government sought to harness funds that secular diaspora Indians might hesitate to send through religious institutions, and it sought to create an exception, to open new channels of diaspora philanthropy, allowing certain types of donations to flow while constraining others through the stringent FCRA rules. The global Indian being hailed for her participatory engagement in 2012 was a particular, secular, transnational individual seeking an alternative to giving money to a temple, a mosque, or a family foundation. Politically, this was the Congress Party's constituency, and such secular giving counteracted the growing diaspora power of the BJP, which relied on discourses of religious nationalism for its support (see Mathew and Prashad 2000; Bhattacharjee 2016; Bhatt and Mukta 2000; Sundar 2004; Anderson and Damle 2019).

A challenge, according to the IDF-OI director, was a perceived lack of "mutualization" for the small investor. This is an interesting term that refers to a repeated commitment to Indian investment benefiting both donors and the state. The model was the mutual fund, and the Indian government saw the possibility of building a partnership: "We must provide for mutualization and make the philanthropist feel that the thousand dollars that they give is helping to change the lives of many people. Give them a sense of participation," the director explained. In this new development model, it was not the participation of the poor that was sought—this new model of participatory engagement targeted the diaspora's elite.

Through this model, the government sought to address national developmental needs. Civil servants realized that small, diaspora investors couldn't see the visible impact of their giving because contributions were fragmented across geographies and causes, so the government channeled the IDF-OI donations into a few key areas of national development, including those affecting primarily women, girl children, water, rural public health, and noncommunicable diseases. In practice, then, IDF-OI was more than a window. It sought to organize India's development agenda. IDF-OI did not support the rights-based or activist forms of development that oriented the previous work of many NGOs. Instead, it imagined a new knowledge economy that realized a new mode, of "diaspora experience" in addition to financial capital. It conceptualized diaspora philanthropy as reaching "beyond the narrow confines of monetary resources," and drawing upon a reservoir of social capital, particularly from Indo-Americans in the arenas of "knowledge sharing, knowledge transfer, technology transfer, and driving entrepreneurship." The Silicon Valley innovation of the 1990s in the United States was driven by Indian and Chinese workers, and a large number of Indians were now returning to India. IDF-OI worked to develop a three-tier system of "mentoring," including an internship program, a scholar's program, and a distinguished visitors program, to get its diaspora to return.

The government was trying to "mobilize diaspora resources for a global diaspora connect" on a massive scale. Indian diaspora philanthropy wasn't only about channeling funds to India. The theme for Pravasi Bharatiya Divas (or Overseas Indians Day), sponsored by the government in Jaipur in January 2012, was "global Indian inclusive growth." The foundation director explained, "Unless we are able to ensure globally equitable prosperity you are going to have a situation of either conflict or dissonance." At this same conference, the Prime Minister of India at that time, Manmohan Singh, announced that the government would reduce the restrictions on foreign direct investment and offer voting rights to NRIs. Raising resources was not a problem. The challenge was a persuasive one of diaspora return. It was about building a diaspora community—a kind of global Indian loyalty and a global/national identity. The foundation director had just returned from this Pravasi Bharatiya Divas event when we met. At this event, he hadn't been trying to raise funds, but by way of conversation, he mentioned IDF-OI to the people he was sitting next to. He said, "Each of you can be a champion . . . you can write the next chapter of India's story." In fifteen minutes, six people had pledged five million dollars. This was the philanthropic corridor the state sought to open, and which the FCRA regulated. Each person pledged a specific sum, to a specific cause, and in a particular geographic region. The condition for each pledge was that they would determine how the money would be spent. One person said he wanted to set up health clinics in five villages in his *panchayat*; one wanted his pledge allocated for the education of girls; another wanted to set up water reservoir tanks in Rajasthan.

IDF-OI aimed to function as a credible portal for philanthropic flows from the Indian diaspora to India. As a benefit, it vetted the receiving organizations. These financial tributaries were governmentally directed, and the funds flowed through governmental banking instruments, which were highly monitored and regulated. IDF-OI had an internal mechanism that facilitated financial control, and funds from the diaspora to India through IDF-OI did not support projects that challenged governmental objectives; they built and implemented those that supported governmental objectives. Perhaps we should not think of the governmental structure here as a window (as in IDF-OI), but as an *aqueduct*, a managed bridge that opens and closes selectively to manage flows from a body of water, such as a reservoir, and transport them over an obstacle, such as a ravine or a valley. In the case of the Indian diaspora, the reservoir was filled not with water but with resources; monetary wealth and knowledge. The obstacles to be traversed by the aqueduct leading away from the diaspora and toward India were borders, including India's national border. Thus, the aqueduct conveyed resources that had been backed up and collected in other nations, and then channeled them in calculated ways both regionally and in terms of practice: that is, with no outbursts, or activism. A very controlled version of the nation's expatriates giving back to the nation was being manicured and manifested, curated and sculpted, by the government, which feared terrorism and political interference, but also needed resources in the form of global investment and labor to survive. The government turned its attention in a dual direction: inside India via strategies of development and welfare schemes, and outside India via making it possible for certain kinds of input to flow freely into the nation from without.

Crackdown: Renewal Time

The licensing renewal clause of the 2010 FCRA, which said that NPOs had to renew their FCRA licenses every five years, became effective in 2015. That same year, the GOI cancelled the ability of over 9000 NGOs, including the Ford Foundation, to receive foreign funding and put dozens more on a state-sponsored watch list and accused Greenpeace of interfering with India's national development. This was given as justification for freezing the latter's accounts (*New York Times* 2015, May 7; Jain and Mohan 2015). Greenpeace India was barred completely from receiving foreign funding (*The Guardian* 2015). Civil society groups went to the media and accused the government of a crackdown, as the government defended its actions in the name of bureaucracy and national security. The weeding, according to the government, was merely an exercise of transparency: an effort to weed out ghost NGOs (those no longer in existence), errant NGOs (those not filing proper bureaucratic returns), and threatening NGOs (those endangering national security) (Sharma 2015b). The dramatic crackdown on NGOs by the Government of India and its advocacy aftermath centered around the FCRA. The cancellations of 2015 followed the leaked IB report that accused NGOs like Greenpeace of interfering with India's national development, "trying to take down India's coal-fired plants," and plotting against national security. The cancellations sparked a civil society frenzy, inspiring engagement, protest, push-back, and eventual amendments by the Government of India to the law. However, this is not a story of progress—there is no end to the dynamic back-and-forth; it is a story of a recurring process—a revolution of rules. It might be better to conceive of it as a heated conversation, a dialogue between unequal partners, and to consider the FCRA a nodal point through which negotiations took place. As the FCRA was used as a tool of statecraft, it galvanized the nonprofit sector in its advocacy efforts.

The 2015 crackdown targeted international organizations. The Ford Foundation, which had started its work in India in 1952 at the invitation of Prime Minister Nehru,[11] was not registered as a society, trust, or charitable company in India, and the government asserted it must be registered. What distinguished Ford from other international NGOs was that it had not applied for a "liaison office" in order to function as a nationally registered branch of the international organization. An international organization such as Oxfam, for example, operated in India as Oxfam India, which was registered in India as a society and was governed by an Indian board of directors. In this way, international NGOs partnered and funded their Indian NGOs with foreign funding regulated by the FCRA. In this model, the government functioned as a circuit breaker, facilitating flows of resources of which it approved while maintaining the capacity to cease approval for funding if an NGO engaged in activities deemed against governmental interests. Though the government targeted some international NGOs, it also worked with others, and depended on civil society groups to ameliorate problems of development afflicting many Indians. As the government steered civil society, which it perceived to be unruly, through the FCRA, civil society worked to keep the government in check (Jain 2015). The list of organizations that lost their FCRA permissions in 2015 included hospitals and universities that neglected to file their annual FCRA returns. The governmental sweep was bureaucratic housecleaning that the press described as a governmental crackdown (Sharma 2015b).

The international press showed concern over the assertion of governmental authority regarding Ford, Greenpeace, and FCRA. An article written by *The New York Times* Editorial Board (2015) argued that the Ford Foundation was tagged for its political activities by Modi's government. Once Ford was put on a national security watch list, it could no longer give funds to Indian groups without prior permission. The article called the crackdown political payback, noting the Gujarat state government's complaint against the NPO (Sabrang Trust) that had received money from Ford. The trust worked on behalf of victims of the Gujarat riots and sought to bring charges against PM Modi for enabling the violence. The government had earlier accused the director of the NGO of embezzling funds meant for a museum in honor of riot victims. These antagonistic politics were fought in philanthropic corridors. *The New York Times* Editorial Board (2015) called the crackdown a political vendetta, reporting: "The state asked the ministry to investigate the trust for 'disturbing the communal harmony here and carrying out anti-national propaganda against India in foreign countries.'" NGOs critiqued the government and asserted a space of dissent. In retaliation, the state audited NGOs.

Greenpeace was also targeted by the government regarding the funding of its activities in India. While the media and the NGO cried political foul, the government argued in favor of bureaucratic procedure. After Greenpeace had its FCRA funds frozen, the press reported that the NGO pleaded before a court that the Indian government did not have the power to freeze domestic contributions through FCRA.[12] The government froze the funds as a form of political targeting. An e-newsletter circulated by one NPO delved into the Greenpeace FCRA issue, arguing the suspension of funds was due to a political crackdown.[13] These funding freezes affected the nonprofit sector, which reacted with outrage, as the government repeatedly framed NGOs as threatening national interest.[14] In the leaked Intelligence Bureau report, the government accused Greenpeace of interfering with national development and of "trying to take down India's coal-fired plants." Greenpeace had its FCRA registration suspended twice, including its domestic accounts that received local donations and which made up 70 percent of its funding.[15] Greenpeace's India program director told the media: "I think the crackdown's coming from the top and so now even the bureaucracy's not open to any form of engagement." The director also remarked that previously some channels were always open "at least somewhere in the party." This suggested that it was a "clamp down on dissent." As a result, some NGOs were going underground and toning down their campaigns.[16]

When the first batch of five-year FCRA registrations were set to expire in 2015, 30,000 NGOs, foundations, and societies dependent on foreign contributions faced a unique challenge, and a looming deadline that NGOs considered a ticking time bomb. Many wondered how the government would deal with the flood of registrations. Members of the voluntary sector worried about the future. It was not technically, their problem, but their operations could be curtailed if the government could not follow its own rules and regulations. In anticipation of the deadline, NGOs filed

paper forms and gathered their accounting records in order to apply for
the first-time renewal process through the post. The Ministry of Home
Affairs determined that it would have to process renewals in ninety days.
Then, on June 17, 2015, the government proposed new rules (replacing the
FCRA rules of 2011), which digitized applications and required more compliance stipulations for NGOs (Mohan 2015). In the "GOI Amendment to
the FCRA" Circular dated June 17, 2015, the GOI requested a response by
July 1, 2015, via mail or email. It was a request for feedback from the public,
namely the NPO community that would need to abide by these rules.

One could analyze the sequence of events as not only the draconian
crackdown depicted in the media but also an effort to rule a social sector
that by its very nature resisted rules. Some NGOs channeled their advocacy efforts toward the government itself, seeking to alter governmental
procedures, as in Right to Information issues (see Pande and Singh 2007;
Sharma 2013, 2014, 2024). Apex organizations representing other NGOs
sought to negotiate with government bodies on behalf of the entire sector
by lobbying for a separate ministry to oversee the voluntary sector, sitting
on the (now defunct) Nehruvian inspired Planning Commission, and participating in specially appointed governmental offices. Others chose to go
underground altogether and remain ad hoc activist groups without registering with the government or seeking international donations. Still others
registered under the category of charitable company, under the Companies
Act. There were different paths an institution could take in response to
the increasingly restrictive environment. NGOs organized and agitated
in order to affect changes to law. They protested to shape particular demands, and used the media to voice their concerns. Anil Choudhary of
INSAF—one of the NGOs whose funds were blocked by the MHA, and
which filed a PIL case against the government and its FCRA law in 2013,
and won—said: "This Act is part of statecraft. Whoever is responsible for
running a state at a given point of time uses such act/rules to control dis-
senting voices."[17]

As the new rules were passed, NGOs struggled to comply with requirements, and to educate the sector about rule changes. In the new rules,
the FCRA oversight and regulatory monitoring of civil society groups was
to be conducted electronically, increasing the potential for governmental surveillance. Other new rules included changes to form names, which
increased the potential for bureaucratic errors, and specific processes for
banking notification and reporting (see Box 3.1).

BOX 3.1. Processes for Banking Notification and Reporting

- Online submission of forms.

- Receipt of FCRA contributions had to be posted on NGO websites within seven days of receipt.

- Banks had to send information about FCRA transactions to the central government within 48 hours.

- End-of-year income/expenditures reporting had to be submitted online.

- New form number changes: FC-4 replaced FC-6; FC-7 became FC-5; FC-8 became FC-5; FC-9 became FC-6; FC-10 became FC-7; FC-6 became FC-4.

- New regulations regarding gifts from relatives (form FC-1), while form FC-2 was prior permission for foreign hospitality.

- Form FC-3 was an application for registration/prior permission renewal for acceptance of foreign contribution by an association "having [a] definite cultural, educational, religious, or social programme."

Source: Draft NGO Report Reviewing FCRA, 2010, and Its Rules (n.d.).

The dizzying shifts in the identification numbers assigned to governmental forms, and form requirements, created confusion for NPOs seeking to follow the law. Other changes involved new restrictions, including the banning of activities deemed "against national interest," the inclusion of social media handles, and specific approved categories of permitted activity via FCRA (see Box 3.2 on the next page).[18] New, acceptable categories of social engagement for nonprofits were identified in the amended law.[19] NGOs had to account for expenditures against a list of eighty-one "purposes" in their annual return (before the amendment there had been fifty-six categories). The new list had three overarching categories under which all activities fell (see Box 3.3 on page 105).

In an article titled, "Should the Social Sector Get Its Own Set of Laws?" (Manku 2015a), a journalist interviewed the president and co-founder of a policy research NPO, who remarked that the FCRA was irrelevant and pointed out a loophole: one could create a fake software company and re-

---

BOX 3.2. Categories of Approved FCRA Activity and Procedures
for Implementation

- A declaration had to be signed for forms FC-3 and FC-4 certifying
  that organizations receiving FCRA funds were not conducting
  activities "against national interest."

- Form FC-4 required certification by a chartered accountant, and
  forms FC-3 and FC-4 required the inclusion of social media
  information (FB and Twitter handles) of NGO staff.

- Specific approved categories of activity appeared in this
  amendment, making politics out of bounds for FCRA funds.

- A separate form was required for funding political activity: form
  FC-6: "Intimation to the Central Government of receipt of foreign
  contribution received by a candidate for election (politics)," a form
  that "must be certified by a Group A Gazetted Officer of the
  Central/State Government or 1st class."

- Form FC-7 was the application to use for seeking permission for the
  transfer of a foreign contribution to another unregistered person.

Source: NPO workshops (2012–13).

---

ceive foreign funds. Legally, one didn't have to report these funds under
the FCRA if their source was a for-profit company. He recommended replacing the FCRA with a FEMA-like law: "An ineffective law is as good
as no law," he added. "The best way to gauge a law is by answering the
question whether the law serves the main purpose it was framed for." The
Supreme Court advocate who represented Greenpeace India in the Delhi
High Court in 2014 after the MHA blocked funds to the organization
citing violations, said: "It is unjust to treat all kinds of societies, charities
and non-profits on par because questions will be asked if the working style
and financial flows are different"(Manku 2015a). Manku notes that the
situation was more complex when nonprofits that were registered under
different laws came under the single umbrella of the FCRA. For decades,
civil society had been at loggerheads with government because of the challenges posed by this one-size-fits-all approach. "How can the same law
[FCRA] be used to govern a body like the Port Trust of India and a rights-

---

BOX 3.3. Activity Categories

- *Service Delivery*, which was not controversial, included construction, welfare, education, income generation, agriculture, religion, disaster relief, theater/films, women's empowerment, seminars and awareness camps, cultural activities, national celebrations, development, and sports.

- *Civil Rights Advocacy*, included activities in the following areas: human/tribal/indigenous peoples' democratic rights, caste and religious discrimination, justice, national resources, climate change, public accountability, child rights, public health, internet freedom and cyber security, violence against women, sex worker rights, the criminal justice system.

- *Research*, a new category that included: research, seminars, conferences, publications, and lectures. Research was considered a realm of social engagement that could threaten the status quo. Activists, intellectuals, and critics came under governmental scrutiny.

Source: NGO Circular on GOI Proposed Amendment to FCRA Rules (2015).

---

based organization like National Foundation of India, which helps raise money for grass-roots organizations?" asked the leader of an NPO in the article. There was an urgent need to "re-work the legislative and regulatory frameworks for NGOs in India."

> A "social" organization could be hauled up for printing pamphlets or organizing protests or talking about livelihoods. On the other hand, the Ice-Skating Association, was also a non-profit but minus the "social" tag, can carry out similar activities without drawing official notice. So even though both fell under the same law, it is up to a MHA official or the political party in power at the centre to decide which activity to label anti-national and which not to.

Philanthropy for rights-based issues had increased globally. The soft power of advocacy-oriented NGOs that had the ability to affect national laws was being restricted by the FCRA, and funding for rights-based advocacy was targeted.[20] The 2010 FCRA cap of 50 percent of funds going to administrative expenses affected rights-based groups, which used staff for programs of education, advocacy, and outreach. Some organizations that had their accounts frozen took the judicial route. INSAF and Greenpeace filed PIL cases against the government to get their FCRA funds unfrozen (Ashok 2015). Communication between civil society groups and the government took place via bureaucratic, and legislative, means, yet their dialogue was not one of equal partners; the state always maintained the upper hand. "Controlling the source of funds is like starving a sector, weakening it," said a chartered accountant who worked with the nonprofit sector (Mohan 2015). "They [the FCRA department] don't answer calls, don't reply to emails. For annual reports submitted, they never send receipts or acknowledgment, and if the application is rejected, rarely do they give reasons" said an NPO director.

Advocacy Responses

A few days after the MHA published the draft amendment to the FCRA in 2015, it called for comments by July 1. On June 30, an NPO hosted a discussion with thirty NPOs in New Delhi to plan a set of recommendations to submit to the MHA. The revised FCRA set off a flurry of government-oriented advocacy in the nonprofit sector. The FCRA encouraged the Ministry of Home Affairs to provide increased scrutiny over foreign-funded NGOs, under the auspices of the interest of India's economic security. Integral to this were issues of transparency, whereby the government made large NGOs receiving foreign funds through FCRA visible to the government itself. Transparency and rule tightening could be seen as punishment for the gains accrued by civil society groups through enacting legislation such as the Right to Information Act (2005). In the rules of the 2010 FCRA, NGOs were required to provide details of foreign funding within forty-eight hours of receiving it, to "ensure transparency." The oversight was part of the new measures, which some argued facilitated tighter integration between the Ministry of Home Affairs and the Reserve Bank of India for increased monitoring and state control (Aurora and Sharma 2015). The concept of "rule" took on a double meaning: *to govern* and a *rule of law* (Mohan 2015).

During the 2012 to 2015 reform of the FCRA, three advocacy organizations in New Delhi, which I will call Society 1, Society 2, and Society 3—all of which were "apex" NPOs (membership and/or service organizations oriented toward the voluntary sector itself)—initiated forums to respond to the changes on the horizon for the FCRA. They assisted civil society organizations with navigating the regulatory reform taking place through law. Society 1 was a membership organization that sought to speak for the nonprofit sector to the government and to lobby for what it called a "more enabling environment" for CSOs. In a response to the IB report leaked to the media, Society 1 published a circular documenting the outcome of a workshop held to address what it considered to be a "sustained attack on civil society and the voluntary sector in India."[21] It addressed specific concerns emerging from the leaked IB report, including the pervasive culture of secrecy around governmental control, stating: "NGOs are easy targets. They are managed by the FCRA department and the IB, both of which are inaccessible to the common citizen. Reports are leaked to the media but never shared in public." Society 1's circular challenged the state to consider who was best suited to manage the public good. It addressed a perceived history of suspicion between the government and NGOs,[22] and pointed out that most leaked reports were futuristic. NGOs were not found guilty; they were assumed to be guilty.[23] Society 1, through its report, challenged the government for its assumption that NGOs were subcontractors and not partners in development.[24] The report outlined eight specific suggestions, in the form of queries to the ministry. All such circulars and reports contained specific recommendations for the government.[25]

Society 1 convened a workshop to organize a collective response to the draft rules of the 2010 FCRA. In June of 2015, it sent a letter to the Ministry of Home Affairs documenting the results of the meeting, convened by the NPO with representatives of thirty "prime voluntary organizations." The meeting was organized in order to draft recommendations to send to the MHA regarding the proposed amendment to the FCRA rules. It addressed issues the NPO considered critical, that had been incorporated in the proposed rules. The sector felt the rules contained clauses that were restrictive, difficult, and intrusive. Issues highlighted during the meeting included the points shown in Box 3.4, which Society 1 organized in their response, containing detailed requests for rule adjustments.

Society 1 sought to both educate its constituency about the forthcoming rule changes and mobilize a collective response. It held a series of FCRA clinics in a nationwide outreach initiative. Because organizations could apply for renewal six months before the renewal due date, the first wave

---

BOX 3.4. Requests for Rule Adjustments Resulting from Workshop

- Regarding *uploading financial data* every time an organization received funds: the proposed rule stated that receipt of funds must be displayed on a website within seven days. NGOs in rural areas would likely face difficulty complying with this rule, because they were based in locations without internet density. Though earlier this rule was applicable only to NGOs receiving funding of more than Rs 1 crore, the new rule could make NGOs vulnerable to local harassment if financial data were to be made public (Sharma 2015b).

- The NPO requested the creation of a robust *grievance redressal system*, with direct communication between the ministry and NGOs. The NPO argued the proposal to move processes online would make it difficult for NGOs that had trouble with their password and login regarding FCRA accounts. Noncompliance had already resulted in the inability to file annual returns, with subsequent FCRA suspension and/or cancellation. Since most of the FCRA cancellations in the "chilling crackdown" were due to bureaucratic noncompliance, this was an issue of concern. For example, if an NGO had moved and neglected to inform the FCRA office, its FCRA license would be cancelled. Society 1 had worked with the Ministry of Home Affairs in 2012, after the initial cancellations due to bureaucratic errors had occurred, to get the NGO licenses reinstated.

- The NPO demanded *accountability* on the part of banks, and the MHA and voiced the need for three-way communication between banks, the MHA, and NGOs. In the FCRA provisions, banks were required to notify the MHA when they received foreign contributions, but Society 1 recommended that they also notify NGOs.

- The NPO argued for the exclusion of Facebook and Twitter (*social media*) addresses of the chief NGO functionaries and working committee of an NGO on the FCRA forms, arguing that this was an invasion of privacy.

- The NPO requested translated versions of the draft FCRA rules and other communications by the MHA in Hindi and in other languages, citing a governmental English bias. There were limitations of central governance in a multilingual nation such as India. The centrality of the government presented the locality of the hinterlands as a problem of translation.

- The NPO requested extending the date of soliciting suggestions in favor of *more dialogue*. The deadline of only fifteen days for feedback was too limited.

Source: NPO Draft Study Review of FCRA, 2010, and Its Rules (n.d.).

of renewals was anticipated in November 2015. Organizations with multi-year projects could renew twelve months before the renewal due date. What did Society 1's FCRA workshops consist of? On the first half day, a session was held on compliance requirements of the FCRA law. After lunch, there was a session on resolving questions and answering queries. Participants were encouraged to bring relevant papers on which to ask advice. Workshops were held in seventeen key cities and were sponsored by four organizations. They were geared toward senior leaders, managers, and other members of voluntary organizations dealing with FCRA issues. It was not expensive to attend (450 rupees, which paid for the workshop, lunch, refreshments, and resource materials). Seats were limited to fifty; workshops were small.[26]

In an online newsletter to its membership, the communication director for Society 1 articulated why the sector had become alarmed regarding renewals. The provision for FCRA renewal stipulated "the use of an online form followed by a download of its hardcopy which was to be accordingly submitted through post to the Ministry of Home Affairs." However, as the date approached, the online portal did not open on the MHA website and no notification had been released. Many organizations went ahead and filed renewals, but "what about those hapless organizations isolated from the communication grapevines of a metropolis?" the newsletter asked. This MHA lapse was perceived as "bureaucratic evasiveness" by the staff of Society 1, a form of structural violence resulting from bureaucratic indifference (as described in Gupta 2012). Later in the newsletter, evasiveness was interpreted more broadly as authoritarianism, which required an activist response in the form of "educating the masses on why civil society matters."

FCRA clinics addressed the confusion and anxiety that the prospect of FCRA renewals had created in the sector. A report on FCRA clinics, published in Society 1's e-newsletter, mentioned the additional stressor of unreliable FCRA "brokers" (described as "touts who are trying to exploit the situation"). The FCRA clinics sought to remove regional disparities in access to information, as organizations in the capital city of Delhi had more access to information regarding legislative reform than those in remote rural areas. Yet, Society 1 and its sister organizations sought more than information sharing. They aimed to review and comment upon the law itself: "Furthermore, while the MHA is conducting FCRA renewals, [Society 1] and [Society 2] are in the process of reviewing the law itself and documenting organisations' experiences in working within the ambit of the new law," and the clinics were helpful in identifying issues for the feedback-giving process. This was FCRA activism and its dialogic structure at work.

The work of other NPOs in Delhi overlapped with Society 1's efforts. Their directors participated in workshops and were invited to speak at forums. The community agitating for legislative reform was a tight one, and its members knew each other. Society 2 was a completely virtual NGO. I met with its director as he described his activism as "informational/communicative." Through an online forum, Society 2 members could discuss the hairy details of FCRA rules. Many wrote in with "what if" questions; some wrote with sophisticated critical analyses of the FCRA rules themselves. Like Society 1, Society 2 called out to its membership, asking for feedback on the proposed rules. It collected this feedback and also wrote a letter to the ministry on behalf of its membership, with recommendations. Thus, an interesting aspect of this online NGO was that it was, strictly speaking, a virtual forum, a web-based blog, in which NGO members could assist each other with information about navigating the changing legal landscape. This was particularly relevant to the altered calculus of laws regarding foreign donations. For example, under the revised Companies Act of 2013, NGOs had to consider sources of donations, as donations to companies must also pass through FCRA approval if the charitable company was registered as a Section 8 company. Subsidiary companies were considered foreign companies if they displayed a shareholding pattern with more than 50 percent of shares held by foreign entities. A member wrote a question on this topic, on an advice column in 2015, asking if a subsidiary of a foreign source was also a foreign source:

> Dear Sirs, we are an organisation in [x state] working on healthcare. We have a donor which was not classified as a foreign company and as per the company's directive we have been considering this money to be Indian money. We now have a confusion [after] reviewing the New Companies Act wherein the subsidiary company seems to become a foreign entity due to the shareholding pattern of holding company. Our donor is the subsidiary company: therefore, the following are our queries: 1. Are all the funds that we have received since 1/4/2004 classified as foreign donation under FCRA??? 2. if they are considered foreign donation and we have FCRA but have not deposited this money in FCRA account, what are the consequences? 3. what is the corrective action that can be taken?

The responses (by six members) on Society 2's forum explained that the NGO had till December 31 to rectify the error, and explained how to file the correct forms. Accountants of charitable organizations wrote in to this forum with queries and had a dialogue on how to approach changing legislation. It functioned as a support and advice community/column. As with Society 1's workshops, it also functioned as an advocacy group, collating responses to its members regarding the FCRA amendment and sending a written response to the Ministry of Home Affairs FCRA department.

Society 3 was set up to help other NGOs. Its primary focus was educational, publishing short information bulletins, disseminated on an email listserve, on the nitty-gritty of legislative reform. It also conducted workshops for NGOs. Incorporating a wry sense of humor, Society 3's advice reports were written to alert and educate the NGO sector on changing rules, laws, and requirements. Run by a chartered accountant and scholar (an Accountability Guide), with expertise in nonprofit management, it was a valuable reference for Indian NGOs. The reports covered the political terrain of NGO engagement in real time and through the lens of accountants and the law. The reports were presented in the form of updates, or capsules, on the changing regulatory landscape.

One capsule explored what it called the "FCRA cocktail." It discussed the danger of mixing foreign and local funds in an FCRA account and described the case of Greenpeace, in which local and foreign funds were frozen because they may have been mixed. The capsule warned readers: "Lesson for NGOs: Draw a very thick line between FCRA and non-FCRA bank accounts. Don't ever cross this line." Another capsule alerted the sector about FCRA cancellations for not filing forms for FCRA funds: "How to make sure your name does not figure on the next list [of cancellations]? 1) check if FC-6 is showing online, if not, verify if Ministry received FC-6; 2) check if FCRA shows correct address; 3) pray every day . . . always helps!" The capsules were good natured and good humored. One capsule warned against governmental takeover of assets: "if land [was] bought with non-FC funds and the building was purchased with FC funds, or if a vehicle was purchased with joint FC and non-FC funds, then the government can take over the non-FC assets without court orders." Another explored how the FCRA 2010 capped administrative expenses of foreign contributions received during the year, and noted that if an NGO's administrative expenses were likely to exceed 50 percent, then it must receive government advance approval. The capsule detailed one of the reasons for the suspension of Greenpeace's FCRA license: "the association has incurred more than 50% of the foreign contribution on administrative expenditure during the financial year 2011–12 and 2012–13, without obtaining prior approval." "If your NGO is involved in advocacy, organising, or other forms of social awareness, your 'administrative expenditure' may well be over 50%. Keep watching it and get prior approval if you can't keep it below 50%." Advocacy and rights-based organizations, which were staff heavy, tended to incur these high administrative expenses. The devil really was in the details, and the rules.

The capsules, as a collection of missives, read as a chatty newsletter, a humorous advice column focused on how NPOs were to deal with the FCRA. Two capsules listed seventeen donors that appeared on the government's prior approval list—climate or environment focused, rights-based, and religious. Another discussed the advantages of NGOs' registering as Section 8 charitable companies through the Companies Act, instead of as societies or trusts. The reasons given were quicker registration, access to the benefits of a charitable trust or society, and clearer governance rules. A further capsule announced that the FCRA office had fixed the fifth day of each month for open meetings and problem solving with the NGO community, and another placed the "chilling crackdown" in the historical context of earlier FCRA cancellations: "The last one year has seen more headlines about FCRA cancellations than the previous 30 years. Is FCRA cancellation a new phenomenon, or is this being used maliciously by the present government to clamp down on civil society? The facts do not support this popular view."[27] The Accountability Guide working with Society

3 argued that large-scale cancellations of FCRA registrations were not malicious, rather, they were a housekeeping exercise; the bulk of the cancelled registrations represented NGOs that had become defunct, had stopped received foreign contributions, or were not filing their FC returns. And yet another capsule explored how NPOs could register as for-profit companies to avoid FCRA scrutiny, and cautioned against this route, given the intricacies of the law. If a for-profit company was involved in social work, or programs with foreign contributions, it also would require FCRA or prior permission, and the exemption for FCRA was only for business, not charitable or public-sector work. The intricacies of the regulatory reform were mind-boggling.

To address this in another form, the Accountability Guide held workshops for the nonprofit sector. A workshop announcement, "Meet your new In-laws this August," was written in the same humorous yet informative tone as the capsules:

> Their names are: FCRA, FEMA, Income Tax, Service Tax, and CSR. Each of them has a different understanding of who you are and what you do for a living. The introductions will be performed by [the NPO director] over three days, with wit and humour, as well as insight and empathy. You will get to understand why and how FCRA was born 40 years ago, and the mid-life crisis it is going through now. You will learn how to make sure you and your grantees do not enrage it beyond endurance. You will also be introduced to FEMA and RBI, which have the final say on branches and extra-marital liaison offices. You will then meet Income Tax and find out how to remain in its good books. You will learn about the goodies it can offer, and the havoc it can wreak in your fiscal life. Hopefully you will also be able to avoid its Cyclopian eye of Transfer Pricing on transactions with your sisters abroad. Also, keen to meet you is Service Tax, a little known member of the family. Understanding his psychology will help you continue your mission of service to the poor and vulnerable, without getting axed or taxed for it. You will also get to say hello to CSR, a rich cousin, who might grow up to be your best friend in need. Other family members you will want to meet include the new Companies Act, who can offer you a safer neighbourhood, if you don't mind the higher cost of living.

The three advocacy NGOs, run by Accountability Guides, served the nonprofit sector and aimed to address the legislative reform that threatened to strangle civil society. Civil society organizations as activist agitators sought to redefine the law as it moved from a Bill to an Act, in the interstitial spaces where change was possible. They worked to educate their constituencies in the nonprofit sector who might not be aware of the new regulatory terrain. As advocacy organizations, they did not agitate for reduced regulation by the government; they demanded better regulation. They were not immune to the critical refrain that NGOs are poorly managed or inefficient institutional mediums for providing basic social services. They sponsored governance workshops, and publications on best management practices for their members. They too wanted to see the voluntary sector purged of the "bad apples" but urged the government not to throw out the entire bunch.

Conclusion

The FCRA began in the Emergency, and continued through different political eras of party rule, instituting a space for statecraft and advocacy. By asserting what was legible to the state as accepted FCRA activities, and articulating what was not, the government gained public legitimacy. Implemented by civil servants in the Ministry of Home Affairs, the FCRA focused on issues of domestic security, on defending national borders from "external" political influence, and redirecting NGOs to raise funds domestically. As much as the FCRA was a tool of statecraft it was also a fertile site of advocacy and a philanthropic corridor to be regulated. Faced with the threat of cancellation arising from the revised FCRA, NGOs in New Delhi came together to organize, to speak back to the state, and to propose alternative governance structures. The FCRA crackdown inspired civil society groups to band together and lobby for themselves as a group. Debates over the FCRA involved public issues of social welfare, and through struggles over the FCRA NGOs lobbied for the political space to provide public welfare and called upon the state to keep its social welfare promises.

The FCRA was not the only philanthropy pathway being explored by the government. Sources of diaspora philanthropy were wooed as the FCRA rules became more punitive, and the Government of India, whether through the initial attempts by the Congress Party with the 2010 FCRA revision or the strict amendments implemented by the BJP in 2015, created a longer story of regulatory control, which scrutinized certain types of foreign donations for specific, rights-based advocacy activities. By 2017, the impact of the revised 2010 FCRA was felt in the sector as a culture of fear. As one NGO director remarked in an interview in 2017:

> [The government will] find an excuse to cancel on some very flimsy ground usually. Usually, you don't even know why [an organization has] been canceled. I mean that Médecins Sans Frontières got canceled. They're a huge humanitarian organization that provides medical services during relief. And they just said: "You go to the bank, and you can't withdraw your money or bank accounts are frozen. You never get a letter. You never get a meeting with anyone who will tell you why."

MSF had come to this NGO director the month before to discuss this issue. Amnesty International, Greenpeace, all of them were at risk. I asked if Greenpeace's FCRA had been reinstated, and she explained,

> No, no. You never get it back. . . . Raising funds in India is extremely important because the only regulation that bites is FCRA. If you're raising Indian money, there's no other law that says what NGOs can do or not do. So, they [another NPO] are now, because they are a campaigning organization in a way and they don't have a lot of partners like us and a footprint in the States, they need fewer sums of money. Interestingly, their fundraising within India actually went up very dramatically. So, there are enough Indians who are wanting to support them.

"Then they can exist?" I asked. "So they exist," she said, "and they're doing fine."

This would later change with the 2023 Finance Bill that proposed to regulate domestic, inter-charity philanthropy. It was easy to imagine the government had an agenda, but the government was not a single entity. It was comprised of different, often competing, bodies, institutions, and offices. Still, it was hard not to interpret the regulatory shift as a move to encourage NGOs to raise funds domestically, especially if an NGO wanted to focus on social issues and controversial topics. Another director said the government didn't like dissent or conflicting opinions, and the media and civil society were being scrutinized and oppressed. The government also depended on foreign donations from overseas Indians. "The only reason they don't just shut FCRA and just stop foreign funding, which would really affect pretty much all of us because we then fund all the smaller organizations, is their own organizations get a lot of money from overseas Indians."

The FCRA had gone almost completely online by 2017, from being paper-based to portal-driven. This made it easier for the government to monitor, manage, and administer: "So, it's now easier for the department to crackdown and see who filed and who didn't," said an Accountability Guide who supported the government's aversion to foreign political interference but argued the threat was also internal. NGO workers were an alternative, political, power base, and the fear of anti-national sentiments expressed by the 2017 BJP government mirrored other global authoritarian and populist shifts. Perhaps all political parties are against foreign influence; this was the basis for the FCRA during the Emergency in 1976. The BJP, however, was "digging out information about NGOs and making it available to public, to authorities." It was putting NGOs, and the people that ran them in danger, if not physical danger then the danger of having their work be "seen in a different light," and potentially misinterpreted. A Professional Critic explained: "I'm not saying that what NGOs do, everything is fine. There are certainly areas where NGOs need more supervision. [. . .] But at the same time, they should broadly be left alone, otherwise they can't function because they're really fragile. And that's where I think we have a problem."

This chapter presented a portrait of regulatory reform of a specific law, the FCRA, including the advocacy responses it inspired in the nonprofit sector. From the 2010 revision that limited activity deemed "against national interest," to the 2012 rules articulating its processes of implementation, to the "crackdown," closures, and renewal processes of 2015, Indian NPOs have scrambled to understand, follow, and protest the law. In this process, the FCRA reform oriented the advocacy repertoire of the NPO sector. Traffic lights, bridges, windows, or aqueducts, philanthropic corridors are spaces of statecraft. The FCRA, alongside the government's quest to both control and woo diaspora philanthropy, became an arena for NPO engagement that shaped the nonprofit sector.

FOUR

Navigating the Rules

Failed projects, failed organizations, failed economies, personal and professional failures. Fear of failure stifles the voice, muffles the mind, stops creative wheels from moving, and intimidates the imagination. For an institution, failure brings on the shame of closure and social death. What is failure, and how can we assess its power without falling into the grip of its own self-definition? Can we evaluate failure without using its grammar? Can we possibly analyze it from another angle to experience it as an entity in its own right? When one speaks of failure, often one implies utility: one fails at tasks, strivings, tests, aims, and goals. Plans fail. Building designs fail. States fail. Failed states require intervention. Receiving an F on an exam means one needs help (remediation). Failure triggers action. System failure, social failure, organ failure, body failure—death. Perhaps it is modernity itself that is the engine that determines perpetual motion and its opposite: stasis, inertia, failure.

Nonprofit organizations are public in nature. They are not privately held; they are shared by citizens, the state, donors, and beneficiaries (stakeholders) with competing interests vying for attention and resources. This discursive competition—including the power to define an institution on its own terms—produces stress in nonprofits. These tensions at times explode into culture wars, negotiated through the court of public opinion and the media to determine whether an institution is "good" or "bad." When institutions like NPOs fail they are closed down, collapse, or are remediated. Institutional transformation and nonprofit growth and development are often discussed in terms of success and failure. NGOs are judged by size and economic success: that is, their ability to raise funds and to scale up. As an Indian philanthropist noted, "funding is so closely tied to the vision of success that social organizations are forced to find ways to claim success, not necessarily for societal outcomes but for continuity of funding" (Nilekani 2019). What if we used a different evaluative lens, beyond outcomes, focused on the process itself? What if we built failure into the process of doing nonprofit work, supporting projects that begin and end, that do or do not meet their goals, yet that stumble upon unexpected arenas of need and new challenges? What if funders gave a wider berth to nonprofit institutions that experimented with the nonprofit form itself? In the world of nonprofits, failure is a common counterpart to the discourse of development and of progress, and in this discourse sometimes nonprofits must fail in order to succeed. For some, failure is part of successful attempts, part of the process of striving, moving, achieving, and goal setting.

To be legible to the state, and to communicate with it, nonprofit organizations must develop certain types of bureaucratic and institutional literacy. To be legible to the market, they must be structured, and behave, like corporations. Nonprofits must be legible to state governments because governments license their institutional forms, and regulate them as nonprofits, through registration laws that function as institutional birth certificates. Without registration with the state as NPOs, they are not nonprofits; they are civic groups, or social movements, or loose associations and collectives. The category of the nonprofit is a particular institutional category that not only structures communication with governments, it also facilitates and legitimizes funding flows. For some groups, particularly radical activist ones, becoming a nonprofit is itself an act of failure. Some have argued that one cannot protest the system from within, as this position involves co-optation (INCITE! 2007). Nonprofits fail for several reasons, but first and foremost is lack of resources. Because nonprofits do not earn profits, they depend upon philanthropy, grants, donations, and membership dues. As donor-dependent institutions, without funding they cannot exist. When they lose resources, they fold, fail, and cease to operate. Another stumbling block for the institutional health of nonprofits resides in tension with government bodies regarding political activity. As laws were reformed in India, being political came to be a liability and, for organizations on the cutting edge of social transformation, the invisible fence separating nonprofits from political groups was crossed as civil society organizations strove to make social change.

Navigating the regulatory rules was an act of improvisation for non-profits. As nonprofits improvised in relation to regulations that constrained them, the limitations became part of their institutional identities. Improvisation was a component of everyday life, of navigating categories—such as "nonprofit-ness" for institutions.[1] Responding to constraints through improvisation was a way of responding to the environment with decisions. In the process of improvisational negotiation, nonprofits pushed back to resist regulations when they became too restrictive. It was not just the rules that confined and defined the category of nonprofits, but the dynamic engagement with the rules—pushing against them, challenging them, asserting them in defiance—that created the nonprofit form, and the nonprofit sector, as discursive categories. Nonprofits demanded rules to facilitate their sector, and resisted when the regulations became too restrictive. Legally, nonprofits were defined by these constraints through the operations of law.

Audits in the Public Sphere

In 2013, urban myths regarding bad nonprofits circulated widely in the newspapers. These were not stories about those who broke the rules, but narratives criminalizing an entire sector. The narratives were deployed as explanations for why the nonprofit sector required increased regulation, a sort of informal political commentary similar to critiques of corruption leveled at the government (Gupta 2012; Sharma 2008; Parry 2000; Roy 2011). As the anti-corruption movement gained ground, large protests spread into the urban streets (Sharma 2024), and governmental failures to address infrastructure problems were targeted by the public and the media, especially regarding claims that incompetence and corruption had slipped into the nonprofit sector, which had "mushroomed" (a word used in the press at that time). NGOs were called paper NGOs (that is, fake); parliamentarian-wife NGOs; shell companies; vehicles for money laundering. NGOs were being given as wedding gifts, included in dowries, bought and sold. What were the evaluative mechanisms for determining failure in the nonprofit sector? Many in the sector itself spoke with me about the need to get rid of "fly-by-night" NGOs, and the importance of sorting the good from the bad. The situation was offered as an explanation for why India could not develop and why regulatory reform was required. One civil servant described fly-by-night NGOs as a barrier to diaspora philanthropy. Small diaspora donors, he said, were "once bitten twice shy" as they encountered "fly-by-night operators, masquerading as nongovernmental organizations." Diaspora donors put their money where their hearts were, but then discovered their funds did not go to the intended purpose. The civil servant spoke of improving the "credibility at the back end" and of "delivering the cause" that was dear to donors' hearts.

As I traveled through the nonprofit sector in Delhi, I heard stories of actual NGO failure. These were often told as fantastical stories in a "can-you-believe-this" or "I-told-you-so" sort of tone. Some stories were terrible, and I hesitate to narrate them because they were secondhand stories, recounted by those who experienced problems that I could not verify. Nor did I try. But this is neither journalism nor am I seeking to write an exposé. As an ethnographer, I am concerned with the ethos of a group, the norms and rules that govern some activities and stifle others. As with any industry, members of the group—insiders—can be the worst and most gossipy critics of all. One NGO struggled with plagiarism. Was this a "bad NGO" or a "bad employee?" What could be said about it, as the small nonprofit did not have resources beyond the internet and there was pressure to produce, was that some young staffers were pushed to cut and paste. All the result required was a citation, but then the work would not have been their own. Another employee of a nonprofit outsourced her work and paid someone to write her reports. Yet, the NPO itself sometimes outsourced reports to scholars, and this was considered acceptable. What was the difference? Authorship? Some nonprofit workers I met with called this NGO a failure, a nonstarter. It was not what people expected it to be—it didn't live up to its expectations. I wondered if perhaps the expectations were not realistic. Could failure in some cases be a matter of unrealistic expectations? NGOs were considered utopias, angels, and Gods, bound to experience failings in the mortal world. Other scandalous stories included the buying and selling of NGOs, advertised in the newspaper and on Quikr.[2] All the tales of nonprofit malfeasance referred to uneasy relationships with the market. But NGOs were not oriented toward profit, and the regulatory frameworks regarding bad NGOs were meant to "weed them out." This was part of the larger conversation taking place in Indian middle-class society in Delhi regarding corruption. Scams were ubiquitous and had become a political issue inspiring activism through the anti-corruption movement, and via laws such as the Right to Information Act. I was so struck by the pervasive and persistent conversations about scams, that I started to keep track. Nonprofits did not have a monopoly on scams by any means. Corporations were also being scrutinized.

In Box 4.1 is one list I began on a particular day as I navigated the city. Some happened to me, others to friends and family. These were minor negotiations (scams) that entered my personal life as an ethnographer on a single day in April 2013, which I offer as a snapshot (via fieldnotes). Stories of scams filled the daily newspapers and were as commonplace as the weather. The government and its required bribes for development projects was also a regular character in the ongoing list of scams, as were stories of retired government officers starting NGOs and siphoning off funds.

In this context, of endless negotiation, what were the implications of NGO failure? Who determined it? Donors—as in, we won't give you future funds because you have failed. Or, governments—as in, in order to get a license, to register, or to maintain a license the institution must meet certain criteria. Given these external evaluative mechanisms, there was a movement in the nonprofit sector for nonprofits to take over the evaluative mechanisms themselves, through self-governance. Several organizations with which I was in contact in Delhi were actively involved in working with nonprofits to increase their self-governance capacities. Two voluntary organizations held capacity-building workshops with nonprofits and published materials on governance to educate the sector. Another worked specifically in the credibility realm. It provided certificates of compliance for nonprofits after an extensive audit. NGOs sought this certification to provide financial credibility. A director of a large NPO required nonprofits it funded to join the credibility-granting NPO and become certified. Another arena for assessment was an annual report produced by the auditing company Bain and Edelman, considered a reliable source and used as a credibility indicator. Because one could not measure the success of a nonprofit via its profits, assessment occurred through indicators and audits (see Merry 2016 for an ethnographic analysis of indicators).

I met with a former civil servant who had a broad perspective on

BOX 4.1. List of Minor Negotiations (Scams) in 2013

- Gas cylinder: Indane gas. Each family allotted x number of cylinders per year. If one is not using, someone in gas company sells cylinder in our name on black market. We pay Rs 450 per cylinder. Black market is Rs 1200–1300. Got text about cylinder.. What happened. A family member had to go to Indane and complain. Then they received a cylinder without a receipt. Something fishy. Government official had started NGO in order to funnel money from government programs, through own organization. (Happened to family.)

- Getting petrol at petrol pump: someone pretends to put it in car but puts some into bucket. You get charged for entire amount but don't receive it. (Rumor.)

- Fruit seller: shows you good fruit. Gives you rotten fruit in sleight of hand. (Me, always.).

- Friend's school: trying to push her daughter out to make vacancy for family that will make big donation. Daughter was sick and had death in family so missed school one month. School harassed parent and tried to get her to withdraw child. The school then threatened to keep the child back a grade, which was illegal until class 8. Family called contact in Indian Police Service who suggested contacting the media, which had more power than schools. (Happened to friend.)

- Everything is negotiated. Kickbacks. Shopping and bargaining. Asking for a discount for absolutely everything. Some shops now hang sign—"Fixed Price"—to avoid haggling. Haggling culture, getting an edge. (Happened to me.)

- The Citibank in the local market is no more. Turns out the folks that loaded the automatic teller machine loaded Rs 1000 bills into the 100s slot and then withdrew money. Swindled Citibank out of loads of cash. Now Citibank is a boarded-up corner shop area. So, it goes. That bank was a pain anyway. Finally closed my account.

Source: Author's fieldnotes.

governmental, nonprofit, and corporate approaches to development. He
had worked in all three sectors, including a harrowing experience with a
corrupt, UN-funded, and government-sponsored nonprofit. Though I did
not have an opportunity to verify the details of his story, I include it as an
exemplar of the many stories I heard as people argued that the nonprofit
sector needed regulatory oversight. Members of the voluntary sector also
echoed these concerns, and it became a common refrain. This development agent—who had first worked for the government, then the nonprofit
sector, later the corporate sector, and eventually returned to the nonprofit
sector—was deputized by the government to monitor a large, government-
funded UN project focused on artisans. In his efforts to monitor the project, he saw that the organization was not doing the proposed project but
had created a performance of development for monitoring in the form of
reports. As a career civil servant, he was aware of the limitations of governmental work, but was idealistic about working with the NGO. His
idealism was shattered when he learned a factory had been set up to manu-
facture artisanal products, and village women were paraded as the artisans
(and paid for that service) as needed. The NGO used its funding to support
itself, not the women it claimed to assist. He was dismayed that no real auditing or monitoring was being done. The fakery was not in the NPO but
in its credibility mechanisms, which were manufactured. When he began
to monitor the projects, he met with resistance; the group rejected his requests for reporting mechanisms. He thought about restricting funds but,
he said, "Money has to go because they'll start crying: 'Artisans will die if
you don't give an order.'" It was after working there for four or five months
that he started to explore the situation himself and realized the work was
not going to artisans. The NGO had started a small garment factory in a
city, and the funds went to hire factory workers and purchase raw materials. The artisans did not know funds were supposed to go to them. He
went to the villages and spoke to the artisans who were unaware—it was a
structural problem and a business, and the fake monitoring was beneficial
to the donors and the NPO. He said:

> They are happy their project is running. NGO is happy they are getting
> money. Consultants and monitors are happy because they are getting
> their money. Once again donor agency is happy, they are getting reports
> from consultants and monitors. Everybody is happy. Whoever has voice
> is happy. The money, which is being eaten in whose names, they even
> don't know that the money is being eaten in my name.

With all his experience in government, he considered the problem structural, and he blamed a lack of accountability mechanisms. The drama caused
the civil servant a great deal of heartache, and health problems due to stress.

He moved into the corporate sector where he thought the profit motive
was clearer and did not allow for such misbehavior, lies, scams, and scandals. He thought the category of Section 25 companies (later Section 8)
offered an accountability structure. His new position was in a corporate
development company establishing service centers consisting of internet
kiosks in villages for e-governance. The project had been given to the nonprofit sector, but it had failed to meet its targets, and nobody had been
trained to use the computers. NGOs received their funds but there was
no one to guide the process. They could not provide the e-governance services, or any other service, on the internet, so "everything collapsed." It
was another case of NGOs taking the money and not following through,
with people being left high and dry. He spoke of how, in 2008, the government had developed a public-private partnership with a corporation, developing a business model and charging fees for services. The fee structure
was motivation for the corporation to get involved in development. This
entrepreneurship model worked better, in his view, because profit was an
incentive, a type of accountability, and proof of service in the corporate
sector. Companies made money when entrepreneurs made money, which
meant services were delivered to people. In the government there were
bribes, and NGOs were unreliable and had failed, but the motive of profit
was enough for this civil servant to move to the corporate sector. After
years of working in the corporate sector, he took up another position in
the nonprofit sector. These sectors were not mutually exclusive and often
intersected, with labor and expertise flowing between.

I recount this story to emphasize, not that NGOs and the government are bad and that the corporate sector of social entrepreneurship is
good, but that the three sectors work together as a trifecta in the public
imagination—with one sector moving up in the moral evaluation range of
indicators and others falling behind. In this moral rubric, the corporate
sector is good only because it is not the government or the nonprofit sector.
Or the government is bad because the nonprofit sector is good (closer to
the people and not corrupt). This relational map for evaluating actors
working for the public is always in transition, always being rethought, and
always open to analysis in the court of public opinion. When nonprofits

fail, it is sometimes because they are nonprofits in relation to other institutional forms, ones that are proposed as more viable, regulable, accountable, and credible forms, such as corporations. Corporations do not have
to vie for serving a vague public, though they are increasingly being pressured by voluntary groups and governments to be more socially oriented.
Nonprofits could not exist as a "sector" without the relational, moral, and
structural comparison with corporate and governmental approaches to the
same social problems, such as infrastructure, poverty, women's empowerment, public health, and public welfare more generally. The comparison
was a normative evaluation, and a moral audit that took place in the public
sphere. Nonprofits are often held to a higher standard because of their association with public good instead of profit (as in the corporate sector) or
politics (as in the state).

To combat the perception of the nonprofit sector as scandalous, and failing, a frenzy of activity took place among NPOs. New dangers emerged,
of being political, and efforts ramped up to help NPOs follow the rules
and establish their credibility. These efforts were aided by the NPOs specifically oriented toward evaluating and certifying nonprofits. The poor
reputation of the sector was troubling to nonprofit leaders tasked with articulating the credibility of an entire genre of institutions, and many NPO
leaders felt responsible for setting the record straight. There were implications here as well for the reform of regulatory frameworks that was taking
place. NPOs were losing their ground, and the authority to determine the
frames in which their work was understood. NPOs were evaluated in three
arenas: by donors when seeking funds, by governments providing permissions and licenses, and in the court of public opinion, constituted by the
media and the public.

The Danger of Being Political

Being political was becoming a liability for NPOs, especially if they received funds through FCRA. The tension between critiquing the state and
working with the state to change it generated strategic conversations in
the voluntary sector. A political NGO could be considered a "bad NGO,"
resulting in its FCRA license being revoked and its funds frozen. The
issues of political engagement prompted self-censorship in anticipation of
resistance from the state. This was in 2013, before Narendra Modi was

elected, and tensions increased after Modi's election. As Aradhana Sharma's 2024 work on the political party Aam Aadmi Party (AAP) points out, the anti-corruption movement was an example of this type of danger. AAP emerged as a political party out of the anti-corruption movement, demonstrating the potentially porous boundaries between these categories. If NGOs were shapeshifters (Bernal and Grewal 2014), one could say that this particular group shape-shifted to another leg of the state-market-nonprofit three-legged stool. There were distinct implications for regulatory frameworks in this transformation, as the state could no longer regulate the political party in the same way it had regulated that party as a nonprofit or social movement. AAP critiqued the state while proposing itself as an alternative. As in other parts of the world, such as the United States, Turkey, and Egypt, other groups on the politically Right-leaning end of the spectrum also moved from the field of social movements to that of party politics. It marked an increase of populism, and a shift from the nonprofit sector to the political realm. Regulations were set up to limit political activities, and because of this, some NPOs opted out of registering as societies or trusts, becoming charitable companies instead, which were regulated under the Companies Act.

Activist Donors had plenty to say about this shift. I sat with a philanthropist in the leafy neighborhood of central Delhi in 2012. We were in a Lutyens building left over from the colonial era, the graceful simplicity of the low white structure offset by a gigantic banyan tree outside the window. As we spoke, I was acutely aware that they[3] were the richest person I had ever met. Class distinctions did not disappear in the nonprofit world; they took on hues. This philanthropist dressed in an understated yet sophisticated manner, their language refined and resolute. I described my project as an ethnography of shifting regulation, explaining that I sought to understand how the government changed laws that affected the nonprofit sector in India, while the voluntary sector worked with the government to alter lawmaking efforts in a manner suitable for the sector itself. The philanthropist had been deeply involved with the social sector since early 2000, setting up some foundations, serving on the boards of others. Their perspective on the sector was that of a funder and a strategist. They saw a tectonic shift in the sector that was generationally related to leadership and vision. They thought out loud about the history of the NPO sector in India, and how many of the senior leaders of NPOs came out of the cataclysmic events of the 1970s and '80s that had also prompted international aid, events like the aftermath of war in Bangladesh, famines, and earthquakes. Times had changed. They reflected on how, after twenty years of liberalization and the aging of the NPO-sector leadership, the generation of people interested in citizen-sector work or social work "were quite different from their leaders and gurus." Their thinking had changed, and they lived in a market-oriented India, much different from the socialist India that pre-dated the 1990s.

There was a generational issue at work in the realm of NGOs, and different decades produced distinct issues, as well as eras of civil society activism. The social sector had changed in concert with historical events. The Activist Donor argued that the emergent generational chasm affected the nonprofit sector in regard to doing what they called "political work," and they considered it a form of de-politicization.

> Younger people are less interested in doing that kind of political work. I think there has been a kind of de-politicization in India over the last two to three decades. [. . .] The kind of people who come out of colleges, idealistic young people, and go and work in rural India are fewer, because they are focused somewhere else. They are also more pragmatic I think. . . . a lot [of] their work used to be against the system, antagonistic to the system. Now I see a lot of people trying to work to change the system from inside.

The nonprofit sector was being corporatized, and the market-oriented society influenced who gravitated toward the nonprofit sector. They said, "There are supposed to be three million NGOs but even if we assume those numbers are highly inflated, most of them are single-person, two-people, three-people NGOs anyway, but I think they are shrinking. They are changing. Their future is much less solid. They are isolated." We spoke of Anna Hazare and the anti-corruption movement, which was active at the time of our interview, and they asserted the anti-corruption movement was not solely a Leftist movement. Middle-class India was agitating for change; the movement was made up of young, urban, middle-class Indians. The movement was not about class, or class consciousness. It focused on transparency and bureaucratic justice. They reflected, "the question about the model of development is still very much alive. It's not taken for granted that the state in a sort of pre–Cold War kind of communist form is the way to go or that markets will solve everything. The debate is very alive as to what constitutes citizenship, what constitutes rights." The model of the Congress Party, which was in power, was a growth model, but the model had not been realized in terms of development. The Activist Donor's work on development filled this gap, and promoted sustainable ways of life, but at the moment protest was interfering with governmental infrastructure and development. "So, you can see a rumble in the belly," they said. Protests focused on land and a lack of governmental transparency.

The government was becoming increasingly nervous about NGO activity, and it was "striking back." They mentioned protests over the Kudankulam Nuclear Power Plant as an example. "What is it that the government is really afraid of?" they mused. They considered the possibility that the government was taking back what it had yielded to the NGO sector in the 1980s, and wanted NPOs to become extension agents of governmental programs. Nonprofits worried about this, though many had been extension agents of the government. Perhaps this was why the government had begun to perceive the NGO sector as a threat. It depended on them and integrated NGOs into its development programs. "Usually in India we've seen historically it has been civil society models that get adopted by government," they said. "There are many many examples of that, but today the state is taking back the ground it yielded it [to] NGOs and perhaps even to corporations, and in some sense it is taking back that ground. How successful it will be I don't know."

They were concerned. They considered the 2 percent CSR program emerging in revisions to the Companies Act to be "outsourcing governance." On the one hand, the CSR provision promised a new income stream for development. "But what development?" With this new structure, the government could decide the terms of development and the project foci. Business philanthropy had a long history in India (Sundar 2000), though this type of philanthropy typically was connected to the environments in which businesses operated. In 2012–13, the 2 percent initiative was being developed and had not yet been implemented. They wondered,

> Would it be better that the corporations spent that 2 percent looking inside the fence at their own business practices and their own harmful practices, at the basic impact they will have just through their business, not just in their local communities but maybe to some grandmother living on the other side of the world? And would that money not be better spent inside, improving the systems of business that cause harm in the first place? I don't know. That's my feeling, that tomorrow's company has to be more like that.

They were open to critical conversations. Whether or not civil society had become the handmaiden of the government or of corporations, the government was not a static entity. There were also people from the corporate sector working with government to transform it.

The sticking point had become funding for political work. The government was restricting the capacity of foreign agencies to support political work in India, a position this donor was not against. "If there is political work in India, let them raise local funds and do political work. . . . They are not saying stop doing political work, but they are saying let it not get funded from outside. [. . .] And you are welcoming Walmart and you are welcoming France's and Russia's nuclear industry into India, but then you are saying no to the development-side aid on the grounds that it is political." How one defined politics was determined by the government in terms of charitable purpose. In one sense, everything was politics. The donor concurred, "The moment I chose to engage in even to solve a child's hunger is a political activity." The question of politics dominated the 2010 FCRA, which made it illegal to give foreign contributions to charitable organizations that were involved in political activities, and these events had created a culture of fear:

> There is a culture of fear in India right now in the NGO sector. We are always watching our backs, our accounts. I mean I don't have that problem because I'm in a very small minority of Indian foundations so we have less to worry about, but everyone else is dependent in some way or the other. All the NGOs who are receiving money are in some way or another dependent on foreign money which has been coming into India for so long and they are all nervous, because the Indian money is not ramping up fast enough for political work. Some of the philanthropy that I do is purely in that space, in the political social space, in the rights space, and in the justice space, but most of the new philanthropists, they, I mean their worldview is a market-oriented worldview, many of them. They believe that markets will work and they come from a conviction that it is better markets that will work to lift up our poor from poverty. So much of their philanthropy is coming from that belief and they are doing social enterprise or impact investing or even they are, you know, [the] basic services they are setting up are market-oriented solutions.

The foundations that emerged from the business community were market focused: "They are capitalists and that has served them well and that is how they have created their wealth and now they believe that that is the

way for India to become wealthy. So, or, they will support education because education . . . [can] create employment opportunities." In this landscape, rights-based work was more difficult to support. All NGOs were
dependent on foreign money and most of the new philanthropy was geared
toward market-oriented solutions, not rights-based work:

> Those institutions and NGOs that are still around and that want to do
> rights-based, justice-based work are going to find it very hard because
> Indian philanthropists will not support that work and the foreign phi-
> lanthropists are being driven out. Which may not be a bad thing because
> that work has to be supported locally. So the case has to be built for
> justice, political rights, you know all that sort of thing: equity, transpar-
> ency, governance issues. It's probably all right for them to have to find
> that money here or create membership-based organizations so it's like
> retail fundraising, so then you get more and more people into the politi-
> cal struggle. Rather than act, you know, from your ideological position
> but funded from outside. I'm not sure it's not a bad thing.

The philanthropic tide shifted toward domestic funding for highly sensitive and political issues, and this would later come under the regulatory
radar as well. If, in the past, transformative efforts had followed colonial
models of economic transfer, in some ways the governmental initiative
forced a new political economy. If the NGO sector had previously been
funded from "outside," the government now pushed its domestication. I
wondered out loud if the nature of rights-based work was being rewritten, and if what constituted rights-based or justice-based work was being
reformed. My research project had started while I was thinking about very
boring things like taxes. One can talk about rights and theories, but I was
really interested in people who did this kind of work and what they worried about when they filled out their tax forms, and when they tried to
get FCRA permission. The donor said, "Most of our NGOs are so small
and they are so focused on the passion side of their work that they quite
often ignore the process side of filling out stuff and auditing their stuff and
keeping every record till the last rupee and paisa. There are a lot of issues
there. We have to build that capacity quite a bit."

The Activist Donor worked to build the financial and accounting capabilities of organizations, especially those that were not capable of fitting
into corporate models.

> As a foundation that is set up to enable NGOs to do what they know
> how to do best, we have had to grapple with these issues and because of

the way government is forcing us, we have no choice. We have had no choice. Our choices have got reduced and reduced and reduced even as a philanthropic organization. We are now [requiring] our grantees to do utilization certificates. I hate that word. [. . .] They have to send you back information in a particular format that tells you that your money was utilized, so it is a certificate which protects me [as a philanthropist] and I don't want it. I wish I could just give away the money and not have to deal with any of this, but I am bound by law.

Such certificates were easy to replicate, and the donor's foundation foreclosed this possibility with audits, which added costs to its operational expenses. The donor lamented about the additional costs of conducting external and internal audits:

We have to hire external audits; we have to have internal audits. We have to go the whole hog which is not how I envision doing my philanthropy, but I have no choice anymore. [. . .] It's very costly. Our money is going up on that end of it. So, we are now supporting, as part of the grant we have to give an extra grant to them to make sure they can comply with all this. So the whole thing is getting corporatized, shifted in a certain way and I think this is one more way of government being able to handle the sector better.

The government, seeking to regulate the sector, reformed it in a way that it could become legible to the state, for purposes of governance and control. They were quick to add that all blame should not be directed toward the government; the sector had become irresponsible too.

I mean any time you point a finger somewhere three fingers are always pointing back at you. So, our sector has become quite irresponsible. We can hardly say that there is no blame on all sides. So, there was a shake-up needed of some kind but now of course the pendulum always swings too far [to] the other side and I hope it settles back somewhere in the center. But our NGOs did need a bit of dose of a reality check, some feedback loop as to how far you can go.

Credibility Is Legibility

A few months later, I met a Professional Critic—the director of a large NGO/foundation that was both grant-receiving and grant-giving; it funded smaller "partner" NGOs. Though regulatory reform caused anxiety for nonprofits without bureaucratic literacy, this one was large, established, and capable. We spoke of rules and exceptions to rules, and if there were state initiatives for nonprofit regulation. Those that could not fit, the misfits, the institutional aberrations, risked being labeled bad NGOs. As the government moved toward a corporate model for nonprofit regulation, anything drawn outside the lines encountered scrutiny. The director was a veteran of the voluntary sector, and had been working in it for thirty-five to forty years. They explained that government was tightening the FCRA because it feared NGOs for three reasons.

> [First, the government is] really scared of NGOs. They think, they know how corrupt and how bad the government is in India so they're worried about a Tahrir square kind of happening. And when they saw all those numbers come out, large numbers, you know? During the agitations against corruption. And they never feared agitations as much as they fear now. They know that with the internet and all of that. Because they know how bad they are. They know themselves how bad they are, more than we know.

The second issue was that "there is evidence that terrorism, money for terrorists, has been funded through NGOs." And the third, was that "the government thinks NGOs should be like babies who don't cry. So, NGOs that don't raise any issues but sit and serve as delivery where government failed, cannot do it, make the government look better." The government was opening its borders to facilitate certain types of capital flows, such as foreign direct investment from its diaspora, while it also sought to encourage corporate engagement with social development and welfare through the 2 percent CSR provision in the Companies Act. The director was annoyed with the regulatory reform, describing how the government had asked six large bilaterals to leave India: "They said you can work in India but only through government. You can give grantmaking through government to NGOs." They thought it was partly a function of global positioning, in which the government wanted a legitimate seat at the global political table:

> This was a planned move to ask. You know because India wants, we want a seat in the UN, we don't want to look like a beggar nation. We want to look like an emerging economy and giver so how can we have all this aid. So now we are telling all of them who managed to, like DIFID and USAID, that you can go.

The foundation director was also skeptical about the 2 percent CSR provision in the 2013 revised Companies Act. The director then rushed off to another meeting, and I sat to discuss the philanthropic environment with her staff. One assistant mentioned that later in the week, seven "thought leaders" were coming together, including the General Controller and Auditor of India, a member of the Planning Commission, a principal secretary from the Ministry of Health and Family Welfare, a development economist, philanthropists, and a Member of Parliament. The conversation was slated to cover how the changing economy in India was affecting India's philanthropic culture. The NGO was concerned with creating an environment to enable philanthropy in India, and to develop a culture of philanthropy. Both the "public" and the government lacked trust in the voluntary sector, partly related to issues that people called "transparency." They discussed improving structures and processes beyond audits and toward transparency.

Their goal was to create philanthropic trust in the sector, yet the nonprofit sector was extremely diverse. There were so many different kinds of NGOs that one could give to: big and small. There were portals and initiatives that had structured giving in India, such as GiveIndia. Because NGOs worked closely with the government for decades, the shadow of governmental bureaucracy hovered over the sector. People trusted neither the promises of the government nor those of NGOs. Corruption existed in all sectors: neither the state, the market, nor the nonprofit sector had a monopoly on shady practices. As a result, the nonprofit sector was in crisis. I suggested to my interlocutors that perhaps the international NGO, which was modeled after a corporation, might have to be re-thought. In contrast to the governmental and nonprofit sectors, the corporate sector in India garnered respect. It had produced the middle class, and an aspirational culture of consumerism which was hopeful. Unlike in the United States, where the corporate sector was less trusted after the global economic collapse of 2008, in India at the time of our discussion, the corporate sector was considered more transparent and reliable than either the government or nonprofit sectors in the relational trifecta of the government, nonprofits, and the market.

Helping NGOs Follow the Rules

Because regulations were in constant motion, Accountability Guides took it upon themselves to help NGOs follow the rules. It was hard work to teach others to stay within the boundaries of the law. One chartered accountant with whom I met was a translator of the rules, a broker of sorts. He saw his job as being to learn the rules and to advocate for them. He had written a training manual for the government. I sat with him in a small office on the second floor of a storefront building on a crowded street in North Delhi. Upstairs, above the street, noises of the crowd receded as he described his job to me, his clientele, and the challenges he faced. He worked in a very narrow arena: helping nonprofits navigate law. He saw himself as an educator, a broker, and a CPA. After the interview, my head was spinning with acronyms for laws, new initiatives, rules, and struggles to move through the legal and bureaucratic terrain of regulating the non-profit sector. As a chartered accountant who worked primarily with the volunteer sector, he described 99 percent of his clientele as NGOs from the "grassroots," large NGOs, and foreign agencies or foreign organizations setting up their offices in India, and the services he offered differed accordingly, from audits, to advising on tax laws, to trainings for NGO personnel and "chief functionaries" on "their financial management of NGOs and the laws." He also did evaluations and appraisals for funding agencies. In this manner he interacted with NGOs from both the financial and programmatic angles. He saw them as being intricately related. "Many times people tend to look at finance and program from two different perspectives, but they do not understand that they are two sides of the same coin. Unfortunately, the two sides don't like to see each other," he said.

I had reached the interview early, and he kept looking out the window nervously, sweating. It was hot and I was sweating too. In the middle of the meeting, two elderly nuns arrived. It turned out that the accountant had double-booked his meetings. I had arrived early, and they had arrived late. He took a break from talking with me to speak with them, and I sat in an adjacent room listening. It was strange to hear him advise the sisters from Ireland, an in-practice example of what he had been telling me. I felt uncomfortable, as if I were eavesdropping, but it was fascinating. The nuns had arrived from a regional office and sought language and information about the FCRA. He instructed them in what information to tell the civil servant, and what information to fill out on the form. He told them what not to write down. The tendency is to write too much, he explained, and *sarkari* (government officials) won't understand. He explained that this could cause problems. It was an issue of jurisdiction, he clarified. The sisters were thankful for the consultation, and when they left, we returned to the interview. His tone was different with me as a researcher versus his calm and compassionate explanations of the practical ins and outs of forms with the nuns. I thought about how one needed a translator for the bureaucracy, an expert in the archaic forms with secret, numbered, ever-changing names. I was struck by his patience. How he had talked about what to fill in on each form box, why this and not that, and what the opaque bureaucratic categories really meant. How he explained the details and the rules. Failure to correctly fill out the form meant possible rejection of a FCRA license, which could mean not being allowed to receive foreign funds, which could mean financial and/or social death for a nonprofit institution. It would mean nonprofit failure. The nuns had been worried, and he had reassured them, advised them, and sent them on their way.

He evaluated programs for financial review, which included verifying how an organization spent its funds. Sometimes it required field visits to see projects. The programmatic angle was integrated into accounting practices, and this was important to the accountant:

> Some certain things we take for granted, you know. Sometimes we do not actually understand even the difficult conditions in which the [NGO] has to work. I was sitting at my desk and thinking, "Oh, I can describe certain ways of doing things," but when I get out to the field, I find that there is no banking facility available there, I might say you [pay] by check. But there is no banking facility available there . . . [and] to carry the money to the place is so, so very difficult. And things like that. You know you have to go by road, and you have to walk it down, go up a hill, climb down a hill and then reach the village, then there'll be instances where you'll start in the morning, and you reach the village in the evening. And because we look at everything from thumbs up things, you know, that you are at a [height] and you can just get down, swoop down, you know, and get things done.

It was important for the Accountability Guide to understand the conditions and contexts in which NGOs worked. He spoke of evaluating a watershed program for a donor agency. If they were to send you when the watershed was absolutely dry, perhaps you would find the truck in the field and think that they were foolish, but if you had actually worked in the program, then you would understand the relationship to the water and the sand and catchment area, and why there was a runoff, and why "a particular thing is important."

MANUALS

With this expertise, he had been working with foreign agencies to help them navigate Indian laws. He performed evaluations for them and helped write financial manuals for NGOs; he had also done evaluations and interacted with 100 NGOs. Each donor agency came with its own manual for implementation, but for the accountant the basic tasks remained the same. "A debit is a debit; a credit is a credit." He decided to write something applicable to everybody, then tailor it to specific requirements. He created evaluation systems. Creating a general process of audits was an act of translation across institutional contexts, and this was a form of nonprofit advocacy.

To write the manual, he visited NGOs and interacted with the NGOs' auditors, and then wrote it in an accessible format for the NGOs to use. He tried to avoid overly technical language, came up with a draft, field-tested it, had a workshop with the NGOs and their auditors together, and then developed the final edition. When we met, he was in the process of revising a manual to reflect changes in the FCRA and the Direct Taxes Code (DTC; Bharat 2009), which was also being revised to include nonprofits. As the laws changed, NGOs scrambled to keep in compliance with the laws. A key component in the changing regulations was the proposed shift in the tax code from the term "charitable activities" to the term "permitted welfare activities." The accountant was deep in the distinctions between the rules and the laws. "The Act is 2010, but the rules are 2011, but both are—both are hand and glove, both have to be operational together. Ok, I can't keep the rules separate and the laws separate, but I personally feel that they still committed certain mistakes, that the rules are not consistent with the Act, and they're still in the process of amending the rules," he said. After the rules had been passed, they were amended.

In the case of the FCRA law, it came under the Ministry of Home Affairs in the Government of India. But why the Ministry of Home Affairs and not the Ministry of Finance? Well, it was due to the nature of foreign donations, he explained, and their relation to the "sovereignty of the country," and "whether the money is coming in for developmental activities or the money in coming in for terrorist activities." He discussed the history of the FCRA from 1976, and its relation to the Emergency under Prime Minister Indira Gandhi. It was a story repeated by many of my interlocutors, over and over, so as to remember and understand, and also to educate me, the outside researcher, of the history. He discussed how the registration provision appeared in the FCRA in 1985:

> So, in the year 1985, they said everybody should get registered and, surprisingly, in the year 1985, whoever applied for the registration got the registration. Ok, so there are various people now today who have the FCRA, but they do not know they have FCRA. They've not been reporting; they're not receiving any money. So, this is what happened. [. . .] So now what they [the government] did was, the biggest bombshell we've had is this year. On 7th of August 2012. 7th of August 2012. They cancelled 4,138 registrations overnight.

It was shocking when the government cancelled the registrations of NGOs without any explanation, bureaucratically. In 2005, there had been a previous purge of 8,673 NGOs for not submitting FC3s for the 2001–2005 period. The FC3 form required annual reporting on "how much you received, from where you received [it], where you utilized [it], etc." In 2005, they put 8,673 organizations under the category of "prior permission," which meant they had to receive prior permission from the government to receive funds. He gave the example of the requirement of listing donor-specific amounts on the prior permission form.

> If I have a project and I apply to [x], and this project is worth, say, 1,000 Norwegian kroners, OK. So, I give this project to the embassy, the donor gives me a commitment later, says that OK "You go to the Ministry of Home Affairs, take the permission, we give you the money." So, I ask the Norwegians, you give me permission to receive this 1,000 kroners from [x]. The permission would be donor specific, that is [x]. The permission would be amount specific, but the permission is not time specific. Time would depend on the, on the project.

One had to keep requesting permission every time one sought a donation. This posed particular challenges for accountants like this one, but he found solutions:

> We tell them that you make a larger project, and you take the permission once. Like, if I've taken a permission once of 1,000 Norwegian kroners then I reach that 1,000 limit, I don't need permission. I can't cross that 1,000 permission. So, it is donor specific, amount specific. I cannot take a permission to, say, receive money from [x] and go and receive money from [y]. . . . even though it is the same amount.

RULES CHANGE

I include these detailed examples of navigating the rules to demonstrate their complexity. Now, factor in that the rules were in constant motion—a shifting horizon line. It was not only a lot of paperwork, the requirements ensured that new NGOs would not get registration. First, they had to receive prior permission for the FCRA governed the capacity for NGOs to receive foreign donations. The other laws by which NGOs also had to abide, such as registration laws, which were board certification but did not give an organization "the right to live," the accountant clarified. "Let me tell you one thing. The main laws for any NGOs is first you have to get registered, trust society or [charitable] company. That is your board certification, but that does not give you the right to live—in very simple terms." The right to live. An NGO without funding did not live; it died. It failed to thrive. He continued, by emphasizing the distinction between foreign and domestic funds to NPOs:

> It doesn't give you the right to live. Ok. If you want to live on Indian funds, you get registered under the Income Tax Act. Ok. Then you are income tax exempt. Ok. Get registered under the Income Tax Act, which is properly called, which is properly called 12-A. 12-A is actually a section in the Act, but it is called a 12-A registration. Once you have 12-A registration, you file a return every year and if certain conditions are fulfilled your remaining income is not taxed, not taxed at all. So, Indian money. [. . .] But if you want to work with foreign funds, you have to go to Ministry of Home Affairs. Ok, so, even if you wanted $1 you have to go Ministry of Home Affairs to get the permission, ok. Now, a new organization will not get registration. For a very simple reason, they've got certain internal guidelines that say your organization should be at least three years old.

The regulations and restrictions of the 2010 FCRA focused on spending foreign, not domestic funds, though this topic would later be debated and revised in the 2023 Finance Bill.

A new organization had to get registered, but there was a three-year waiting period before new organization could do this. In the interim, it sought "prior permission" in the probationary period. "Because they're suspicious," the accountant clarified, "they want to check you out. They want to check out some things, this that and the other, only then they give you [permission], as I told you this law comes with the Ministry of Home

Affairs." It was a security problem. "The moment I apply to the Ministry of Home Affairs, my application will go to Intelligence Bureau." I was surprised there was so much anxiety and bureaucracy surrounding donations. "The Intelligence Bureau will do a thorough background check of who is running the organization, what were they doing over the year, what are their plans, and things like that, and after they give you a clean check, the Home Ministry will give you the thing [permission certificate]." One could apply for prior permission but in order to do this, the institution had to be three years old, and the latest condition added to the list of requirements was that the institution should have spent at least ten lakhs rupees [one million rupees]. In other words, one had to be a big NGO to get prior permission. One had to have spent one million rupees on activities over three years in order to apply for prior permission to receive foreign funds. It is worth repeating that these restrictions and rules did not apply to NGOs receiving Indian funds. The government had become increasingly strict regarding foreign funds to the nonprofit sector, and there were other complications as well that made it difficult to receive funds. To receive foreign funds, there were several steps to be followed: find a donor and arrange for a commitment letter (the money hadn't yet been transferred), then apply for permission to receive the funds. If the NGO found another donor during the same three-year period, it had to take a separate prior permission. Permissions were donor specific and amount specific. NGOs hired this accountant to apply for permissions because the process was so complicated. It required specialized knowledge to understand the parameters. Once filed online then paper copies of supporting documents were to be submitted within thirty days of the online application. The accountant saw the online application process as a positive move, as an application was filed online a file number was generated. Of course, it sped up communication between government departments too: "The moment I submit it on my Home Ministry website, is automatically going to IB [Intelligence Bureau]."

Once the file went to the Intelligence Bureau, it became a different sort of inter-departmental issue, according to the accountant. He gave the example of an NGO in a small town in another state, besides Delhi—Uttar Pradesh, for example.

> UP. If I'm sitting in some corner near the Nepal border, what will happen is my application will go to central IB. Central IB will send it to State IB. State IB will send it to District IB. District IB will send it Local

LIU. At Local LIU, guy who does all that passport verification and all that will come in and check you out and then the report will travel back physically.

Suddenly the process seemed a little less efficient. I shall point out here that the state governments did not have anything to do with this, except for the state government intelligence units. I realized, during this conversation, that there was a tension—or fissure?—I'm not sure what the best word would be for it, between state-based regulation regarding the registration of nonprofits, and the central regulation of funds received from foreign sources. For example, trusts and societies were registered in particular states. Meanwhile, the federal or central government governed international fiscal transactions. The Registrar of Societies had nothing to do with FCRA, or at least, it didn't at the time of my interview.

Given these changes, the accountant was busy writing his manual. He envisioned it would cover all the legal Acts applicable to NGOs, including all technicalities and procedures but it would not use technical language. He sought to present the information in "user-friendly form," listing the dos and don'ts and indicating opportunities. He was waiting for the Direct Taxes Code to be announced, so he could include it in the manual. Waiting for the laws to be rolled out was like chasing the horizon line for the Accountability Guide. The sector knew they were on the way but when? And what? Everyone was waiting. The new tax code promised to have obligations for nonprofits in the Income Tax Act.

MOTHER NGOS AND LIAISON OFFICES

The accountant also had written training manuals for the government to explain its NGO structures, specifically, the relation of Mother NGOs and Field NGOs to government development schemes located in different ministries. The accountant didn't want publicity. He laughed as he told me that he could convince his friends that the finance manual was his, because he used the name of one of the NGOs with whom he had worked. I had not heard the category of "Mother NGO" before. It was a way for the state to deal with a number of NGOs through a single institution. The Mother NGO fed smaller NGOs, and the budget would be presented jointly. The Mother NGO was responsible for making sure the field NGOs were doing their work.

Anyone can apply for a Mother NGO, like if I'm a big NGO and I'm working, say I'm working in Lucknow and you know there are several NGOs [to] feed the poor and all that, so I apply for my status as M NGO. So, when I apply, the government really checks me out, whether I'm capable of handling, whether I've got the [monitoring capacity] or not and it makes me one [a Mother NGO]. Once it makes me one, then it tells me that I can have so many Field NGOs.

This process of checking, monitoring, and accountability measuring changed with the 2010 FCRA, which included rules regarding banking regulations. He explained that with the old FCRA they would not allow NGOs to operate multiple bank accounts, "but in practice people were operating multiple bank accounts." If an NGO had an office in Delhi, which they used as their bank account when they registered with the Ministry of Home Affairs, they could not receive funds in any other Indian account. However, issues arose if the NGO operated in another city. It could not open a bank account there. "How do I expect you to operate in Lucknow if they don't permit you to open a bank account?" he mused. Some NGOs opened accounts without permission and used them, which created problems. It was difficult to monitor the accounts:

> In a sense, we are telling NGOs to take certain precautions when opening the account. It should not be construed like, as an account receiving the funds, like you receive the money here [. . .] and at the end keep a minimum balance in that account, never receive any money directly to that account, never put any Indian funds into that account, so that every entry can be traced from my parent account to that account.

He knew of organizations that had thirty bank accounts and the government did nothing. "I know of organizations who opened a second bank account, these guys went there and asked them to close that bank account and would not allow them to operate. OK, so different treatment can happen to different people." Within fifteen days of the opening of an account, an NGO had to inform the Ministry. The problems lay in the inconsistency in implementing audits, not the lack of audits. The issue was one of "field verification" and governmental suspicion. Sometimes the government asked local police for reports as well. The amended law had passed the previous year (2011), and it was being tested.

CREDIBILITY CERTIFICATES

Local magistrates were tasked with vouching for NGOs and ensuring nothing was wrong with them. A certificate was to be sought from the local district magistrate, but there was confusion regarding the rules. This increased bureaucracy required bureaucratic literacy, and NGOs were considered suspect if they were not bureaucratic enough. Though the certificate was not mandatory, the accountant explained that most people didn't know this, so they ran around trying to get the certificate. The law as written did not require submission of the certificate. However, he also mentioned that, in his experience: "if you are in a state which is touching any of the international boundaries, any of the international waters or Tribal areas, the government, central government, will definitely do a verification." Boundary areas required enhanced security. Again, this was a rule that applied only to NGOs receiving foreign, not Indian, funds.

NGOs were also considered suspect for not requesting permission to receive foreign funds. Earlier, if an NGO did not apply for and receive FCRA registration and was caught, the government would freeze its accounts, send a central investigation team from Delhi, and then the NGO would have to apply for "condonation of that offence." The offense would be condoned, and a penalty would be incurred, called a "compound." The problem with this, for NGOs, was that when they did apply for registration, they had to answer the question "Have you received any money without prior permission or without registration?" and they would have to write "yes." He showed me a "compounding chart," and explained that he would be often called in to advise NGOs in these circumstances. A steep financial penalty for NGOs was imposed for ignorance of the law, via compounding.[4]

As we spoke, he offered me kulfi (Indian ice cream), as it was his secretary's birthday. We sat and relished the cold desert on the steaming hot day. The sanctions stressed the sector. They were part of the new FCRA law; compounding did not exist in the older version of the FCRA. Also, in the new FCRA there were strict regulations regarding the passing on of funds from one NGO to another. In this manner, through the banking regulations, the process of centralizing control of FCRA funds had begun. The revised FCRA initiated an increase in centralized banking surveillance of the nonprofit sector. An effect of this was to formalize the sector and bring it in line with bureaucratic procedures found in the money-regulating world of larger institutions such as corporations. Nonprofits were no longer outside state capture, and the procedural incorporation by the state used the nonprofit sector to define itself as a regulatory body, and a legitimate protector of public funds. An important regulatory restriction governed the passing of funds:

> Passing on of funds means that now the [FCRA] Act is very clear on it. Earlier, the definition said, the definition said that foreign contribution means, you know, it said that, you know, either through one or more persons—let me try and explain to you. You are a foreign donor, I'm an Indian, Indian entity, and I'm registered here, OK. You transfer some funds to me. Out of that, I transfer some funds to another, Tom, who's running a[n] NGO, and Tom further transfers some money from that to Harry, another NGO in India. I'm registered. I'm registered. Tom and Harry also have to be registered under the Ministry of Home Affairs otherwise they can't take the money from me, even though it is Indian, even though it comes in—I'm giving it to them in Indian rupees, because that foreign money remains foreign till it is finally spent.

Routing restrictions were also in the FCRA but people were not aware of them:

> People were routing funds. Tom doesn't have FCRA, Martin has FCRA. So, what he does is he makes Martin the applicant, OK, and the money is utilized by Tom. He gives all the vouchers to Martin, plus gives him a commission, OK, and he gets his money. Martin is very happy, that you know, I'm able to support you, you pay me my fees. That is called routing.

An entire economy was developing through the routing of funds, but the FCRA Act was very clear.

> It says no person who is registered and can't get a certificate or obtain prior permission, [and who] receives foreign contribution shall transfer such foreign contribution to any other person unless such other person is also registered under the prior permission. [. . .] Now what happened is, an interesting thing happened here. The law says you cannot unless you are registered or you also have a prior permission. Martin cannot transfer any money to Tom unless Tom is also registered and has taken prior permission. When they came up with the rules, they made a mistake. In the rules they wrote, if Martin has to transfer to Tom, Martin should take first permission from the central government to transfer funds even though he's registered. [. . .] Immediately they came out with a revision or an explanation—No, no, no, no, no, if Tom is registered, you don't need to take permission.

The government realized it had made a mistake in the rules, so in April 2012, it changed the rule itself. The law was revised through practice and eventually via amendment to the rules.

> There was lot of controversy regarding this in the old law. They did never mention anything, so what people used to say is, they used to say, the money has come from abroad into my Indian account. I earned this interest in India, in my Indian account, how do you say it is foreign? So, what many of the guys used to do is, used to transfer interest to their Indian funds and use it. OK, so, therefore, a couple of years back what they did was they changed the annual reporting form itself and it brought in this one line where I was supposed to write down interest earned in my savings account and interest, OK. But the law did not say it, it was only the form. Now, in the new law, they're very clear about it. They said interest earned is foreign contribution; there's no two opinions about it.

These were important details: interest earned was considered a foreign contribution. In the FCRA, the primary exclusion was for political organizations, which were excluded from receiving FCRA funds. Yet part of the confusion, which increased the potential for breaking the rules, was that rules kept changing, and nobody except this accountant, and a few others in India doing similar work, understood them. There was an absurdity in trying to follow the rules that nobody understood.

We talked about the relationship between the Direct Taxes Code (DTC) being discussed in Parliament and the FCRA. The accountant was reluctant to discuss the DTC, because it was not yet law. He was well aware that when it became law many things would change. We talked about the Income Tax Act and the way it regulated charitable organizations (or, those registered under 12-A of the Income Tax Act). He anticipated that in the new tax code—in progress and under debate—there would be provisions that would prevent carry-over of funds from one year to the next. The accountant was adamant that I needed to understand the FCRA and its delineation of a foreign source. The FCRA was law, unlike the tax code in progress, which was too fuzzy to really discuss from the perspective of an accountant tasked with helping NGOs follow the law regarding a foreign source that was not exclusively money:

> If you receive any fees for any work done it is not considered foreign contribution. I'll give you an example. I'll give you an example. Say, foreign contribution comes into the picture only when I receive some money from a foreign source, OK. Foreign source. Foreign source means a gov-

ernment of a foreign country, a foreign national, or an agency of that country or an agency functioning in that country, etc., etc. . . . Now, source, this is very, very important. It's not currency. It's not currency, OK. So, therefore, you as a foreigner come to my orphanage, give me 100 rupees, I cannot accept it because I'm registered or I have foreign contribution, yet, 100 rupees because you are foreign source. You're foreign, so therefore, therefore, we have these small small NGOs who are not registered under FCRA functioning—they have more self-help groups, the men are making cards, jam, you know those things. Once in a while they come to a fair, Dilli Haat [Delhi artisan and crafts market], you know Dilli Haat, they set up a stall there. They can sell something to me; they can't sell it to you, because you are a foreign source. You have to be registered.

These were the intricacies, the weeds, and the details with which this accountant populated his daily profession, understanding the shifting legal terrain and training and teaching, guiding NGOs. He continued, "So, as law it was not permitted. I am an Indian NGO; I'm running a seminar, I have Indians coming in and applying registration. You come in and apply, I cannot take you, because accepting any money from you is accepting any money from a foreign source, which is a violation." I asked, even if I pay in rupees? He clarified, in the affirmative, that currency was not the source, accepting funds from foreigners was the source. This had been rectified to address fees from foreign sources, "including fees charged by education institution or toward cost of goods and services and expended by such person in ordinary course of business or trade is now not considered a foreign contribution. [. . .] If I'm a[n] NGO, I don't have FCRA, I can sell pastry, you can pay me, no problem, because it is outside the permit of foreign sources." It was in the ordinary course of business or trade, which lay outside the purview of the FCRA. However, if I wanted to deposit ten lakhs directly in an NGO-bank account, the NGO would have to have permission through FCRA. He thought this was good, as people were unknowingly violating the law. For example, he said: "You come to my orphanage, you like my work, you give me 100 rupees. Literally speaking, it is foreign contribution, OK, it is foreign contribution."

If an NGO received more than one crore rupees, it had to put the information in the public domain. NGOs were putting their annual returns on the web. This was an effect of RTI (requests for public domain from citizens from the government flowed also to the NGO sector). Perhaps it was payback to civil society, which had demanded the RTI law. But this new provision had consequences. He didn't think it had to do with RTI, and instead attributed it to local competition: "many times what was happening is, I file my returns, I'm working in a small remote place, and I don't disclose it to my neighboring villagers what I am doing, so people were [requesting] to the Government of India and asking to disclose this information." They'd go to the central government to find out about the next-door village. Hence the government required recipients of more than one crore rupees to put the information in the public domain.

One could not invest in mutual funds with FCRA funds, because it was a speculative activity, and was in contravention to the Income Tax Act: "they consider any mutual funds as speculative activity. They say the money has come for use; the money has not come to earn money on it." This was an important distinction between the nonprofit and commercial sectors. In addition, commercial organizations were, generally, regulated under different laws and parts of the government, though this was not true in the case of charitable companies. Commercial organizations were regulated under FEMA (Foreign Exchange Management Act). The accountant remarked that the 1976 FCRA was at one point renamed FCRC (Foreign Contributions Management and Control), but the last "C" was controversial, the Accountability Guide explained, and it was changed back again. Names mattered. Another change in the law, connected to issues of transparency, was that "you cannot have more than 50 percent of the funds fund administration. And they have defined what other things we do in our administration." He considered it problematic. "They have defined it, virtually everything goes under administrative expenses." Advocacy groups and those that spent funds on training were at a disadvantage with this new regulatory framework. He suggested to NGOs, that they propose the project to the donor "in such a manner [that] as many as possible expenses get absorbed into the program cost." The legislative guide was vague, though not unlike trends I had seen in the nonprofit world more broadly toward supporting programming instead of administrative costs. The government could target areas of concern for further scrutiny. Because the FCRA was administered via the Ministry of Home Affairs and was concerned with national security, particular geographic areas or sources deemed governmental threats would receive further scrutiny with increased surveillance. While earlier it may have been a rubber stamp, this time it was a microscope. "It literally means that, Martin, you cannot work in the Northeast without my prior permission. Martin, you can't receive this money from Tom without my prior permission." The government now had the potential to blacklist institutions and donors. It also affected funding flows and the roles of banks in relation to the nonprofit sector. "Banks will have to report the assets of different organizations of a particular nature. Now, this is, you know, they say that any organization, if they consider you of political nature, they can debar you. But this becomes very, you know . . ."

POLITICS

How did one define politics in the FCRA?

> Rule 3 deals with political nature. If an organization has a wild political objective, understood. [. . .] Group with objectives of political nature in which community participates in political activity, understood. Front organization of a political party, understood. But I don't understand this, organizations of farmers, workers, students, youth whose objective as stated in the memorandum or activities gathered through material evidence includes Step towards advancement of political interest of such groups. In fact, here, it also said, you know this was in the draft, larger social economic, that means if I'm making SAGs [social action groups] and all that and through them, I'm capacitating them, that means it can be construed as a political activity.

Social Action Groups fit into this as did any organization that habitually supported public causes, social movements.

> So that means, I have to be very, very careful if I'm in your charity, nobody will harm me. If I'm in your religion, nobody will harm me, as long as I don't convert. OK. But if I do any advocacy, [. . .] I have to be very, very careful. Like, for example, if I take a moment and ask people who demand water, drinking water, safe drinking water, it can be construed as a political activity. [. . .] I remember in one of the meetings a guy from [x], he asked me [to] campaign for water; he said do it with Indian funds, don't do it with foreign funds.

In other words, campaigns could be financed with Indian, not foreign funds. NGOs were very concerned about this. Everyone I spoke with was talking about it. He continued, "Like, for example, you have a Right to Education Act. If I am promoting that, I can be construed as I'm trying to make some political interest. So, this is where, so this political nature is a very vague term."

What about foreign NGOs wanting to set up an Indian NGO? There were two channels for this process. One was a foreign NGO wanting to work in India, they could go to the Reserve Bank of India and under FEMA set up a branch office or a liaison office.

> Say, for example, [x], when it came to India and formed [x], it formed a liaison office, OK. Médecins Sans Frontières, when they came to India, they had a liaison office. OK. Medecins Sans Frontières. [. . .] They set up a liaison office, but there are restrictions on a liaison office; there are re strictions. Like, [a] liaison office can only, like you can't be a funding agency. You can only liaison, you can, you know, what you call select your partners, things like that, and then, you know, then you transfer the money. [. . .] No, no issue as long as they are FCRA registered. OK, now, subsequently what happens is, they want their operations to be in India, so they set up an Indian entity. But again, to set up an Indian entity, they will have to form a society, trust or a [charitable] company, which is independent of the parent unit. And, this again, has to follow all the laws, has to register, then 12-A, then FCRA and all that.

There was an issue for foreigners: no foreigners were allowed to be on the boards of Indian NGOs.

> Ministry of Home Affairs is allergic to foreigners on your board. Because they say that they cannot check on [the details] of that person. OK. They have permitted a few cases where you can have a foreigner on the board. They say that the person has to be in India for more than 10 years, you know, this person is necessary because of their expertise, and all that, all that.

The Mother NGO or liaison structure was a franchise model. I looked around his office as our conversation wound down. I noticed that his walls were populated with photographs of him shaking hands with global leaders.

NORMS BROCHURES

One way to overcome the perception of failure was for NGOs to establish credibility and to figure out systemic methods for this. Accountability Guides did so through workshops on self-certification and self-governance, through accreditation via external audits, and through report writing. Self-certification had been a topic of discussion since the 1980s. The sector sought to develop a "code of conduct" for voluntary organizations. One NPO organized its membership and wrote guidelines and handbooks for internal NPO self-governance and good governance.[5] Another organization provided accreditation services for the nonprofit sector. I met with the directors in 2013 and 2017. Much had changed in these five years; aside from the leadership change, the climate for nonprofits had also shifted, with the BJP gaining power via Narendra Modi's election in 2014. In 2013, the director was anxious about being interviewed. They had been interviewed by a journalist who misquoted them in an article on NGOs as "cash cows," and they were reticent about speaking. They spoke of the difficulty of judging an organization, and of determining if it was "good." The consensus emerging from the sector was that the nonprofit sector needed to have its "practices benchmarked" to demonstrate credibility to funders. Since the government was not able to do this, the sector had to do it on their own, and the NPO took on the mandate to "presume norms, standards, and practices." Two sets of norms emerged: "minimal and desirable." The NPO had accredited 300 NGOs in 2013, and 361 had applied for accreditation.

The independence of the process of NPO accreditation was preserved by a third party. When organizations applied for accreditation, the NPO first called for documents upon which a desk review was conducted. Then an assessor was sent to remote areas to visit and evaluate the NGO's operations and to write reports. These visits were not surprises, and once the observations were submitted to the NPO, a conversation began with the NGO and the NPO regarding feedback on the assessor's report. Capacity-building needs were assessed, with the goal being helping the NGOs, not solely rejecting them. Fees were determined on a sliding scale, based on the size of an NGO.[6] The NPO hired assessors from all over India, and NGOs sought to be accredited in order to gain credibility and legitimacy.

When I returned in 2017 to see what had become of the organization, there was a new director at the helm, an anthropologist with a background in international development, and we discussed "norms enforcement and education." I felt we could speak the same analytical language. In order to enforce standards in an industry, the NPO worked to educate the sector and provide symbolic capital and recognizable infrastructural evidence for those who met standards. The NPO also wrote training manuals that were toolkits for trainers; it was an uber-NPO regarding rules and regulations. Accreditation was a "seal of credibility and accountability," certifying that organizations followed norms of governance, including accountability and transparency. By 2017, the NPO had close to 650 members that it had accredited and was inching up to 700. Accreditation was a business in itself, albeit a nonprofit educational one geared toward other NGOs. The director spoke with urgency of the issue and the role of the NPO with a recent governmental directive to regulate the sector more strongly. There was a PIL case active in the Supreme Court, and the NPO had been involved in discussions surrounding committee recommendations for governance of NGOs more broadly. In response to the Supreme Court order for the GOI to create accreditation mechanisms and punishments, the GOI created a committee of senior, retired government officials tasked with making recommendations to the Supreme Court. The PIL focused on NGO funding, demanding the government help with the regulatory framework for civil society organizations, develop accreditation mechanisms, and determine punitive actions for organizations that did not follow the rules. The NPO was asked to present its accreditation system to the committee, which recommended vetting of organizations be done by Daarpan, an NGO-portal in Niti Ayog (formerly the Planning Commission).

The landscape was rapidly shifting to a world of online portals, and as it had with the FCRA, which had moved online, the NPO now helped NGOs navigate the portal world. The process of institutional formalization, of standards and certification procedures integrating the nonprofit and governmental sectors increased surveillance. New requirements mandated board members (and their spouses) disclose properties. Efforts to "weed out paper NGOs" superimposed an infrastructure of surveillance on an informal sector, and centralized regulatory processes. If an FCRA certificate had not been renewed, then an NGO could no longer receive foreign funds, and some of the non-renewed NGOs were large: with 100 to 150 partners and 400 to 500 staff members. When such nonprofits were shut down by the government, they also shut down their funded programs for smaller NGOs. The government was opaque in its response, refusing to answer why renewals were denied. As everything moved online, there was no human to whom one could appeal. The online shift had eliminated the problematic industry of FCRA brokers, but some circumstances required talking to somebody to sort out problems. NGOs that had their FCRA cancelled either had to shut down due to lack of funds or fundraise locally. If the renewal application was cancelled, the organization had to stop its work. Nonprofits scrambled to keep up with the rapid pace of regulatory change that left small, less bureaucratically literate institutions in its wake.

The idea of a norms brochure fascinated me as an anthropologist. I thought of village anthropology and whom one might ask about norms:

who were the keepers of the book, the elders or the religious leaders who developed and maintained norms? Some groups were developing institutional instruments to work with the government and other NGOs. Norms brochures were guides to NPO behavior, as were governmental corporate social responsibility initiatives. The CSR provision in the Companies Act outlined directives to corporations and nonprofits on how to do (i.e., implement) social welfare, and in this manner, institutional policy and law were forms of norm-setting. It took education to change the sector, to get institutions to comply with accreditation requirements, and it took incentives, like access to potential flows of philanthropic capital for organizations deemed "credible." Though the former director had been involved in conversations with the government about integrating the NPO's accreditation into governmental programs, in 2017 the director saw more value in having civil society participate in what they called a "self-revolution," and they were wary of becoming a service provider for governmental agencies. Service providers were not interested in change; they were hegemonic reproducers.

Conclusion

I began with a question of failure, and the role and threat of failure in NPO assessment. Through the experience of reformers—a former civil servant, an Activist Donor, and Accountability Guides, we see how they navigated, and helped the others navigate the landscape of rapid regulatory reform. Through instruments like norms brochures, capacity-building workshops, and credibility certificates, these actors strove to protect the nonprofit form from threats of demonization in the public sphere, and to educate NPOs about the rapidly changing rules, which if not followed could result in suspension of licenses, freezing of funds, and institutional closure (failure). The revolution of rules included a moving horizon line due to politics, which increased institutional pressure to attend to the rules as they changed. The changes in rules occurred in multiple laws, including the FCRA and the proposed changes to tax law, and focused on monitoring the routing of funds and facilitated centralized regulatory oversight.

FIVE

The Power of Association

As laws changed rapidly, the Indian nonprofit sector in New Delhi came together to address rules and amendments and to strategize how to communicate with the government in order to have input in revising the laws as they were being passed. This process was a dialogue that took place in workshops, and it was built into the lawmaking process. These workshops are social spaces and active subjects whose participants included NPO representatives (Professional Critics), civil servants (sometimes retired representatives of the state), and accountants and lawyers for the nonprofit sector (Accountability Guides). Through such workshops, national policy for the nonprofit sector was produced by nonprofits. I begin with NPO leaders' historical attempts to draft policy for the nonprofit sector, which did not result in law but inspired subsequent efforts to navigate regulatory reform through workshops. I then explore the process of regulatory centralization that occurred as a cluster of laws were revised. In the decade that the reform occurred, it became difficult for NPOs to navigate the thicket of rapidly changing rules.

Workshops were a context for individual voices to become collective intervention, and organizational sites of association where nonprofit reformers came together to strategically navigate legal distinctions as they rapidly transformed. Distinctions regarding public versus private and for-profit versus nonprofit organizations and state versus central subjects were key frames of analysis in the workshop discussions I observed, and as a space for advocacy, workshops produced collective strategies to navigate the revolution of rules. The regulatory distinctions that workshop members analyzed and discussed appeared in revisions to a constellation of laws, including tax law, the FCRA, registration laws, and the Companies Act. Due to shifting legal terrain, workshops were arenas of nonprofit advocacy through which understandings were developed, challenges considered, and strategies formed. In 2012, when these workshops took place, there was still a healthy dialogue between the government and the NPO sector, and civil servants and nonprofit leaders and workers attended the sessions, though this dialogue would later be curtailed. Through the regulatory reform of nonprofit law, governance of the nonprofit sector became increasingly centralized. Workshops occurred in process, at a point when laws were proposed, and as feedback was requested by the government. They were convened to structure collective feedback, but they produced a setting in which the nonprofit sector united to lobby the government for supportive regulation. The voluntary sector did not seek less regulation; it sought better regulation.

I attended many workshops during my research, some of which lasted multiple days. This chapter presents a mere sample of a much larger communicative ecosystem in which the sizes, topics, and attendees of the workshops varied, and the structure and aims remained consistent. I reference the *workshop*, a social space and a physical setting, as a proper noun, a nonhuman actor, and an institutional form. Workshops were structured as information sessions, debates, brainstorming sessions, and opportunities to hear multiple perspectives. After each workshop, an organizing NPO compiled the issues and concerns and would report—on behalf of the entire NPO sector—to the government, either in the form of a petition or through meetings with a government minister (for example, the Finance Minister in the case of the Tax Workshop discussed later). The aims of workshops were to request change in regulatory processes, and this was how they created their collective voice. After communication to the government resulted from workshops, the ball was in the government's court to adjust rules and regulations. Workshops began as a communicative forum and became an active subject that assisted nonprofit self-regulation and facilitated communication with donors and the state. I saw some of the same people at all of the workshops I attended: leaders of prominent NGOs in India; civil servants open to dialogue; and NGO-members brought to Delhi from the other parts of India to weigh in on processes of legal reform. NPOs in Delhi depended on the perspectives of their national membership, and these member organizations depended on the Delhi-based NPOs for representation. The results of this relationship were that workshops spoke on behalf of the sector. Fear of being targeted by the government was growing in 2012, and workshops structured group representation by institutions, whose job of advocacy was crucial for protecting NGOs that dared complain against the government.

In Favor of a National Policy on the Voluntary Sector

One NPO with which I spent time working had been holding policy-making workshops for decades. In the NPO's archive room, I found documents from 1994 of similar workshops and task forces. Though taking place in an earlier era, the conversation between the nonprofit sector and the government had been a long one, changed in tone but with many of the same issues on the agenda. These conversations took place over and over, across years and political parties. As I read through documents with earlier iterations of these processes, I was struck by history's repetitions. One report, published in 1995, discussed a task force on reviewing and simplifying rules, Acts, and procedures affecting voluntary organizations, and documented a workshop held in 1994. The introduction began much as did the workshops I participated in nearly two decades later, articulating the need for voluntary-sector organizations to be considered on their own terms as separate from other types of institutions. The report targeted registration laws, the FCRA, and the Income Tax Act, and set up task forces to address them. Nearly twenty years after this report was published, as I attended workshops in 2012 and 2013, the same concerns were being addressed. If resolution had not occurred, why were the same strategies being followed? This was more than an exercise in futility. The instrumental process of workshops was a political strategy unto itself. To understand workshops in the nonprofit sector, we must understand them as exercising the *power of association*, one of India's constitutional rights, and freedoms and a UN declared human right.[1] Workshops were processes through which debate and political consensus occurred, as in the 1994 Workshop, where voluntary development organizations came together to express their need to identify themselves as a type of entity separate from other types of organizations. They articulated this need in response to governmental "strictures and long drawn[-out] procedures" in the Societies Registration Act, the FCRA, and the Income Tax Act.

From this 1994 workshop, three task forces were set up: on registration acts, the FCRA, and the Income Tax Act.

The "National Policy Workshop Report" documented how an NPO, on behalf of task force members, submitted a report to the government, in November 1994, which was delivered to the Secretary of the Prime Minister's Office and the Finance Secretary. The aim of the report was to request and initiate a process for amending existing laws. It sought to initiate a conversation, both bureaucratic and political, between the voluntary sector and the government. A campaign pressured the government to amend the Acts just mentioned, and revisions to the laws were proposed. When I attended workshops in 2012 and 2013, the conversation continued, regarding the same issues and the same laws. Another report in the NPO archive documented an action plan for voluntary organizations and the government through policy.[2] The action plan had resulted from a two-day convocation of 100 voluntary organizations from all over India, inaugurated by the Prime Minister and the Deputy Chairman of the Planning Commission. VOs mobilized and organized the poor, and delivered governmental services via development projects and public works, including roads, schools, health centers, irrigation projects, and water and sanitation programs. The policy paper reinforced the partnership between VOs and the government in service delivery and development provision.

In 2007, another attempt at national policy creation was initiated, and a report, "The National Policy on the Voluntary Sector," was produced by the government's Planning Commission, in conversation with the voluntary sector. The national policy proposal is evidence of the government–VO collaborative relationship that existed in the early years of economic liberalization. These documents were also attempts at institutional self-regulation by the NPO sector (Sidel 2010; Dadrawala 2003). "The National Policy on the Voluntary Sector" (Government of India 2007) was a policy paper that did not result in law, though it remains an artifact of the communication dynamic and a vibrant inter-sector conversation that existed between the voluntary sector and the government. The National Policy proposal was referenced in workshops I attended as something that never came to be, an attempt. It stood as a historic horizon line for NPOs, outlining both past efforts and the scope of possibility for collaborative engagement, and a reminder of what once was. It was a positive step, the result of NPO efforts in dialogue with government officials. I briefly analyze some of the contents of this policy, as a starting point, and as context for the ethnographic analysis of workshops that took place five years later, in 2012–13.

The Preamble (Section 1.1) stated: "This policy is a commitment to encourage, enable and empower an independent, creative and effective voluntary sector, with diversity in form and function, so that it can contribute to the social, cultural and economic advancement of the people of India." The "Scope of the Policy" (2.1) described the diversity of VOs included in the policy, with organizations engaged in: "public service, based on ethical, cultural, social, economic, political, religious, spiritual, philanthropic or scientific and technical considerations." It mentioned that VOs included formal and informal groups, community-based organizations; support organizations; networks, and federations, as well as professional membership associations. It articulated that to be covered under the policy, VOs should have the following characteristics:

(a) They are private, i.e., separate from Government;

(b) They do not return profits generated to their owners or directors;

(c) They are self-governing, i.e. not controlled by Government;

(d) They are registered organizations or informal groups, with defined aims and objectives.

The "Objectives of the Policy" (3) included creating an "enabling environment for VOs that stimulates their enterprise and effectiveness and safeguards their autonomy":

- To enable VOs to legitimately mobilize necessary financial resources from India and abroad;
- To identify systems by which the Government may work together with VOs, on the basis of the principles of mutual trust and respect, and with shared responsibility; and;
- To encourage VOs to adopt transparent and accountable systems of governance and management.

Because many of the promises made by the Planning Commission in the dynamic dialogue between the NPOs and the Government never came to fruition, the policy document is a historical artifact outlining a relationship that came and went. It was a hoped-for proposal, a utopian outline of possibility. In 2007, there was scope for hope. A future to be dreamed into policy documents.

A section focused on "Establishing an Enabling Environment for the Voluntary Sector" offered mechanics for the VO–GOI partnership, including safeguarding the autonomy of VOs while ensuring their accountability. It encouraged legal reform and attention to the complexity of registration laws that constituted NPOs as state subjects (4.2). It discussed how VOs could register as societies, as charitable trusts, or as nonprofit companies under central or state laws. Some states adopted the Societies Registration Act with amendments, while others created independent laws. Laws relating to charitable trusts varied across states. Over time, many of these laws and their corresponding rules became complex and restrictive, "leading to delays, harassment and corruption," the policy paper documented. It recommended that the Planning Commission act as a nodal agency interfacing between the government and the voluntary sector. It argued that the Planning Commission would, in the policy, "encourage State Governments to review prevailing laws and rules and simplify, liberalise, and rationalise them as far as possible." Finally, to facilitate registration of nonprofit companies, it proposed the government "examine measures to simplify procedures under Section 25 of the Companies Act (1956), including those for license, registration, and remuneration to member-employees." In this section, in retrospect, many of these requests came to be in the regulatory reform that ensued, though not in the way the NPO sector desired.

A central, all-India statute law for VO registration was proposed to serve organizations operating in different parts of the country and abroad in the proposed national policy (4.3). It proposed that this could "co-exist with prevailing central and state laws, allowing a VO the option of registering under one or more laws, depending on the nature and sphere of its activities." It outlined processes for encouraging VO accountability and self-regulation and suggested governmental oversight: "The Government will encourage the evolution of, and subsequently accord recognition to, an independent, national level, self-regulatory agency for the voluntary sector." It proposed to help "bolster confidence in the voluntary sector by opening it up to public scrutiny" (4.5) by putting information about publicly funded VOs in the public domain. And it outlined guidelines for the management of public donations (4.6). It identified public donation as an important source of funds for the voluntary sector, and one that could increase sustainability. It focused on tax incentives:

> Tax incentives play a positive role in this process. Stocks and shares have become a significant form of wealth in the country today. In order to encourage transfer of shares and stock options to VOs, the Government will consider suitable tax rebates for this form of donation. The Government will also simplify and streamline the system for granting income tax exemption status to charitable projects under the Income Tax Act. At the same time, the Government will consider tightening administrative and penal procedures to ensure that these incentives are not misused by paper charities for private financial gain. (4.6)

A subsequent section proposed the government review the FCRA and simplify its provision regarding VOs: "from time to time, in consultation with the joint consultative group to be set up by the concerned Ministry (as suggested under Section 5.4).

A section on development partnership identified "shared goals and complementary roles," between the voluntary sector and the government, noting "formal processes of consultation and strategic collaboration" as well as project funding through shared schemes." This was a collaborative model, produced through a collaborative vision. It said: "The Government will encourage setting up of Joint Consultative Groups/Forums or Joint Machineries of government and voluntary sector representatives," and that "The expertise of the voluntary sector will also be utilized, by including experts from VOs in the committees, task forces, and advisory panels constituted by the Government." The "strategic collaboration between the Government and VOs" was to take place "through national level programmes that are long-term in duration, and utilize multiple strategies," including "project funding." This was more than mere bureaucratic-speak, or hollow promises. It was a proposal for legal formalization of an existing relationship between the governmental and NPO sectors. The National Policy also included a section on philanthropic reform (6.1, "Strengthening the Sector") that argued Indian society had an established tradition of philanthropy, and though tax concessions enabled donations to charitable institutions, there was untapped potential in channeling "private wealth for public service." The policy was aspirational, pro-VO, and VO–GOI collaborative. It was written at a time when some of the voluntary sector leaders sat on the Planning Commission, when a porous border existed between the voluntary sector and the state. By 2012, the relationship was changing.

A Question of Profit: The Thicket of Distinctions

How do you fail as a nonprofit? Make a profit. (Joke, true.)

NPOs navigated a thicket of distinctions in law, as regulation was based on whether an organization was public or private, for-profit or nonprofit, and NPOs used workshops to navigate this constantly changing regulatory landscape. I attended two workshops in 2012, one on tax law and the other on nonprofit law more broadly. The *Tax Workshop* analyzed VO struggles with rapid legal reform, and was a brainstorming session. The *Law Workshop* was a structured debate regarding a specific proposal to create a multi-state registration law: the Multi-State Societies Registration Bill (Kassam et al. 2016, 26). Members of the Law Workshop debated the proposed law, where the sector should turn, and how it should self-advocate. Both workshops were sites of solidarity and disagreement, arenas where ideas could be hashed out and discussed. They were policy-forward discussions and attempts to write the horizon line of policy. A running thread in both workshops was the question of profit in nonprofit sector regulatory law.

The Tax Workshop was attended by forty to fifty people, including chartered accountants, civil servants, and NGO types. Experts were brought together to explain the proposed Direct Taxes Code (DTC), and its proposed amendments, regarding how it would affect NPOs and the charitable sector. The meeting was at once educational, advocacy, brainstorming, and planning. The goal was to come together as a group in order to take a clear and coherent list of demands to the government—with the request that the rules of the DTC be amended. The meeting was detailed, wading into the weeds of tax law, with certain provisions discussed, analyzed, and debated. But the conversation was also wide-ranging and circular, addressing government-NPO relations, NPO-government and corporate relations, and the categories of charitable purpose and profit as defined in the law. The role of regulation and the rules were also discussed. Government officers spoke from the perspective of the state, including the recently retired Director General of Income Tax Exemption, who was humorously introduced as "the cause for the problems." He introduced himself as a compassionate person who would help attendees see the battle from the other side. At this point, the dialogue between the government and VOs was friendly. Chartered accountants (Accountability Guides) explained the nitty-gritties of their responsibility to follow the law as written, and described where the rules became tangled and difficult to navigate. NPOs complained to the civil servants and expressed their confusion with the laws. They outlined their problems working with tax officers and came up with recommendations for how the state could alter its practices in relation to the NPO sector. Attendees drank tea, took phone calls, talked past each other, disagreed, and agreed. It was multi-vocal and productive. This was the practice of advocacy and self-regulation, and the two were intertwined.

The Tax Workshop opened with a plea for members of the workshop to come together, and one NPO leader, a Professional Critic, expressed the urgency of unity and self-advocacy. He argued the nonprofit sector was poor at articulating its accomplishments, especially compared to the corporate sector, which lobbied well and whose members stuck together. He suggested nonprofits learn from the corporate sector, and tell the nonprofit story better, by emphasizing what nonprofits contributed to India beyond the GDP. He cautioned attendees that without unity the nonprofit sector would become an endangered species. Another leader chimed in in defense: "We are not doing anything wrong. We are facing some problems, difficulties. We will iron them out, sort them out. Before we leave this place, we will tell you the solutions. First, let us have confidence that we are all in the right path. A clean and clear conscience."

CHARITABLE PURPOSE VERSUS ACTIVITIES

A theme of the Tax Workshop was the relation between tax-exempt status and nonprofit status, as expressed through the category of charitable purpose and activities. The category of the trust was the workshop's starting point. Of particular issue was section 2, subsection 15, of the Income Tax Act on tax-exempt status, which defined NPO relationships with the government. This tax-exempt status was considered a government subsidy, one leader emphasized, which supported charitable purpose. Another NPO director discussed the notion of trust in tax law and its relation to charitable activities (previously known as charitable purpose). Because many NPOs in the room worked for the poor, he explained, they were taking up the responsibility of the government. The bone of contention focused on the category of charitable *activities*. Categories of charitable *purpose* were defined in in the Income Tax Act, Section 2(15), not charitable activities. Charitable purpose included "relief of the poor, education, preservation of the environment, medical relief and the importance of advancing any other object of general public utility." One person used public toilets as an example of general public utility, available to anyone, and how charging funds for maintenance might take this utility out of its tax-exempt status and put it into the world of business, commerce, and trade. How would a VO maintain a public toilet? If they charged five rupees for maintenance, it fell into the category of commerce and business, which was in conflict with the law. Some argued this could be brought to the court, where it would be challenged regarding its charitable purpose. Charitable purpose did not refer to the *type* of activity. At what point did an activity become non-charitable? The chartered accountants in attendance, the Account-ability Guides, led the workshop discussion, elaborating upon distinctions between charitable and noncharitable. It was the *purpose* that was charita-ble. This interpretation and understanding of the law required the special-ized knowledge held by chartered accountants. Determining whether the objective of charitable purpose had been achieved was based on judgment of a veritable gray area:

> The Income Tax Act says you are working towards achieving the ob-jective. How do you achieve the objective? Your decision, your choice. You might have one judgment of income tax [?] don't do that. It leads to a tangle. They said, the objective of the trust is to pay for communal harmony, peace prosperity everywhere. This trust achieves everything [. . . .]. How does it achieve is not relevant; a Muslim is doing by going to a Mosque, a Hindu is doing by doing puja to Hanuman. The objective is to achieve peace, harmony, prosperity. How do we achieve this objec-tive? It's your decision. The Act does not constrain you from following whatever way you want to achieve that.

It was charitable purpose that was defined in the Income Tax Act, not charitable activities, which appeared in the proposed revision to the Act in the Direct Taxes Code Bill. With the proposed DTC Bill a regula-tory shift was underway—from charitable purpose toward charitable ac-tivities, and this distinction had implications for nonprofit practice. NPOs in attendance voiced concern that an organization could be suspended for not following the rules regarding charitable activities, some of which didn't fall within the nomenclature of poverty, environmental protection, or monuments: for example, gender issues and child abuse. "What about old people's homes?" someone asked the accountant. "These are people that don't have recourse; they don't have children." NPOs had historically stepped in to fill the gap, and the gap was being closed by the government through changes to small rules and laws. These concerns regarding proposed rules would later be brought to the Finance Minister for discussion, as an action item created by workshop participants.

Members of the workshop discussed the intricacies of dealing with the income tax officers regarding the interpretation of income tax policy. One VO director explained how even if you were not correct, if the income tax officer took a different stance, then you would be "sitting on a lot of charitable money and then the issues of time and anxiety, just fighting the case." The proposed DTC Bill stressed the sector because some did not understand what was allowed and what was not. If a categorical mistake could be used to close down an NPO, then a deeper understanding of categories of acceptable regulatory requirement was required. The government determined these categories through law, and government officers such as civil servants were tasked with evaluating practice, sanctioning nonprofits when laws were not observed. One NPO leader, a Professional Critic, argued the space of interpretation was dangerous, particularly for organizations working with marginalized groups like Adivasis and Dalits, groups that the government considered threats in certain regions of India. The "law has to be framed in a way that the individual [tax officer] cannot refuse it," one person said. Another added, "the problem is the red light. What is the red light we do not know. That is the problem. The red light is there, ok, but if the red light is looking like blue to some and yellow to some, that is where the issue is." Some in the Workshop expressed concern that the Finance Minister would not be amenable to representation by the sector, and some argued that he had been particularly hard on the not-for-profit sector. Others pressed the issue of whether there was space for communication. (Notice that I have begun to capitalize "Workshop"—as its collective voice is being formed.)

HOW TO HANDLE MONEY

A provision in the proposed DTC Bill was to require NPO accounting systems to be on a cash instead of an accrual basis, and this presented unique challenges to the operating budgets of nonprofits. A recommendation emerged through conversation in the Workshop to request the proposed rules be revised. Professional Critics and Accountability Guides argued the world was moving toward accrual accounting, but that the DTC required cash accounting. The Workshop recommended 10 to 15 points to be included in the petition to the government. They suggested cases where NPOs were rejected or penalized in the income tax realm should be included. The process of the Workshop involved discussion, disagreement, debate, agreement, and clarification as participants developed their collective strategy. Attendees contributed specific experiences to use in the petition in order to make specific points. As they contributed their own stories, they brainstormed how the law should be written differently. Suggestions would be sent to the Finance Minister on behalf of the NPO sector in an aggregate voice as nonprofits. A woman spoke about her work in the microfinance sector, which had been under close attention by the government. There were organizations of different legal forms doing microfinance, and she argued for NPOs to be considered their own sector, a public "third sector." Some organizations did microfinance in the nonprofit mode, whereas others did microfinance through a for-profit model.

THE NEGATIVE LIST

A retired tax officer explained that tax subsidies via tax-exempt status were considered expenditures by the government. This was why the government sought to control the tax-exempt nature of NPOs, and it was done through what he called a "negative list" of activities, those that were not allowed. He argued that legislation regarding trusts was poor, and with the amendments it had become even worse. If one ran a trust and paid taxes the government paid no attention. The question arose with the request for tax exemption, because then the government lost revenue. Tax exemption was considered government spending, which required regulation. When the government sought to regulate the activities of a trust, it could create a list of allowed activities or activities it did not allow. The first option was very difficult, so it created a "negative list" of unallowed activities.

After he spoke, the room erupted in conversation, questions with many people talking, and discussion returned to taxes and accrual accounting. Grants didn't become expenses until they were used, so an accrual basis worked better for nonprofits. However, worldwide in nonprofit accounting, whatever income was received if earmarked and on an accrual basis was not counted as income until it was spent. This was difficult for the government to accept because if the government received money for a future project, it could not be regulated on accrual basis. Was the regulatory focus on accounting and when funds were spent, or on revenue and when funds were received? The two approaches appeared to be in contradiction. Perhaps this was a technical problem of translation. NPO workers in the meeting expressed the need to translate their context to the government in order to make laws work for them, and to amend the rules.

The income tax officer pressed his point, articulating that the natural way of working in the tax department was to view funds when they were received. The problem of accumulation, and accrual accounting, arose when funds were received for future projects, which was difficult for the tax department to consider. One attendee exclaimed that this was no different than what the department had to handle on a commercial basis: "All companies under the Companies Act used accrual accounting. All we are saying is that internationally, accrual accounting is the more scientific way. Number two, the Government of India has declared a few years ago that even government accounts need to go on accrual accounting from cash accounting." Nonprofits lagged behind in accounting trends. An Accountability Guide emphasized the government treated NPOs differently from corporations because it considered the tax exemption a government expense, which it was responsible for overseeing. The tax-exempt status was a subsidy that fell upon an account log in the category of expense management. For the NPOs, it was revenue management. Different departments. Different perspectives. Different mindsets. Different perspectives on the nature of the law as it was being made.

The difference between for-profit companies and NPOs was that NPOs had beneficiaries, who were public. Tax exemption, as a government subsidy, was considered an investment in the sector. A heated discussion ensued regarding the problems that this mistranslation created, particularly in relation to governmental oversight in relation to donor requirements and audits. A few spoke to question if there was a larger bias at play, in favor of the corporate sector. One said:

> Because if you look at the corporate sector the government bends over backward. Tax exemptions, tax holidays, budget foregone. All of these aspects. NGOs are coming in, but there is a development deficit where the government is not providing sources for the poor, elderly, or destitute, or for children. In that instance, they are stepping in to fulfill an

obligation of the government which it is unable. Therefore, India must be proud of its very vibrant civil society because what distinguishes us from China? Other than the democracy [. . . .] Why are you having this bias against [. . .] you have FDI [foreign direct investment] in retail, you have liberalized the economy, you are bending over backward to accommodate every foreign company that comes into the country. You are giving them such largess.

A Professional Critic suggested taking up a Supreme Court petition (PIL) on the inherent bias of the government, which interfered in the NPOs' capacity to do advocacy. "It is a larger question that we can take up in a Supreme Court petition or something, because there is a bias. There is an inherent bias [. . .] Therefore, this leads to all kinds of harassments on the point of legislations and laws." While NPOs had been funded "99 percent" through foreign philanthropy, this was shrinking and "coming down by 40 to 50 percent." The NPO sector was "doing the job otherwise government should have done it, and we are being hit." It was doing the social welfare work of the government and being penalized through increased scrutiny.

The nitty-gritties regarding regulation, and cash versus accrual audits, propelled the Workshop to gear up for a fight with the Finance Ministry. They discussed the importance of making the government understand the issues: that projects could last for five years but funding was one year at a time. Donor income was not income until spent, as in accrual accounting, yet the government considered it on a cash basis. Accountability Guides explained the difference in detail to the Workshop members. The DTC Bill did not account for this concern and the Workshop decided this must be communicated via lobbying. There was confusion in the room about the law itself—what it was, what it proposed, and what was allowed. The educational, self-regulatory aspect of the Workshop was itself a form of advocacy, which resided in the power of association. This effect of the Workshop coexisted with the Workshop's goals of creating a petition to lobby the government.

An accountant suggested tests to determine eligibility for tax-exempt status. He proposed regulatory instruments:

The present law is unnecessarily very complex. The basic thing is what are the tests to be applied to get the registration and to get tax exempt? What are the tests that the government or the department should apply? If those tests are simple, accurate, we will also have a comfortable time. The department will also have a comfortable time. We should decide about what are the tests that should be applied, and that should be brought into the law. Like, once I said that instead of defining charitable purposes or just productivity, you should put a *negative list*. That becomes absolutely important.

What is the difference between an NGO and a company? Just think about it. The company also has funds. I think the only difference is this, that in the case of this, that in the case of the company the profit goes to the shareholders. In the case of the NGO the profit is redeployed, so if your second test is that [. . .] no amount of income should go to any of the trustees or managers. I think that is a very good test.

The distinction between companies and nonprofits was essential to their regulation. Workshop attendees argued the nonprofit sector was "doing 70 percent of the government," and that government-created trusts were also totally tax exempt. One attendee remarked, "The substantial justice should always prevail before the technical justice." Another member proposed a potential solution: a website where nonprofits could go to speak to the government about these technical issues, to enhance communication and eliminate unnecessary penalties due to bureaucratic confusion. The tension in the room stemmed from the opacity of governmental bureaucracy. Even if income tax officers appeared to agree in person, there was always another person reviewing the issue, and NPOs did not know where they stood. Confusion about the rules created stress, as did the whimsy of bureaucratic implementation by governmental representatives.

A large part of the Workshop focused on trust law, but the conversation also touched on decreased foreign funding for NPOs and the need to raise funds domestically. India had a large sector of individual givers, many of whom were religiously motivated, though these practices were out of regulatory purview (Bornstein 2012b). How was one to categorize charitable activity? Were greeting cards created by a charitable organization and sold for a fee a business to be taxed? Where was the line to be drawn? Much of the work supported by the government through NPOs was done through government tenders, and this process and the language of tendering was sometimes interpreted as a business. "The moment you apply as a tender, it is a business income," one attendee remarked. This was a real problem. And then there was service tax, a separate topic also discussed. Attendees addressed their questions to the government officers in attendance, who did their best to clarify the governmental logic of the law. "The mindset of procurement—unless that changes it will remain a problem. This is the main problem. What is business and what is not business?" one person exclaimed in an exasperated tone. Many talked at once, many weighed in, some brought up problems of subcontracting. Donor issues were also brought up regarding project-based funding. There were arguments and disagreements, diversity in the room. It was not easy to come to a conclusion about what should be done; the Workshop was a process. Details, details, details, in the weeds of the law and what should be done, what were the hiccups, what needed to be changed, what did not work. The Workshop came together to communicate with the government about the law.

Corporations were shadow figures in the Workshop. Some corporations wanted to "route their CSR through NGOs," and others were forming their own NGOs, entering into tenders with the government and being given work. The CSR provision in the Companies Act (2013) was mucking up the boundaries. The Workshop discussed how a distinction should be made by the tax officers. Again it came up that there was bias on the part of the government against NPOs and in favor of the corporate sector:

> That's what the bias is. Compared to the corporate sector on every stage. On one stage you are handing out largess, resources, everything to the corporate sector, and on the other side you are strangulating the non-profit sector which is really working in human service. When will you recognize this? It is high time we all stood up and said, "This is our contribution to the country." High time.

The question was one of profit. Did the sale of books by an NPO constitute profit making, pulling its regulation into the commercial sector? Was a violation of these categories an act of corruption? "Anything will make people corrupt. Me sitting over here can't make people honest. We can make only rules," the tax officer exclaimed, referring to charitable purpose, "So, I am suggesting, purpose will be rule, purpose will be same." The details, again, emerged regarding the boundaries of acceptable expenses, and whose responsibility it was to regulate them. Another speaker commented: "The only problem which will come—I don't know to what extent the government can unplug that—is when you can make a rule for the companies which are Indian companies. Now we have multinationals. If they have the law, their law is permitting them. That's where the problem starts." There was always a space beyond the regulatory frame. Some spoke of litigation. Others cautioned against it: "One word of caution I do always tell all the NGOs, you should only embark on litigation where the law is well certain, transparent, clear. Otherwise, your money, energy, time. It really saps your ability to pursue situations. Just keep that in mind as a very golden principle in running the organization." Most NPOs didn't have expenses for litigation; only as a last resort did NPOs go to court.

It came down to the mindset of the assessing officer "You are right that way, he must distinguish which trust is genuine." The police were harassing NGOs, especially in Tribal areas where NGOs were doing work in health and education. Those NGOs were being scrutinized by the police—apart from the income tax issues, the FCRA, and the CBI, now the police. "All of this, so much harassment to people who are doing service." The increased surveillance produced fear. "Why police is coming? They are checking whether you are recruiting Maoists," one suggested. Another explained that FCRA was being restricted in Tamil Nadu, and there were orders for the police to check every NGO and to examine all their documents. The Workshop moved in and out of Hindi, though not all members of the meeting were from the north where Hindi was dominant. Some stirred their tea, spoke in tandem, had side conversations to debate and disagree.

The end goal was to send a petition to the government. "If somehow, we are able to convince the Finance Minister, who is a very logical rational mind, that these are the problems. That these are the provisions which are causing a lot of controversy, confusion, without adding to the revenue. They can be either removed or simplified like this. I'm very confident," one person remarked. Another added, "To tell him this drafting is doing no good to the country and no good to the revenue. Some are not practical. At least we did our best. . . ." The Workshop decided it was necessary to take the issue head on, given the context: "What is happening is that eventually the voluntary sector is going down in the last few years, and on the opposite side if you see those so-called foundations coming up, because they have resources, they have everything. [. . .] They have money to spend also. They have money to spend with media, money with cocktail parties and all those things [. . .]."

Discussion turned to the FCRA and regulation itself. Details regarding FCRA license renewals were discussed, as were the 4,000 licenses that had been cancelled because of bureaucratic errors due to changes of address. Members of the Workshop were asked about their experiences, and a discussion of proposed changes ensued. This Workshop took place in

December 2012, when the FCRA rules had just been published. An NPO leader discussed their efforts to reinstate NGOs that had had their FCRA licenses repealed for small bureaucratic errors. The Workshop considered the five-year renewal a "retrograde step." They wanted the license to be permanent, as before. Add to this that the ministry didn't have the staff to process the renewals. The NPO representative added that the problem was not with renewal but with process:

> Because the [FCRA] is the only law which is implemented by the [Intelligence] Bureau, which deals directly with citizens. Where you don't provide the information, it's like a machine you put an application on one side, and you don't know what is going to come out on the other end of the machine. Because you have no interaction with what happens in between.

The issue with the FCRA was political, not merely technical, a tax officer explained:

> Most organizations had moved from the service delivery to the rights-based approach. So, this FCRA is one particular clause in the rules that deemed political status, so moving towards a rights-based approach, makes us wonder if you are going to become a political organization, deemed as a political organization. It is exactly what happened in the nuclear power plant agenda [a reference to Kudankulam].

The Workshop discussed exactly how to navigate the rapidly changing rules. If regulation moved to an online system, which document took precedence—the soft copy or the hard copy (required to also be submitted)? What if there was an error, a mistake of calculation in the two copies? Would NPOs be penalized? There was no system for revision in FCRA, even for clerical mistakes.

The problem remained an issue of profit in relation to charitable purpose, and the intent to earn profit, as the flip side of charitable purpose. These categories would be written into law. Some argued the necessity of distinguishing the nature of charitable purpose versus that of business or trade. For example, he said, if an NPO made software which was used by another NPO, and the first NPO received fees for it, there was profit. But it was different from what a software engineer did, because in the case of the software engineer, the general public was not involved. The law, which distinguished between these realms of public/private and for-profit/nonprofit—shouldn't require every case to be scrutinized. "Then there is no law," he said. It was in the scrutiny, and the interpretation through implementation, that bias could creep. Workshop participants sought better legal instruments to facilitate their work, and to distinguish non-profit from for-profit endeavors. The governmental tender system for social development work did not distinguish between the types of organizations doing the tendering, and this was brought up as an issue. Again, the question was of making profit:

> What happens in law, nomenclature is not properly done; it creates lot of confusion. For example, you know charity conveys something else and actually what we see is something else. So, what is profit? Profit is just excess of your receipts over expenditure. So, every organization has to make profits, it's not a question of not . . . the question is where the profit is being used.

Societies and trusts were nonprofit, but so were Section 25 (later Section 8) companies. In all three legal forms, any profit made was to be put back into the institution, not distributed to shareholders. The defining characteristic was one of intent, as with charitable purpose, which was proving to be a gray area in legal implementation, and in the rules. Some spoke of the professionalization of the sector, away from informal development work, and how charity had become institutionalized. The fundamental issues were questions of profit, motive, institutional intent, and whether or not the institution worked for the public.[3]

Regulation Toward the Center

Besides the public/private and for-profit/nonprofit distinctions parsed out in the Tax Workshop, a distinction emerged in the sector between the regulation of state versus central subjects. A workshop was held in 2012 on a proposed new law that would regulate nonprofits across states: The Multi-State Societies Registration Bill (MSSR Bill). In the workshop, the Bill was lauded by some and opposed by others. It was smaller workshop, though similar in structure and cadence to the Tax Workshop described above. Although it focused on the single bill, conversation roamed, and incorporated discussion on related issues in registration laws, tax law, the FCRA, and the Companies Act. The cluster of laws, at the heart of regulatory reform, made its appearance in every workshop I attended.

The *Law Workshop* was also oriented toward strategy and problem solving. It was convened at the offices of an Indian foundation, and in attendance were lawyers and chartered accountants for the nonprofit sector (Accountability Guides), as well as NPO leaders (Professional Critics), and a retired civil servant (representing the state). We sat around a large conference table and discussed giving feedback on the Multi-State Societies Registration Bill, for which the government had given a fifteen-day window for feedback before it went to Parliament with the possibility of becoming an Act. The distinction between the time a Bill was being drafted, and when it was released for consultancy with "stakeholders," was opportunity for the NPO sector to affect the law. It was a small window, a sliver of time when experts came together to brainstorm and mobilize. In addition to convening this meeting, the organizing NPO wrote a desk study report on the Bill, that analyzed its components, which was presented to the Law Workshop. At the end of the Workshop, proposals were taken to the government minister on behalf of the sector. The Workshop recommended the organizing NPO reach out to its membership and get their feedback as well. Herein lay the dialogue. The organizing NPO sent its membership—of NPOs across the country—a letter with a plea to send comments. It suggested members write directly to the Ministry of Corporate Affairs, which was tasked with the MSSR Bill process, and it provided an address. It offered to collate feedback, which it would attribute to member NPOs and then send along. The NPO then released a report on concerns regarding the MSSR Bill (2012), which proposed to regulate NPOs in India through a central statute.

The report detailed specific provisions, their issues, and made specific recommendations. Like the Tax Workshop, the minute details of each section of the proposed Bill were dissected, analyzed, torn apart, and alternate solutions were proposed. It was a similar process with a more focused lens and sharper instruments. The report provided a summary and analysis, voiced concerns and offered recommendations. It went section by section of the 63 sections of the MSSR Bill, with detailed commentary on the Bill's requirements and proposed alternative recommendations. It used specific legal cases as examples, and included examples of accounting treatment of project grants under the proposed Bill. The final section of the report included "Annexures" regarding the detailed format of receipts and payments, income and expenditures, project grants, and other categories found on balance sheets.

Three months before the Law Workshop occurred, the organizing

NPO published a collaborative report with another NPO, which had re-
viewed the MSSR Bill and outlined the concerns shown in Box 5.1.

The media covered the issue as well. An article in the *Financial Express*
(Sinha 2013) noted:

> The proposed bill, being prepared by the Ministry of Corporate Af-
> fairs (MCA), empowers the Centre to take over, suspend, penalize,

---

BOX 5.1. Multi-State Societies Registration Bill Concerns

- A common law and framework for the entire country was needed,
  but it was not provided in the bill.
- The geographical area may not be the ideal yardstick.
- The proposed bill lacked in scope and in criteria for central
  registration.
- Interstate activity would be treated as an offense.
- There could be no activity pending registration.
- Registration would not be granted in the absence of multi-state
  activity.
- A society may be dissolved by the government even for failing to
  amend its rules for three months.
- The government would decide the beneficiary organization in case
  of dissolution.
- An investigation could be initiated on the recommendation of its
  inspector.
- An investigation could be initiated on the recommendation of a
  single member of the society.
- Power was given to the inspectors to investigate *suo moto* (on their
  own accord) or on complaint from anybody.
- The government may constitute a new board or take over without
  providing the organization any opportunity of being heard.
- The government would allot unique identification numbers to board
  members and governing bodies.

Source: NPO Report (2013).

---

confiscate, cancel, impose fines and investigate societies or properties. All societies will have to be mandatorily registered in accordance with the provision of the proposed law. Moreover, the Bill proposes to treat all multi-state societies as corporate bodies, all such societies will have to file annual reports, balance sheet and details of office bearers with MCA-21 of the MCA.

The article cited NPO recommendations for "a single regulatory authority for all societies, trusts, and NGOs for transparent regulation. A common law and framework for the entire country is needed, which is not provided in this Bill."

In the course of my fieldwork, the NPO had asked me to write an analysis of their analysis document. This was the recursive dialogue of advocacy, of which I was a part as a participant-observer anthropologist. I often weighed in during meetings, sharing my comparative perspective of the nonprofit sector in the United States and adding information from the research I had done. It was a dialogue of intellectuals, nonprofit workers, and it took place in multi-context group think. Like the National Policy on the Voluntary Sector, the MSSR Bill was eventually scrapped. However, workshops were integral to the processes of debate and dialogue between the nonprofit sector and the state in lawmaking, and of democracy. I saw how the MSSR Bill could be problematic for the Indian voluntary sector. It was not clear how the proposed Bill would relate to existing regulations in the Societies and Trusts Acts, the Companies Act, the Foreign Contributions Regulation Act, or the proposed Direct Taxes Code Bill. The Indian voluntary sector was required to abide by all of these state-based registration laws, and central governmental regulation already occurred through the Income Tax Act and the FCRA. The central government sought more regulatory control over the sector, but it was not clear how the MSSR Bill would achieve it. The Bill presented a mechanism for erratic control.

The Law Workshop produced a wide-ranging yet focused conversation on developing outcomes. A debate occurred in the meeting regarding the best way to proceed, and whether to suggest to the ministry that the proposed Bill should be scrapped or amended. The proposed MSSR Bill was a central regulatory mechanism that presented difficulties for the sector. Workshop members analyzed navigating the proposed regulatory framework in relation to other regulatory mechanisms. The Societies and Trusts Registration Acts constituted nonprofits as state subjects, but the MSSR Bill interpellated them as centrally regulated subjects. Similarly, the Companies Act, under which NPOs could register as charitable companies, also centrally regulated nonprofits. The conversations generated by the Workshop continued for a few years, and in 2016, the organizing NPO published a report on registration policies.[4] Like the members of the Tax Workshop, members of the Law Workshop parsed distinctions between the nonprofit and for-profit sectors through regulation. Members discussed how proposed revisions to the Companies Act, which were also occurring, provided additional changes to legal distinctions, through a corporate social responsibility (CSR) provision requiring large companies to direct 2 percent of their net proceeds over three years toward social development. One attendee pointed out that "if the CSR spending actually starts happening, then the NGO sector loses steam because it is set up as an alternative." A new pathway was being built, a new horizon line for social welfare provision. This time, by the government.

Tax difficulty could result in punitive government sanctions, and the Law Workshop's aim was to help NPOs steer clear of this, as well to communicate to the government NPO recommendations for adjustments to the rules. Workshop participants discussed concerns that the corporate sector demanded a tax deduction through the CSR 2 percent provision in the Companies Act, but the provision was already in the tax law. High net worth individuals working in companies sent their money to their own foundations, and as for their corporate clients, "They'll go over this supply chain. They'll also send their negotiation to these guys. So, then they have a huge chunk of money." This was not charity; this was self-interested corporate behavior. One attendee gave an example of a telecom company: "What they do, they ask the government, 'If you give the land, we will put the building, and we'll run the school.' So, government gives the land, they put the building, they fund the teachers. Then they put a [transmission] tower on top. They put a tower on top, and they're basically getting the land free for doing that." Attendees laughed. A few discussed how some companies got their own schools through CSR, in a move of self-interest disguised as tax-exempt charity. NPOs in the Workshop critiqued the corporate sector for its rule abuses.

An employee of the organizing NPO gave a slide presentation of work to date, and mapped the regulatory landscape, highlighting tensions between state and central regulation. The Indian Trusts Act of 1860 had been implemented at the state level, and states then wrote their own laws. There was the Bombay Trust Act for Maharashtra and Gujarat, and Gujarat was now developing its own Trust Act. South India had Endowment Acts that applied to religious institutions. Some states had set up entirely new registration requirements for societies, using registration legislation as a merit guideline. "At the central level and at state level," the NPO employee said, "registrations do not make any provisions for grievances, redress or appeals. The only recourse for civil [society] is the civil courts." Another attendee chimed in to explain that "we have a curious situation in Maharashtra [State] and Gujarat State; all societies compulsorily must be registered under the Trust Act as well." This caused confusion in the meeting, and discussion ensued about how NPOs went about registering in Maharashtra and Gujarat. Because the topic of the meeting was the Multi-State Societies Registration Bill (MSSR), an intimate knowledge of state laws regarding registration was required to analyze the Bill at hand. Another attendee elaborated on the Bombay Trusts Act, which had a dual purpose: to register and to regulate charity. The Societies Registration Act was "currently [. . .] applicable [in] only about half the states. And the rest of them have passed their own laws." He surmised that "when we were under the British, the British had very simple concerns at that stage. But now our issues are more and more interventionist." A question emerged in the room regarding the increasing potential for governmental intervention in NPO affairs.

Regulation of trusts was a gray area. Trusts were not corporate entities, and liability was personal for trusts, unlike societies or corporations: "When there is [a] suit, it is in the major name of the trustees. You cannot sue or be sued in the name of the trust. It's in the individual names of the trustees. So, the liability again is personal. It's a fact many people are not aware about." Societies, in contrast to trusts, had limited liability: one could sue or be sued in the name of the society as a corporate body. The Workshop took a small detour, discussing this distinction. Then the NPO employee continued with her PowerPoint, identifying details of the structure of a trust, including the fact that Indian public charitable trusts were generally irrevocable. She discussed procedures for dissolving trusts and changing a trust's objectives. She moved on to analyze the category of the Section 25 companies under the Companies Act. Section 25 charitable companies were required to apply their profits to the promotion of the corporation's objectives and could not pay dividends to members. The governance of a Section 25 company was similar to that of a society, as the company had members and was governed by directors, a managing committee, or a governing council elected by its members. The Workshop discussed clarifications to her presentation, including the difference between a private or public limited company and its membership, and how the process for getting a license had been simplified.

A workshop attendee brought up the fact that the new Companies Bill (later to become the 2013 Act but then still a Bill) contained the concept of a one-person company. The Workshop debated this new category and how grant makers would see it. They discussed a Supreme Court judgment regarding property held under trust by a Section 25 company in Maharashtra, which had to be registered with the charity commissioner. "Property held under trust, and despite being a Section 25 company, requires additional registration with [the] charity commissioner." This was a Maharashtrian special case. The Workshop worked its way through the details of each of these categorical distinctions, to develop a deeper understanding and in order to advise other NGOs. They discussed the role of the charity commissioner, a position which was not available in all states. Tamil Nadu, another attendee chimed in, had similar regulations for religious places through the Endowment Acts. Another attendee added: "The government has ultimately taken it over. Because there is so much money spending over there." And another quipped, "I always say that it's difficult to compete with God in fundraising." The Workshop members' were good-humored as they waded through the muck of the law in process, much of which differed in specific state contexts. They discussed governmental takeovers and joked that a state takeover was better than one that was priest controlled. At the Kali temple in Calcutta, one attendee said: "it used to be a mess. Only if you get into the temple, they will relieve you of your entire money. You won't even have one rupee left at the end. Then the government took it over." And they all laughed.

When the NPO employee resumed her PowerPoint about the MSSR Bill provisions, she was again interrupted, this time by a gentleman who said:

> There is a problem here. And that's a technical problem. We have been over this earlier also. There is a state subject, and there is a center subject. Now what this . . . and if I may use the word, this law which the government has proposed is primarily trying to intervene in the state subject, on the plea that these societies are stepping beyond the state borders. Without that, you know, this law will not run, sort of pass through the test of the constitution.

That is, the government would not make a law about state subjects alone. They referred to earlier conversations and workshops in which they had participated, where they had discussed the business of charitable organizations and whether they were regulated under states or the central government. Workshops were part of an ongoing conversation for this NPO community of policy thinkers and workers, and the classificatory distinction was confusing even for the experts in the room. One remarked, "I mean of course, there's a confusion that even societies are technically, I mean, commonly, understood as corporations." But societies were regulated by the Societies Registration Act, which was governed by states, not the central government. "So, therefore, you know, you can't say that the society is also [a] corporate body, and therefore a society must be regulated by the center. That would create a conflict." A woman asked, "What are you suggesting?" and he replied:

> So, what I am saying is that it will not be technically feasible for them. Because what they are doing is they're trying to contort, in a contortious manner, they are trying to get hold of as many societies as possible. But that is still leaving a large number of societies. So, your object, which is to ensure that all the societies get an opportunity to register and something like this, is . . . will not be solved. . . . Of course, I am biased because I feel that this law is not properly designed to begin with. So, it will not really serve our purpose.

There were two sides in the debate in the meeting: those that thought the MSSR Bill should be tossed, and those that thought it could be passed and amended. Through the discussion of the structural flaws of the law, the positions of meeting attendees became clearer. The Workshop agreed that there were structural flaws in the proposed law. "There is no uniform design; it is an opportunist law," one attendee exclaimed: "Oh, this Society, it is stepping onto a bus, going to another state. Let me catch hold of this. Oh, this one, oh this . . . has a FCRA registration; let me catch hold of this. It doesn't have the majesty of law. . . . It is, you know, more like a pickpocket." Everyone laughed, and another person said, "Very accurately put!" The Workshop agreed that the legal principal of the law was not clear. Here, the concept of regulation was treated as one of control, and members of the Workshop made a distinction between laws that were monitoring by design and those that were enabling. The Societies Registration Act was an enabling law, not a monitoring one. This was of concern as members of the Workshop contemplated together not only how to propose modifications to the law but also how to communicate these issues to NPOs in the sector who might not have as detailed an understanding of the regulatory provisions under reform as the NPO lawyers, accountants, and civil servants' in the room did. The MSSR law began to appear, in the analytical conversation at the Workshop, as an additional regulatory burden and compliance issue for NPOs. The Workshop discussed why the government was proposing the Bill. "To regulate. Clearly, to regulate." one person said, and another added a thought on regulatory process:

> And that's why the history of this drafting is very important to understand. When a group had drafted this registration Bill for NPOs—and I was a part of it and [one member in attendance] and several others were there—Planning Commission, . . . you know, liked it, and the sector also liked it. After that, it was sent to the MCA [Ministry of Corporate Affairs] for implementation because we had designed it as a corporate body. MCA was not interested. Later on, Ministry of Finance, you know, started going after them, that "Do something; do something." So, half-heartedly, they drafted this Bill.

There had not been a consultation with the NPO sector on the Bill. The Workshop returned to parsing whether to suggest the Bill be improved or scrapped. One participant added, "Should we say, you know, this doesn't make sense to us at all, and you know what, the cost of administering this law will be more than the benefit that we are getting?" Many agreed. There was an issue regarding fees and who would pay them. The burden would ultimately fall on charities in terms of financing the Bill through fees, and through compliance. Another added that most of the societies that were being regulated were "staffed by such simple people that they can get really confused with the simplest concepts. So, to bring in something so complex as this. . . ." The potential for confusion introduced the potential for corruption: "And if you don't register, then that's a good opportunity for a clerk or someone to come and show you the fear of the law." The issue was control, not regulation. The Workshop was all for regulation, and their livelihoods were based on helping NPOs with regulatory compliance, but they were not for the control that was being imposed on nonprofits in the new Bill. The NPO directed the Workshop to come up with an alternative solution. The director had met with the minister, who had said if the NPO sector did not like the law they should propose an alternative. This was the space of dialogue that was available. The question was, would the attendees recommend amendments to the Bill or that the Bill be tossed out? The division in the Workshop became clearer through their internal dialogue. Before they were able to come to a consensus, and a strategic set of recommendations, they articulated their different positions. One attendee mentioned that the problems in the Societies Registration Act were also in the Multi-State Societies Registration Bill. There was also concern about whether or not the government would listen to their recommendations. Advocacy was required. They debated the mechanics of where the Bill was housed, with the corporate minister: "Now, those guys are not, I think, interested in moving things [passing the Bill]. It's like burden on their head," one person remarked.

The Workshop discussed taxation as a form of regulation, and explored the Indian context comparatively, in relation to how other countries regulated their nonprofit sectors. In the United States, charitable organizations were regulated through the federal tax code. In India as well, as one attendee pointed out, the primary objective of NPO regulation was to "prevent leakage of tax revenue" for the government. Both the Tax Code and the Multi-State Societies Registration Bill governed institutions that received tax benefits and subsidies. Both regulatory environments were set up such that "a commercial organization cannot masquerade as a charity and evade taxes. So, that's the primary object. Its primary objective is not to weed out the nonprofits from the for-profits." The Workshop analyzed different countries' models for nonprofit regulation, such as the British model of a federal charity commissioner. "The issue here is that this . . . law [MSSR] is ill conceived," one member added:

> How do you amend this law when the legal foundation itself is not clear? So, I would say that, you know what, our primary Plan A should be that, you know, to say that these are the deficiencies in structure . . . structural deficiencies in these laws, . . . in this law. And, you know, these are the benefits that we are getting, this is what it will cost you to implement this law. So, kindly reexamine that approach.

The Workshop discussed how the MSSR law would present a burden for the sector. One expert suggested scrapping the law, and gave an analogy for the law's structural flaws: "It's like you have one of these security cameras on the door and all the windows are left open [everyone laughed]. So, what is the purpose? And there is so many organizations that are not being monitored. So, your regulatory purpose itself is not being served." Another expert reiterated the technical theme of state versus central subjects. Societies were state subjects whereas the MSSR Bill (and the FCRA and the Companies Act) regulated NPOs as central subjects. A lawyer linked the current debate to an earlier debate on sales tax:

> Before 1957 there were no central sales tax[es]. There were only state sales tax[es]. And a lot of companies used to . . . and then they fought a big case [. . .]. It entered into a multi-state activity. Immediately, the question arose whether the . . . if companies did dealings in more than one state, then what state [would collect] sales tax? Then our central sales tax was enacted by invoking local powers of the central government. So that's where the Multi-State Societies Act lies: the possibly that once you cross over the border of a state then you become a subject governed by the central government, and this is what they want to . . . what they want to control.

Section 25 companies were already regulated as central subjects in the Companies Act. He continued, "Number two, which I have just noticed, that as you are aware, the Companies Act, why Section 25? Because, again, [the] Companies Act is a federal subject. Companies are being . . . because it gets its right . . . its right of business, that is our fundamental right. So, these companies are already registered under the Companies Act." The category of a "central subject" became a Workshop theme.

Emergent in this conversation was how different laws interpellated NPOs in different ways, as state or central subjects. Different forms of governance made certain forms of activity possible, legible, and legal and others illegible, illegal, and impossible. The Workshop discussed the fact that, unlike the UK's charity commissioner, whose office had a website where information about all societies was available, India had neither such a master list nor a central regulatory mechanism. Though this would later become part of the regulatory landscape, at the time of this meeting, it did not exist. One person noted that the "Planning Commission started that but no one [is] registering." Another questioned what value such a list would add to the sector. And a third offered a potent analogy of having a voter card, a passport, a ration card, and an Aadhar card. What was the purpose of yet another identity card? Later, in the 2023 proposed Finance Bill, NPOs would be responsible for registering for a unique ID (*New Indian Express* 2023), but at the time of the Workshop, registration for nonprofits was their identity card. Workshop attendees discussed creating a template to avoid confusion. They considered whether the government would listen to recommendations, or even to an alternate draft of the Bill. Some argued that since the draft MSSR Bill was out, the best strategy was to give recommendations for amending the Bill; to say the Bill was unacceptable without suggestions would not be productive. One person suggested the Workshop clearly identify the fundamental flaws in the Bill and even use the example of the sales tax and central tax and how they were scrapped and replaced by the value-added tax (VAT) as an example of a way forward. Another participant argued the issue was valid and it should be brought up with the government, especially as it was a Bill and not yet an Act. This was the moment when the government requested engagement. The organizing NPO could draw upon the tax analogy in conversation.

The Workshop discussed having a mix of both strategies—critique of the law and a suggestion of a way forward. "Mix of both," one participant exclaimed, "Something like this. We can talk to the Minister of Corporate Affairs and bring our case and those arguments of what exactly we want. In fact, since there is some ownership to that, even we can argue with them on how they want to take it forward. Do they like to meet the states, state meeting, they can organize something like that." The discussion strategy evolved to include working with the Ministry of Corporate Affairs, and even the Ministries of Home Affairs and Finance, to develop champions of their cause. There were NPOs in all Indian ministries; there was no single ministry for NPOs, and while the government sought to create the MSSR Bill and bring it to the Parliament of India as a central governing law, at the moment nothing was clear. Discussion revisited the issue of who would finance legal implementation. Which ministry or department? Did the Bill say anything about fees assessed? Some in the meeting assumed these costs would be covered by the MCA, but then another person reminded the Workshop that MCA didn't want to handle the Bill. "MCA's run by corporate fees. Right?" one person surmised. "Yes, that is right," another answered, "Possibly they will be charging certain fees [paid] by the NGO." Workshop members discussed the role of foreign funding, receipt of which would push an NPO out of being a state subject into a central subject and make it a concern of the central government, which had oversight of foreign contributions to NPOs. Where did the directive for governance lie? It was not clear to anyone in the room, and they brainstormed, supposed, and strategized by sharing information and building a path forward together. There was a discussion of which ministry might take this up, Corporate, Home, Rural Development? They discussed who was at the ministries, who would be open to NPO concerns, and also more strategy issues.

Strategy was necessary because the voluntary sector had taken on the role of criticizing the government. One meeting attendee joked that I, as an anthropologist, would "go gaga over it, you know, telling the world that Indian government is now muting the voice of the sector." Another responded that this was not necessary because the practice "has already been pointed out in this administration." (This was in pre-Modi times, in 2012. Prime Minister Modi was elected in 2014). Another expert pointed out that the right of association was a constitutional right. "The constitution guarantees the right of association . . . [for] doing the work that we do, and taking [us] over is against the constitution, in my opinion."

They discussed the necessity of building awareness of the MSSR Bill with the voluntary sector. Many in the Workshop were concerned that the sector was not paying attention to the MSSR Bill now, but that when it was introduced in Parliament there would be "India-gate agitation" (India Gate was a location for protests in Delhi). The Workshop discussed spaces for discussion, such as during a national convention. They discussed how to move forward, how to create awareness, and what to do. The organizing NPO suggested delivering a communique to its members, asking them for the potential implications of the Bill from their perspective in the fifteen-day window for public comment. This was the period for mobilization. The NPO proposed generating awareness with other NPOs, telling them about the seriousness of the situations, designing a communique giving clear information on what was going to happen, advising what type of petition they should sign immediately, and building a case. The Workshop resolved that the sales tax example be brought up with the government and that contacts in the ministry could be used to buy time so that the Bill wouldn't be tabled in Parliament, though one never knew when it would be brought to Parliament, and this uncertainty presented a planning challenge. One never knew when the Bill could become law. "It's a loaded gun. It can go off any [time]," one added. The fact that the Bill was with the corporate ministry was beneficial to the Workshop, "There is some possibility of making it more human, more professional, as the Companies Act." If it ended up with the Home Ministry (as was the FCRA), the Workshop agreed that it would be a "disaster." They felt the Home Ministry was not equipped to handle such issues, as was evidenced by the FCRA issues. They were not created for such problems of enumeration, unlike the Ministry of Corporate Affairs. The Workshop joked that the Home Ministry was like the "stick and tear gas ministry."

I asked the Workshop about the potential for alternate forms of regulation, such as self-regulation, perhaps even in partnership with the government. They discussed the possibility of there being a place, such as the Planning Commission or a national charity commission, where all NGOs could register, as an alternative to the MSSR law. The Income Tax law did not provide regulations for the sector, and the FCRA was, according to an attendee, "another loose cannon." The FCRA had become more transparent as the ministry was now publishing information on its website, partly due to pressure from the voluntary sector and other struggles being waged regarding the Right to Information Act. The Workshop recalled that the issue of self-regulation had been brought up many times, including during the 1970s and 1980s, and in the National Policy on the Voluntary Sector (2007). An issue the sector faced was its size and diversity—how could it agree on anything? Was "it" an actual "thing"? Diversity posed a problem for self-regulation. The director of the organizing NPO laid out the challenges his organization faced, namely that the sector was broad and hard to categorize, thus hard to regulate: "We have small, medium, large, remotely located, and all those. And there is no one body which is recognized either by government or by the private sector or by the community which gives accreditation." Others in the room concurred that this conversation had been going on since the 1980s and was the emphasis of advocacy NPOs.

Conclusion

Workshop members found themselves in the position of middle management, speaking for those below and beholden to those above. The hierarchical nature of the metaphors used were explicit. They compared international, alternate examples of accreditation, and shared ideas. They returned again and again to the question of cost regarding who would fund these accreditation processes. These experts were problem solvers, administrative masterminds, who collaborated with the government to help figure out nonprofit sector governance. One expert brought up the fact that NGOs would not be willing to fund accreditation unless it had a clear advantage for them. Donors also entered the picture, with their own accreditation systems and requirements. Private agencies had emerged to do accreditation, and the Workshop joked that this was "a scam!"

The Workshop turned to planning, suggesting that the NPO begin a campaign with its membership, and even beyond, explaining the points of concern with the Bill, the "red flags." This would help in motivating the sector to send appeals to the Ministry. The organizing NPO might have to help its membership draft their appeals, as some were unaware of the laws. There was value in gathering the experiences of smaller NGOs, especially if the NPO were to mention that their experiences would be used in conversation with the Ministry to amend the Bill. The NPO suggested conducting a "desk study" to develop arguments to "build our case with the Ministry of Corporate Affairs also and also with the media and all those places." They strategized working with the Ministry of Corporate Affairs, as well as other ministries that might weigh in and influence the Bill. They shared their contacts in government, who was posted where, who was amenable to conversation, who was not. It was necessary to have someone on the inside, who would listen to the sector's concerns, a contact, a friendly ear, an advocate. And then the meeting wound down, over lunch, though some had to leave before that. The attendees discussed, informally, other related issues of mutual concern, including the Tax Workshop, which had very robust attendance They spoke in Hindi and English, noting how law was so specialized few could understand it, and they compared other similar legislative contexts globally, such as the Russian Foreign Agents Bill, and an emergent urgent issue with foreign donors in India, including the Ford and Gates Foundations.

The Workshop closed with a story, of meeting with a civil servant about the impending renewal that was legislated with the 2012 FCRA rules. When queried about how the government would handle the impending FCRA renewal applications, the civil servant said it was his nightmare. He asked the organizing NPO to suggest ways to improve the system and the online filing requirement. Many of the NPOs filed quickly online and then later sent the hard copy. The Workshop discussed the fact that the rules said only hard copy was allowed. The rules were confusing, as the laws changed, even to the experts in the room. They discussed the technical flaws in the system, the snags, and how this translated into a punitive environment for NPOs. One expert framed the problem as a technical flaw:

See, there are technical flaws in the system. I know of many people who are trying to go online and file it there and they are unable to because somewhere or other there is some technical snag comes up, and then you can't move to the next page because, you know, some kind of a technical snag. And several people have faced that. So, I said, just file your hard copies and you'll be all right. Send in by post. Not courier.

The technical process had caused serious problems, and had exposed structural flaws in regulatory reform. The issue of state versus central subject regulation was a structural issue, while the rules and how to follow them were technical ones. Without insider and technical knowledge and bureaucratic literacy, one could make mistakes doing something as simple as submitting documents to the government. He explained why one should never use a courier when delivering documents to the Ministry. Couriers were not allowed inside the ministry. It had to be Indian Post, and Speed Post was best. If an NPO sent the required documents by courier, they would not reach the government and proof of sending would not hold up in court. This was highly specialized knowledge, which the members of the workshop sitting at the table embodied, with their experience, concerns, and strategies. They were a council of advisors for the sector, brought to Delhi to develop a plan with the organizing NPO, which would then be communicated to the sector in order to gather support, and finally, make a petition to the Ministry to change the MSSR Bill. Though the Bill was eventually not successful, the Workshop remained an arena of collective, participatory, democratic advocacy for the nonprofit sector. As much as workshops created spaces for structured debate and strategy formation, many workshops also produced artifacts of association. Some produced petitions to the government or missives to membership, and others produced reports. Reports, as artifacts of workshops, had their own life cycles, political capacities, and mobilizing potential. The next chapter focuses on report writing as a component of NPO process, and a strategy for engaging the public. Workshops helped the nonprofit sector navigate regulatory distinctions—of public/private, for-profit/nonprofit, and state/central regulation. Workshops addressed a constellation of laws, including tax laws, the FCRA, and registration laws for trusts, societies, and charitable companies. They were spaces of advocacy where understandings were developed, challenges identified, and strategies formed, and they were spaces where the power of association blossomed.

SIX

Reports as Mobilizing Technologies

Public Interest Litigation, NPO-generated reports, and research institute reports are all types of reports produced by India's nonprofit sector. Public Interest Litigation (PIL) is a constitutional creation that enables any individual to challenge the government. NPOs were involved in campaigns for social change, and in the particular case of NPO advocacy for the nonprofit sector discussed in this book, they filed petitions as well. NPO-generated reports represented their NPO membership, to speak for the sector more broadly. In this chapter I explore PIL efforts, as well as two NPO reports written using workshop techniques, and research institute reports focused on the nonprofit philanthropic ecosystem. Together, these three types of reports represented a forum for nonprofit advocacy. Reports resulted from research, advocacy, and workshops, and they were nonprofit public goods.

Speaking for the Public

NPOs in India have been involved in processes of national policy development for decades, often in the form of report creation. Development planning in India was historically produced via an institution called the Planning Commission.[1] Initiated as a colonial body, it adopted a Nehruvian notion of central government upon India's independence. As a think tank inside the state, it dreamed schemes for India's future for six decades. When national five year plans were produced by the Planning Commission, civil society leaders participated. For example, the 2012–17 Five Year Plan included a section written by the Steering Committee on the Voluntary Sector, which was comprised of NPO directors. When searching for the Planning Commission on the Government of India's webpage in 2014, I clicked on a link regarding NGOs and encountered a 688-page research report written by an NPO that was seamlessly integrated into the web-world of the state. The NPO-state conjunction was also visible in a 244-page report which had been drafted in preparation for the 2012–17 Five Year Plan by a group of NPOs and Indian civil society experts, funded by the United Nations Development Programme (UNDP).[2] One can imagine how activist-oriented groups concerned with refusing state developmental agendas might be suspicious of NPOs, sitting on the Planning Commission, hobnobbing with civil servants (Kamat 2002; Kothari 1986). One can also see how NPOs and civil society groups could morph into state institutions, and could then become a threat to the state (Sharma 2008).

From within the state some NPOs learned the language of the state, using it to challenge the state itself. If the discourse of the state is rational-bureaucratic, then some bureaucratically oriented advocacy NPOs utilized techniques of the state to challenge the priorities of statist governance, often through the mechanisms of law. Lest one interpret report writing as formal posturing that has little to do with on-the-ground struggles of smaller NPOs focused on social service delivery, resource acquisition, and more urgent concerns of poverty alleviation, recall that in terms of negotiations with the state, report writing existed in the larger, policy-oriented terrain. This political strategy had become an increasingly viable avenue for active engagement as space shrank for civil society engagement. When I was in Delhi, writing reports with an NPO, I was told that one of its board members sat on the Steering Committee for the Voluntary Sector on the Planning Commission. This, according to the NPO staff, ensured the organization a connection between the larger, governmental, policy-oriented report-writing strategies of the Planning Commission and the more local NPO-focused reports written by the Delhi office. As much as reports presented a coherent image of the sector, life in practice was more ad hoc, spontaneous, thrown together, discursive, plural, and consultative. Nonprofit advocacy NPOs in their daily office worlds were filled with debates, despite the representational coherence of their reports. As soon as reports were printed they were out of date, sedimentations of a bureaucratic process, whereas time, and the statistics documented in the reports, had moved on. Reports may become tools of the future but they document the present, which quickly becomes the past. These textual artifacts formed only part of the story, as I am less interested in reports as bureaucratic artifacts than I am in the social processes of their creation. Report-based advocacy was oriented toward other institutional actors like state regulatory bodies, other NPOs, and donors. Through report writing, as a process, NPOs communicated with each other, shared information, networked, and constituted civil society. As with the term *workshop*, I treat *report* as a proper noun, an actor of sorts, which speaks on behalf of the collective.

Some NPOs, though not all, focused their efforts on filing Public Interest Litigation cases. PIL, as a special category of legislation, historically benefited minorities and the poor. PIL was one avenue through which attempts to garner socioeconomic rights from the Indian state on behalf of "the public" were consistently made through the courts (Baxi 1985; Cassels 1989; Holladay 2012; Bhuwania 2014; Landau 2012, 235–37). NPOs involved with PIL cases educated citizens about pending legislation, and demanded enforcement of progressive laws by the government once they were passed. PIL petitions and report-based civil society advocacy, paired together, pressured the state for socioeconomic ("distributive") rights. Some rights-based civil society groups sought to garner entitlements from the state through campaigns, using the judicial mechanism of PIL to enshrine the promise of entitlements into law. A few examples of success in this effort are the Right to Food (2005), and Right to Education (2009) Acts, all of which resulted from civil society campaigns. When laws were passed, that did not mean the end of the social movements behind them. Progressive laws had the potential to exist merely on paper, so in order to hold the government accountable and to encourage enforcement of rights-based laws, civil society groups organized educational campaigns informing the public about such laws. Additionally, and aside from their advocacy work, NPOs provided welfare services guaranteed by these progressive laws, which included work training, infrastructure development, education, and access to information from the state. NPOs reaped the advantages of continued engagement with the state, and their very survival rested upon this relationship. The efforts by rights-based campaigns, through reports such as those related to PIL, indirectly promoted the nonprofit sector, in a self-sustaining cycle.

One must understand the wider context of PIL to contextualize the relationship between civil society advocacy and the law. PIL was structurally innovative as a legal form in that its *locus standi* (the right to bring an action to a court) included the capacity for individuals, such as academics, journalists, and civil society organizations, to file cases on behalf of other groups (Cassels 1989, 499). Unlike the way class action lawsuits are formulated in other countries—where lawyers represent an individual, a group, or a member of a group experiencing rights infringement—in India, civil society groups, nonprofits, and activists can file PIL cases independently. Some Indian civil society groups have consisted of lawyer collectives focused on this practice (cf. Baxi 1985; Bhuwania 2014). PIL's innovation was its procedural flexibility, which encouraged activists to demand redress from the state on behalf of others (Cassels 1989, 500).

Courts historically facilitated PIL cases by waiving fees, providing litigation assistance, appointing commissions of enquiry to investigate and collect facts for cases in order to relieve petitioners of expenses, and recommending remedies.[3] The judicial context of PIL created an inherent, always possible, elaboration of what constituted a right and a rights infringement. As Cassels (1989, 503) notes, "Through an expansive reading of fundamental rights, informed by a commitment to the (non-enforceable) social welfare objectives of the Directive Principles, the courts have sought to read substance into otherwise formal guarantees."[4] The gap between formal legal arrangements such as PIL and existing social realities, was where civil society advocacy fomented. In India, laws could be progressive and innovative, but if they were inadequately implemented, social practices continued to oppress certain groups. Justice in the courts did not automatically translate into structural change for the marginalized. Courts dictated formal justice resolutions, and civil society groups worked to agitate for public rights and entitlements outside the courts and to make sure rights were implemented and upheld.

PIL was both a unique feature of the Indian appellate judiciary and its own jurisdiction, and it was through PIL that the Indian judiciary became a social movement (Baxi 1985; Bhuwania 2014). Led by the judiciary, PIL emerged as a challenge to the legislative arm of the state immediately after the Emergency, when the "court redefined itself as the fount of substantive justice: portraying itself as the 'last resort for the oppressed and bewildered'" (Bhuwania 2014, 314; cf. Baxi 1985, 107). PIL built on the constitutional Directive Principles of State Policy, which set out to deal with social questions of inequality and to promote the welfare of people (though they were not enforceable in court and, as such, were unlike fundamental rights). These Directive Principles were a Nehruvian historical product. In 1950, the Indian Supreme Court acquired a new jurisdiction that permitted the court to hear writ petitions "to enforce fundamental rights against the state" (Bhuwania 2014, 316); hence the Indian Supreme Court became a space for advocacy and activism.[5] PIL was one way to access the Supreme Court and to approach questions of distributive rights; and it was through PIL that petitioners could challenge the state.[6]

Upendra Baxi's early work on PIL, titled "Taking Suffering Seriously" (Baxi 1985), documented the new sphere of the public in judicial activism. Between 1977 and 1979, the term "the people" began to appear in court language. Seeking legitimacy in its post-Emergency populism, the court battled the executive branches of the state as the court became a "people's court." In 1981, PIL opened the Supreme Court to "public-spirited citizens;" petitioners were not representative members of groups, but members of the citizenry at large, suing the state for defaulting on its duty to "the public." Earlier, people's causes had "*appeared* merely as issues argued arcanely by lawyers and decided in the mystery and mystique of the inherited common-law like judicial process" (Baxi 1985, 107; italics in the original). Through PIL, the court gained the constitutional power of intervention. People came to court with "unusual problems" seeking "extraordinary remedies," and bringing "a new kind of lawyering and a novel kind of judging," bringing a "new kind of dialogue in the judicial role" (108).[7]

The activist Indian judiciary created a power triangle between the legislative branch of the state (Parliament), the judiciary (activist courts), and civil society organizations, whereby civil society groups filed writ petitions/PIL cases on behalf of citizens. As Baxi notes in an interview (Sen 2014), the Supreme Court "is essentially acting as an institution of governance." Through what Baxi calls "social action litigation," it deals with "government lawlessness." Baxi notes: "we must today accept the fact that the Supreme Court co-governs the country. Whether it is right or wrong for courts in general to do this is an old question. But our Supreme Court, since 1980 particularly, a little earlier, makes both law and policy." Baxi further argues that the public interest litigation of the Supreme Court is social action:

> Social action is a different concept from the public interest. In a democracy, public interest is guarded by Parliament, not by citizens. There's no direct democracy. All we have is indirect democracy. We elect our representatives and they run the legislature. So, social action is citizen

action and I wanted this to be recognized that it's not lawyers keeping the courts busy. It is people and social agencies like NGOs which take up the cases. (Cited in Sen 2014)

This judicial context encouraged research and collaboration between civil society and voluntary groups, and civil society groups represented collectivities, with PIL focusing on enforcing collective, not individual, rights. Together, NPOs and the mechanism of PIL presented a formidable challenge to state legitimacy, which had the potential to result in law. Examples include the 2012 Right to Food case, in which the Supreme Court ordered state governments to implement a food distribution program, and the Delhi High Court striking down anti-sodomy laws, superseding the legislature. As the judiciary shepherded social transformation via PIL, it legislated from the bench to promote the interests of "the public" (Holladay 2012, 570). The emphasis on collective action and group rights by the courts meant that when civil society groups were involved in advocacy on behalf of particular groups (in the name of "the public"), they could turn toward the activist courts and PIL.

Some NPOs that focused on legal advocacy oriented their efforts toward filing PIL cases, as these cases created the juridical space for citizens to challenge the state and compel the government to enact progressive legislation. Rights-based NPOs educated citizens about pending legislation, and demanded enforcement of progressive laws by the government once those laws were passed. The report-based advocacy I describe fits into this wider terrain of judicial activism, but it focuses on NPOs advocating for the nonprofit sector—as a group (see Comaroff and Comaroff 2006 on judicial activism more broadly). Together, these types of NPOs and activists constituted the arena of bureaucratic and judicial activism where report writing occurred. Once progressive laws were passed by Parliament, development and delivery NPOs were contracted by the state to provide welfare services, including work training, infrastructure development, education, and access to information. In this manner, those NPOs that had become subcontractors depended on continued engagement with the state for their economic survival.

When the Indian state cracked down, through bureaucratic means such as law, on NPOs by freezing their funds, closing them down, or restricting their operations, report writing became a strategy through which civil society groups sought to assert their claims. That civil society groups could challenge the state structurally, through PIL, gave report writing in general in India more weight. The voices and testimonies of citizens and citizen groups were presented in NPO reports, some of which were called "citizen reports." Citizens groups, civil society organizations, and NPOs were all involved in reporting on governmental lawlessness, critiquing governmental processes, and lobbying for their own concerns and constituencies. In addition to lobbying for the rights of others, some NPOs lobbied to protect the interests of the nonprofit sector more broadly, and a primary technology of this endeavor was report writing. This type of legislative activism sought to preserve NPO spaces for social critique. It engaged with the courts and used them but did not exist entirely in the judicial realm. It took place in offices, and workshops, and educational forums, and utilized bureaucratic techniques that mirrored governmental practices employed by the state: writing reports and issuing circulars. Advocacy NPOs lobbied, via law, to challenge the state's monopoly over public good. Report writing, as a form of legal advocacy was situated amid this broader ecology of bureaucracy in NPO work, which also included petitions, public interest litigation, citizen reports, and final reports to donors, governmental bodies, and member constituencies. Report writing was in many ways constitutive of nonprofit labor itself.

Speaking for the Sector

On overflowing shelves and bound together with string in piles of assorted sizes, the reports gathered dust and soot. Each report represented a year, a campaign, and a record of a dynamic discussion. The room sat as testament to the work of a New Delhi NGO's annual efforts expended to produce reports. The room abutted the offices of the NGO, which was focused on advocacy and research, and where I volunteered and assisted with report writing in 2012–13. This NGO was as an apex organization, and it served as an information distribution system and education provider for networks of smaller organizations and civil society groups throughout India. Based in India's political capital, its pulse was policy making and its objective was protecting the space of civil society engagement. Much of this work focused on the legal reform of regulations affecting the nonprofit sector. The report room was a hallway, situated between the offices where workers wrote reports, neutral yet potent, the past surrounding its inhabitants like bricks buttressing the present, mountains of effort lining the walls, artifacts of social engagement.

What is to be made of a room such as this? The stacks of documents in the report room might appear to be the antiquated residue of an outdated form, vestiges of institutional posturing on paper, representing an archaic bureaucratic language. At first glance, reports and report-writing could be discounted as what David Graeber (2016) has termed the "total bureaucratization" of life, but the NPO's reports were more than dead letters; they were advocacy tools, part and parcel of a political process. I analyze report writing as a particular type of bureaucratic engagement that seeks to communicate with the state and institutions in India, such as donors and other NGOs, aiming to affect legal reform. Report writing as a political process generates meetings, workshops, and debates. Through report-based advocacy, a diverse and unwieldy sector of activists, NGOs, voluntary groups, and civil society organizations galvanized themselves into a representational entity. The goals of report writing are twofold: to representationally coalesce what scholar and practitioner Rajesh Tandon (2017) has identified as a diverse and disaggregated sector of Indian civil society institutions into a unified entity ("the not-for-profit sector," "civil society") and to preserve a space for nonprofit engagement.

The NPO's work was similar to that of other bureaucratic institutional settings studied by anthropologists in which documents constitute institutional life, framing and manifesting "bureaucratic rules, ideology, knowledge, practices, subjectivities, outcomes and even the organizations themselves" (Hull 2012a, 253; also see Feldman 2008; Gupta 2012; Gupta and Sharma 2006; Riles 2001; and Hoag 2011). Reports discursively codified institutional worlds, and the process of report writing constructed them (see Latour 2004 for science and law). Report writing was a collaborative process, the result of a temporary discursive consensus, refined and edited through dialogue and forged in debate. Once produced, reports became a medium and a bureaucratic language, a symbolic system that facilitated negotiation between discrete institutional realms, of NGOs, state agencies, and donors. As bureaucratic forms, reports were recursive, simultaneously prescriptive and descriptive, self-referential maps and designs that buttressed and identified advocacy networks and institutional agendas (Riles 2001). Once written, reports had the potential to live on as tools, mobile and mobilizing technologies for the nonprofit sector. Their existence sedimented the diverse and often contentious arena of civil society groups into a cohesive sector, similar to how governmental bureaucracies were aggregated into an entity called the state through document production. Advocacy networks systemically self-manifest by creating reports (for ethnographies of the state, see Gupta 2012; Hull 2012b; Feldman 2008; and Hetherington 2020).

Beyond the reports themselves, we must examine report writing as a social, communicative, and political process. Advocacy reports are emblematic of the bureaucratic processes with which NPOs contend daily. Reports are part of a wider genre of nonprofit textual production, an ecosystem of evaluative documents written for use internally by NPOs and as audit-worthy products for donors. Internal reports and outside evaluations are part of the architecture of proving success for NGOs, and there is a particular practice to writing NPO reports. Anyone familiar with NGOs realizes there is a ubiquity to report writing: of internal monitoring and evaluation, of external assessment, and of outward-seeking advocacy for the sector itself. It is difficult to disaggregate the vectors of these bureaucratic processes, as they are so much a part of nonprofit survival and communicative practice. NGOs report upon their work by doing desk reviews of projects, interviewing stakeholders, making field visits, and organizing focus groups of beneficiaries (Watkins et al. 2012, 303).

Report writing may not look like advocacy, but after a year of sitting at a table working on a report with NPO staff in 2012–13, I began to see its viability as a strategy. Requests made to the state on paper are not outright demands for change voiced in the language of outrage. There is no demonstration of frustration, no performative focus, no satire. In silent contrast, report writing is a form of protest that speaks the technical language of the state: it is rational, bureaucratic, codified, calculating, and it is emulative (Hull 2008). Its arsenal is empirical, utilizing aggregate statistics and narrative cases. Report-based advocacy is a multi-vocal, and democratic social process, though final printed reports rarely retain the messy unfinished character of conversations and negotiations. Most published reports are authorless, much like documents produced by the state.

Report writing in New Delhi got into gear on an annual cycle. Each year, as national budget deliberations ensued, voluntary organizations aligned as a group to agitate for legislation that enabled their work. Groups representing a variety of diverse collectivities and institutional forms, including social action groups (SAGs), nongovernmental organizations (NGOs) and civil society organizations (CSOs), strove to influence the national budgetary process. In these moments, NPOs shifted into high gear. They sponsored workshops with their members to organize collective responses to proposed national budget priorities, and sent recommendations to the Ministry of Finance. A similar process was repeated throughout the year, as Bills, rules, and amendments to laws were introduced and debated in Parliament.[8] Despite these efforts to communicate with the state, suspicion continued to grow in India between the government and voluntary sector (Manku 2016a).

Surveying five years (2012 to 2017) of NPO engagement with the Union Budget in India is to observe an orbit of negotiation between the voluntary sector and the government around a cluster of laws. In 2012, efforts centered around revisions to rules and amendments to the FCRA. Efforts in 2013 concentrated upon the definition of "charitable purpose" in the Direct Taxes Code. The FCRA was again the focus in 2014–15, along with an Intelligence Bureau report that targeted NGOs as anti-national and restricted the political activities of civil society groups, and the new provision in the Companies Act stipulating the 2 percent corporate social responsibility tax. In 2016, revisions to the Income Tax Act took center stage. In this five-year snapshot, we see how civil society groups inhabited a space of advocacy that pressured the government on behalf of the public for laws surrounding civil society engagement.

As the state scrutinized NGOs by increasing reporting requirements and bureaucratic engagement, some NGOs turned to report writing as a strategy. While volunteering with an NPO, I was tasked with documenting the work of the voluntary sector itself via two reports. To write the reports, NPO staff traveled throughout India, conducting research and educating its member NGOs and other civil society groups about shifts in the legislative landscape for the voluntary sector. For example, it held workshops on new reporting requirements detailed in the revised and amended FCRA. During site visits, NPO staff interviewed civil society groups and learned about regional issues facing the sector. Workshops, dialogue, and debate were woven into report writing. Once a draft report was written, it was circulated in advance to the NPO's membership for feedback and workshopped with an invited group of NGO representatives and civil servants in Delhi. The report was discussed, ripped apart, argued against, and put back together, rewritten, circulated to the membership, and eventually published. The aim of report writing involved audiences and participation by members of the state, NGOs, and NGO constituencies (including donors), all of whom were involved in the discussions. Once reports were published and launched, NGOs used them to argue on behalf of their constituencies with funders and with government officers. As NPO staff wrote the reports, they anticipated how their members could use them as a printed product in other contexts. NGOs posted reports on their website for easy download, referencing concerns of the organizations and the sector more broadly. Reports were referenced in conversation, passed around at meetings as calling cards, and used to make arguments in debates. Yet, as the NPO director told me, "The state does not speak, it only listens." Indeed, the state was obtuse and opaque, and as much as the voluntary sector insisted on accountability and transparency, the state remained a mute participant in a forced dialogue. The state had no author, like the NGO reports that declared their urgent observations and aimed their missives from their constituencies.

The NPO saw the changing laws toward nonprofits/NGOs as a problem for its own membership. Bureaucracy and lack of governmental transparency was a particular hindrance for small NGOs, who didn't understand the regulatory laws by which they had to abide. Some had lapsed in their reporting to the government and had lost their legal status under the 2012 FCRA rules. The NPO was working with the government, trying to streamline the legislation for NGOs to make it easier to navigate. In fact, some NGOs found the laws and rules regarding the regulation of foreign philanthropy so onerous that one director I met kept a tax lawyer on retainer to deal with any problems that might arise. FCRA brokers hung around the FCRA office, according to this director, ready to offer help with paperwork. An entire economy of assistance had developed around the bureaucratic quagmire of the FCRA, and in 2013, the government was working to move the entire FCRA process online, eliminating middlemen.

In an unassuming building located in a neighborhood of homes, with the sun blocked by heavy curtains, reports lined the shelves in the room where staff took their chatting breaks when the seminar table/lunchroom was busy. During the year I spent at the NPO, six staff members wrote reports in these offices. Topics spanned the challenges of the voluntary sector: global footprints of NGOs, the status of the voluntary sector, self-certification models, internal governance, private-sector collaboration, the relation of the voluntary sector to the government, and national registration laws. Research studies were assigned to specific staff members. At this NPO, all the staff members writing reports were women. This was not unusual in the sector, as it offered a good first job for educated women after university. Themes of the regional meetings and workshops held by the NPO matched its report-writing themes. On paper, the government made great strides toward addressing social issues with the passage of progressive rights-based laws, but these were gestures without structures of enforcement. In contrast to governmental efforts in social welfare provision, NGOs considered themselves innovative in their responsiveness and flexibility due to their small scale.

MAKING REPORT #1: CHALLENGES OF VOICE

In February 2013, NPO staff met to outline our first report. It should be positive, some argued, outlining the accomplishments of the sector. We decided to break it into sections, each written by a different staff member: (1) history and nomenclature of the sector; (2) contributions of the sector; (3) functions in service delivery, research and advocacy, and entitlements (we opted not to use the term *rights-based* because it might be considered controversial). For the contributions section, we decided to draw upon regional reports written by NPO staff who visited member groups throughout India, as well as sector-based understandings in health, education, and advocacy. It was hard to narrow down what we would focus on, but we discussed how it should represent a clear contribution to society. The report was to be drafted in pieces, put together, presented in workshops, discussed, and re-drafted. A launch was set for June 2013 as we planned the timeline for the report making process. The report-writing process in the NPO produced a new language through which diverse groups could communicate. The language politics of this consensus-building exercise were always incomplete, and emphasized the society-changing aims of advocacy groups working in this realm. In the two sections that follow, I track the process of writing two reports at the NPO, in workshops, meetings, and discussions. The process of writing each report was a social one, filled with debates and constituencies vying for a voice in the unwieldy non-system of Indian civil society.

The Report #1 Workshop was held for one day in April 2013, in central Delhi. Attended by twenty-eight people, it was geared toward the making of a report on the voice of the voluntary sector, and those in attendance were by no means a unified group. The meeting began in Hindi, and within the first five minutes, an NPO member shouted from the audience "English please or speak in Telugu." The NGO community was so diverse that they couldn't speak to each other in the same language. It was because of this diversity that the project of report making required a bureaucratic language of its own. That NGOs from different regions of India, speaking different languages, could come together and discuss common concerns was a feat. The Workshop focused on improving the draft report, and it was scrutinized, ripped apart, contested, and rethought in the meeting as data were debated and more data were requested. The Workshop began with NPO researchers each presenting regional summaries based on site visits they had undertaken to NPO members and networks. Before the Workshop, each of the NPO's field officers conducted a desk study about regional concerns and then held a regional Workshop with local NGOs. They went on field visits and subsequently sent out a mailing requesting feedback. The draft reports were written based on the feedback and site visits. Topics included registration laws for NGOs, challenges that NGOs faced on a day-to-day basis: declining funding, difficulties working with local government officials, a lack of internal governance, a skill gap for NGOs, and competition between NGOs in the field. Uneven development was also discussed, as well as inequities between large and small NGOs, a general lack of stability in the NGO workforce, and interfaces with the private sector. Small NGOs found it difficult to interface with government and the private sector, and suffered from issues of lack of credibility, which put them at a disadvantage. The commercialization of NGOs was an issue, as well as the cancellation of FCRA registrations and licenses by the government. NGO members in the room were vocal about what was missing from the draft reports, and the director of the NPO critiqued his staff in public. Nothing was beyond criticism. The voluntary sector faced new pressures in the form of new governmental policies, amendments to laws, shrinking resources from donors, and competition in social welfare provision from the corporate sector. Though it was difficult for individual NGOs to address the GOI directly (as they could then be targeted), as an apex organization the NPO could do it by representing collective others, as an umbrella institution. Just as regional NGOs negotiated with local government officials, the NPO negotiated with the central government regarding NGO policy.

NGOs faced new problems. Some communities had begun to see grassroots staff in a commercial manner regarding what could they provide. In addition, members at the meeting voiced concern that much of the FCRA funding was going to religious organizations, and there was a request for more analysis of this in Report #1. There was a split in the sector: big organizations were dominating and smaller ones were not ready to learn and associate with the big ones. This too was not in the draft report. But there was a long discussion about what to include in the report, and that nobody would acknowledge the good work of the sector if members of the sector couldn't do it themselves; divisions in the sector gave it a bad name. Another member mentioned that the term *voluntary sector* was misleading, as many civil servants assumed NGOs did not expect money for their work. Someone brought up NGO staff benefits such as retirement issues and provident funds, and another noticed a statistical error in the draft report numbers. Members mentioned issues from their experience, their regions, and their concerns. The conversation was wide ranging and heated—at times confessional, combative; it resisted consensus. Yet, the report required consensus. The conversation waged on throughout the day in multiple languages, switching back and forth. The challenge of presenting a unified front from within the sector was prominently displayed in the debates. The group discussed what the sector was—and some argued it was not NGOs, not government. Struggles for funding were constant refrains: some requested deeper analysis of the material presented in the draft report; others wanted more quantified data. Some requests made by invited members were impossible to meet, though the NPO staff wrote down the comments, taped the meeting, and referred to these requests later, when writing the report.

"Corporates are creating their own kingdoms" one member stated: They created trusts and got government money to become mother NGOs that other NGOs had to go to. A member discussed how Reliance (Corporation) was spending 10,000 crores to develop agricultural cooperatives all over the country, and then was planning to feed them into the corporation. They wanted NGOs to train them, and to use the voluntary sector to legitimize the corporate efforts. The member was troubled by this, and discussed it in terms of co-optation, where corporations hijacked the voluntary sector for corporate aims. This aspect of the dialogue did not make it into the final report. There was too much to include, and the NPO director suggested doing a separate study on it.

Side conversations, and ones that were too heated for Report #1, were placed aside for future studies and later reports. Members discussed whether or not Report #1 should include controversial issues, like competition among NGOs. "Why not?" one member remarked. "What has led to this competition?" That issue should be addressed. The group discussed a spate of new laws being floated regarding nonprofit registration; this too was put aside for another workshop. The conversation was surprisingly organic, a critique of work in progress. As critical as one might be about report-making advocacy organizations, I was impressed by the democratic aspects of report-making processes, which were innovative and experimental. Everything was debated. I had never experienced such a democratic institutional environment. One member mentioned how the context for NGO work was changing and the group "must face the market as it was here to stay." Needs were changing and dreams were changing. "We can't keep on having our dreams and thrust it upon them" one person remarked. There was a discussion about leadership in the sector, as a skill, and how disgruntled staff presented a negative view of the sector to outsiders. The NPO director explained how the report would address and consolidate concerns from eleven regional, state-based studies. One person brought up the issue of governmental corruption; another argued that internal critique was essential for the report, not solely praise.

A tension emerged between focusing on problems by delving deep into each state report, and presenting a positive view by offering solutions to perceived problems. There was also discussion on data: where they came from, how valid they were, and what was missing. The discussion turned to donors, and difficulties. There were donors present in the meeting. Nothing was off the table in the Workshop, though it would not all make it into the final report. The NPO members in attendance gave line-by-line critiques of the draft report. In the Workshop, authorship was relevant. The NPO faced the criticism by its members, and it couldn't hide behind its institutional anonymity. The Workshop was face to face and confrontational. This aspect of report making was markedly different from the authorless anonymity of the final published report, and all day, conversations moved back and forth between English and Hindi. At one point the director of the NPO said, "How can we come together and unite when we can't speak the same language?" The NPO presented, members critiqued, the NPO listened. In this sense, report making was a form of witnessing, and in this sense a form of advocacy. More than documentation, the process was generative. At the end of the meeting, as the time was limited, the NPO director tried to wrap things up. He explained that the goal of the eventual written report was for members to use to share with local and state government officials, and the media, to defend what the voluntary sector was doing. Report #1 could be used for state-based advocacy efforts, and the goal was to be able to speak at a national level with the government. To go beyond the specificities of regional issues, or the detailed annual reports of individual groups. Like the Planning Commission reports mentioned earlier, the NPO reports referenced each other and were referenced by NGO workers as benchmarks for ongoing conversations. As such, they became authoritative institutional texts. Report #1 was a forum for critique and complaint, while its companion, Report #2, documented the accomplishments of the NGO sector. Both were intended for an audience of other institutions, including government agencies and donors. That the two reports were separate and spoke to different audiences signified how threatened the sector was in 2013, which was the run-up to the election year, with India's political helm potentially in transition. Nobody knew where politics would move, and which direction it would turn. It was a year when NGO workers complained of nothing getting done because everyone was focused on politics. In this setting, evidence compilation and report writing became the groundwork for a political argument for one's existence.

The final published report congealed the meeting into a document. It included "citizen's reports" from ten states and the Northeast region.[9] Each communication from "the field" listed challenges faced by the sector in the particular context of each state. A "Comprehensive Report" summarized the findings, which included the overall challenges the NGO sector faced. A cluster of challenges pointed to government-NGO relations, including stringent laws by the government, and "red tapism" where the process of proposal submission and eventual release of funds was slowed by the government. NPOs also faced difficulty in engaging with governmental machinery. The first set of concerns focused on NGO-government relations. The second set of concerns focused on NPO-donor relations. NPOs faced a skills gap, which resulted in limited technical competency being found within small NGOs, and which made seeking donor funds difficult. A scarcity of skilled human resources plagued the sector, and low salaries did not attract professionals. Other concerns focused on the identity and expectations of the sector. Because of governmental and donor demands, innovation and creativity were declining. The report utilized quotations and raw data to humanize its claims. It discussed dependence on donors, and how this restricted freedom of choice regarding activities. In addition, the sector was fragmented, and there was an absence of a collective voice. Confusion about the profit-orientation identity of the sector resulted in other challenges. Finally, NPOs faced competition in the local development sector from outside agencies that were more professionally qualified and could work in a technical manner. Local organizations had shortcomings in regard to information and expertise. Report #1 concluded its list of challenges with a set of recommendations regarding the funding of NPOs, internal governance issues, and strategies to engage with the government and to strengthen the relationship among NPOs. Finally, this report and all the remaining reports contained recommendations for future action.

MAKING REPORT #2: CHALLENGES OF REPRESENTATION

The day after the Report #1 Workshop took place, the NPO held another Workshop to brainstorm another report on the status of the voluntary sector, and many of the same representatives of voluntary organizations were in the room. This Report #2 meeting had a different tone. The Report #1 Workshop had debated the varied multitude of challenges, problems, and complaints NGOs faced in carrying out their work. The Report #2 Workshop focused on the challenges of representing the sector. A funder had supported the report-making process, of which this workshop was a part, and a representative from the funding agency was also in attendance. Report making was an action item funded by donors.

Discussion in the Report #2 Workshop centered on challenges of representation. From the moment the meeting began, there was debate. People wanted to talk about issues, not about the sector, one person argued. Another mentioned the diversity of the sector and how "negativism" was being spread. What is the sector? some asked. There was discussion regarding member expectations for the report. Some wanted to dispel myths about the sector and highlight contributions nonprofits have made to India's development, reflecting on the collective work that had been done without naming individual organizations. There was fear in the sector of reprisals from the government, and no one wanted to be targeted. The NPO, as a membership organization, provided shelter in the collective. It could advocate on behalf of the larger group. Perhaps we could define the sector by defining what it is not, one NGO representative suggested. Members were concerned about singling out particular NGOs as examples: "If we take out certain cases the NGOs will seem like Gods and Goddesses." This would contradict the collective nature of the voluntary sector. Some argued the focus of the report should be on collective efforts, while others argued for the inclusion of more statistical data, which, though hard to get, could inclusively represent the work of smaller NGOs. Some argued that a focus on small grassroots groups should be the desired outcome of the report, to undo the bias toward large NPO representations of the sector.

Capturing the nonprofit sector as a whole was a serious conundrum. If there was no way to systematically sample all the NPOs in India, how could any representation be representative? The lack of statistical data was a concern regarding the legitimacy of the report, and the NPO workers in the room struggled with this issue. The group discussed what the sector stood for and what it was trying to change. Though it was critiqued by the government, governmental policies depended on the voluntary sector. "We need to put our house in order," one person said, "it's almost a last resort." Another member suggested the report would be useful for negotiating with government ministries and in courts of law. There was a need to back up the work being done with some proof, a document, a report. The report should focus on landmark achievements, some argued. "We must have done something right," another said; "Why are we receiving threats?" Though the sector was having an identity crisis, most agreed that being not-for-profit was a focus of all the groups in the room. Others suggested that part of the problem was the desperation to pin down the sector. India had probably the strongest civil society in the world. "No country in the world has what we have," someone remarked. Terminology was important but "with an animal so large, fuzziness is good." Most agreed that the professional aspects of the sector should be highlighted, and that nonprofits were not just volunteers. Another person pointed out the uniqueness of the sector, which was generative and always remaking itself.

The intricacies of the report were debated: how to structure it, which themes to include, and how to encompass India's complex social geography. As I sat through the report making, I was struck by the difference in approach between the writing of the draft report that we (myself and the NPO report writing staff) had done before the workshop and the content generated in the workshop. As NPO members discussed what they wanted the report to look like, the report was being transformed as a tool for membership; NPO staff listened and took note. Not all of the discussion could be included in the final version of Report #2, but the feedback shaped the printed product. NPO members talked about how they wanted to be able to use the report when they met with prospective donors. A solid document would address some of the negative representation that was taking place, some hoped. Yet there was a tension—one that could be resolved neither in the report nor the report-making process—between the pressures for the sector to be professionalized and the ad hoc nature of many voluntary groups, a trait that was the calling card of collective action. People's organizations didn't have to be professional. Members in attendance agreed that the writing style of the report should not be academic; it should be an easy to understand tool for advocacy, right down to having items arranged in boxes. The language politics question reared its head: some asked what language the report should use. It should be a report in two languages, Hindi and English, people agreed, and so two versions were produced. We broke for lunch and continued the conversation informally over the urgent issue of how to represent the sector without losing its core in the process. It was going to be difficult to please everyone in the room with one document, yet this was the task faced by NPO staff writing the report, including myself.

After the workshop, we met to discuss what had preceded this moment. It was a lot to take in and we strategized how to move forward. We divided the report up and each of us wrote some sections. We scheduled a launch date for media and membership. Report writing after the workshop involved a flux of ideas and moving targets. We decided to highlight case studies featuring the work being done in policy formation, service delivery, and rights-based engagement. The regional focus, with which we had written the earlier drafts of the report, ended up being too complex for the representational coherence we sought in Report #2, but we elected to keep that focus in Report #1 in the form of aggregated citizens' reports. Even as I write of this process, I am forced to foreclose discussion of some of the complexity of the negotiations that took place. It was not easy for the NPO staff to represent a complex sector with one document, nonetheless, the report was drafted, edited, revised, redrafted, circulated, redrafted again, and eventually printed and launched. The launch resulted in newspaper articles that helped to circulate the NPO's concerns regarding the sector. I was told it was one of the NPO's most successful reports; it would be useful for NPOs seeking to justify their work. The process of report making through debate and dialogue involved consciousness raising that brought people together.

In its final form, Report #2 was a more static entity than its workshop incarnation, which was necessary for it to become a tool. The report was a bureaucratic document, debate dulled by consensus and formality. With colorful pictures, it could be slapped down on a desk as proof that the voluntary sector was worthy of respect. It came to conclusions and made recommendations. It concluded that voluntary organizations were diverse and vast and that their contributions to the sector had gone unnoticed. It argued that the Indian government did not consider large educational and health-related institutions as separate from voluntary organizations, and it was time for the government to consider them as separate entities. The report also placed NPOs in India in a global context, in consideration of such factors as foreign direct investment; the global recession; India's engagement in the G20, in the India-Brazil-South Africa Dialogue Forum (IBSA), and in the emerging national economies represented in BRICS; and also India's aid to Africa and South American countries. Meanwhile, NGOs were weathering tightening national laws on foreign philanthropy and new state restrictions on NGOs' activities. The voluntary sector had expanded to reach areas the government could not access. The report acknowledged that "Fighting for rights is not always favorable to the bureaucratic mindset," and that "there is corruption in government funding to NGOs. Not only NGOs are blacklisted and penalized but both donors and recipients are scrutinized." The report recommended the Government of India create a voluntary organization council with a new ministry to regulate the voluntary sector, that the government cease distinguishing between foreign and Indian funds, and that it implement the National Policy on the Voluntary Sector (Government of India 2007) and previous Planning Commission recommendations. The policy recommendations were aimed at an audience of state officials comprised of civil servants, Members of Parliament, ministers, and other government employees tasked with regulating NPOs. The NPO heading the reporting effort, like many smaller NGOs, was sometimes understaffed and beset by meager funds, yet I came to see its report writing strategy as a structural one, with long-term aims: to speak to the government on its own terms. The NPO wrote petitions to the government. The director appeared on television and lobbied for the nonprofit sector's concerns. The NPO would not go away. As the director described the tactic to me, it agitated. How? Via reports.

Speaking for the Philanthropic Ecosystem System

Some advocacy NPOs and Activist Donors focused on the philanthropic ecosystem more broadly. Activist Donors supported report writing that analyzed the philanthropic ecosystem and articulated risks and vulnerabilities for donors and advocacy NPOs alike. Civil society groups began to be concerned about the sustainability of civil society itself, partly due to seismic shifts in funding to nonprofit groups. In 2018, one NPO published a report on civil society sustainability, focusing on changing funding patterns. It drew its material from interviews with thirteen prominent NPOs. It produced a report on the nonprofit ecosystem that outlined the different eras in which Indian civil society groups had been active, from pre-Independence to the voluntarism of 2018. The report was written from the vantage point of nonprofits, not funders. It articulated how, over time, civic groups adjusted to changing funding patterns in difficult environments. It linked voluntary organizations and participatory democracy, noting that voluntary organizations provided ideas and cost-effective models for development, as well as mobilized the public for community work and engaged the socially marginalized. They worked for the poor, and as service delivery organizations for the state. Despite the fact that civil society organizations (CSOs) were considered trusted by global standards (such as the *2018 Edelman Trust Barometer Global Report*, for example), in the eyes of the public they were losing trust. It was in this climate that NPOs held their workshops, organized meetings to discuss the sustainability of the sector, and wrote reports.

A third type of report, besides PILs and NPO-generated reports, were written by research institutes on civil society's "philanthropic ecosystem." These reports were system reports: used by NPOs to make arguments for enabling legislative reform. Indian NPOs faced challenges due to the freezing of funds by the state, punitive regulation, and a lack of human resources to be mobilized. Specific structural trends that negatively affected the sector were analyzed in research institute reports. These trends included a bias toward big organizations that had "brand names" and paid high salaries to attract top local personnel, and increasingly restrictive governmental oversight of foreign funding to the sector. There was also a "dilemma of charismatic leadership" in the sector, where a few charismatic leaders dominated the top management of CSOs, resulting in a lack of human resources and skills in small organizations. Constraints on corporate social responsibility (CSR) activities benefited companies instead of CSOs, and these activities tended to be ones that focused exclusively on short-term projects. Most firms working on CSR projects did so through their own foundations and trusts, which excluded small CSOs from access to government-mandated CSR resources. One report noted that just 30 percent of firms collaborated with NGOs to carry out their

CSR work. Those that did sought an NGO with a brand. Overall, restrictions in funding fell into three arenas: foreign, governmental, and private. Foreign funding had been reduced due to FCRA restrictions.[10] The report concluded that voluntarism had become professionalized in India. Though CSOs emerged to question the status quo, current efforts to challenge ruling elites met with backlash via funding restrictions. The Ecosystem Report explored the efforts of thirteen CSOs, documenting how they coped with the shifting landscape, and the descriptive data that follow are from that report.

Though the sample size in the philanthropic Ecosystem Report was relatively small, significant patterns and trends were visible. All the NGOs in the report had to adjust their funding strategies. There was a marked decline in foreign funding (reported by 69 percent of the group), and organizations found a variety of strategies to make up for the lack of funding. Whether through increased funding from corporate social responsibility (CSR; 53 percent of the group), domestic donations, or government funds, NGOs found other ways to support their operations. Decreased international funding created a new space for other forms of support. That said, the alternate funding streams came with their own frameworks, initiatives, and priorities that shaped the work voluntary organizations were able to do. Funding changed the scope of possibility for the nonprofit sector. The main point from the report was the shift from international to domestic funding. The architecture of financial support had been altered, partly through laws, and it had a direct impact on what could and could not be done in the name of legitimate civil society work by NGOs.

Another research institute report[11] was based on over thirty interviews with Indian philanthropists, foreign funders, social organizations, and legal and technical experts. It analyzed funding trends regarding service delivery and rights-based advocacy work. Service delivery organizations were larger, had clear causal connections between funding and outcomes, demonstrated short-term results, and were considered less risky because their work complemented governmental programs. In contrast, rights-based advocacy organizations tended to be smaller, and it was harder for them to demonstrate the causal relationship between funding and results because their focus was on fundamental societal shifts. Their work also took longer, and was risky as it called the efforts of those in power into question. Private resources funded rights-based advocacy work because they had fewer legal restrictions compared to CSR organizations or government. If rights-based advocacy organizations were dependent on foreign funding, then cutting off their funding flow, or at least controlling it, was a sure-fire solution to the "problem" of dissent.[12] The report documented how, as foreign funding decreased, domestic funding increased.[13] Corporate giving increased after the CSR provisions were added to the Companies Act of 2013, and retail funding increased. The lack of foreign funding had been partially met by individual donations and corporate-sector giving, and the shift had a programmatic impact on the types of projects in which NGOs were engaged. Corporate funding tended to favor short-term, low-risk projects with measurable results, and rights-based advocacy organizations suffered in this funding shift. Little domestic funding went toward rights-based advocacy initiatives: they were too politically risky, program results were hard to measure, and the long time frame for results was less attractive to local funding groups.

The research institute reports narrated challenges to the system with an eye toward the potential for Indian philanthropists to step in and fund rights-based advocacy in India's social sector. Both corporate social responsibility funding and foreign funding were highly regulated by the Indian government; domestic philanthropic giving was not. Indian philanthropy had the potential to fill the gap that the reduction in foreign funding had created. However, corporations acting through CSR were not oriented toward supporting rights-based advocacy. This was partly due to the CSR provision in the revised Companies Act, which contained specific reporting requirements that created a chilling effect on supporting work that might involve social risk. The Ecosystem Report offered solutions, including creating a risk assessment framework to help philanthropists address risk aversion; creating recommendations for short- and long-term funding agendas; and creating opportunities to reduce philanthropic risk by supporting ecosystem-level agendas instead of smaller projects and programs. The report, like all reports, did not just critique and complain. It offered action steps.[14] Many reports contained such lists of action items as they were written to inspire advocacy and change. Another report by the same research institution, titled "Enabling Philanthropy and Social Impact in India: State of the Support Ecosystem" (Centre for Social Impact and Philanthropy 2019), argued for investment in a "support ecosystem" for NGOs and social impact philanthropy in India. Its primary premise was that service-sector institutions also needed support.[15] In 2019, when these ecosystem reports were being written, data were being gathered on the impact of the regulatory reform of India's nonprofit sector. By 2024, the effect on the sector was striking. Srinath (2024) notes that by 2024, governmental spending was 95 percent of social-sector expenditure, funneled to NGOs through short-term contracts for social services provision. Work supported through the FCRA no longer went to NGOs working on democratic freedoms or policy advocacy. CSR funding was tied to company interests, and was used mainly for short-term, easy to measure, direct-service programs. CSR funding was also risk averse and did not support human rights or systemic change.

Conclusion

NGOs, civil society groups, and nonprofits in India formed a large and unwieldy category, impossible to accurately represent in a word or a single report. Within this discursive category—loosely referred to as "the voluntary sector"—were organizations that critiqued, refused, and opposed the state as well as those that worked with and within the state, providing state developmental services and realizing state welfare directives. However, due to legal reforms restricting nonprofit organizations from engaging in political activities and increased reporting requirements in regulations regarding foreign philanthropy, the disaggregated sector of civil society groups in India came together in 2012–13 to collaborate. Though some associational groups stood apart from the NGOs collaborating with the state, others worked to change the state itself by lobbying to defend the space for civil society engagement and for regulation that supported the work of nonprofits.

With space for civil society groups shrinking worldwide, nonprofits found creative ways to implement progressive political agendas. As governments globally cracked down on spaces of association and assembly and on freedom of speech—in Egypt, Turkey, and India—nonprofit organizations found alternate avenues to advocate for what they considered to be a public sphere. One of the techniques of this approach was report writing. More than the production of bureaucratic objects and mountains of paper, report writing was a mobilizing strategy involving meetings, discussions, conferences, debates, and arguments. It was a democratic process, which did not stand in contrast to other related forms of protest such as strikes, marches, and Supreme Court challenges through PIL cases. In fact, it was within the larger landscape of advocacy and dissent that report writing could be an effective manifestation of progressive politics. A space of debate was preserved through the social processes of report writing, as debates were translated into reports, congealing a constellation of diverse, sometimes contradictory, institutional forms into coherent discursive entities: the nonprofit sector, the voluntary sector, or civil society. Advocacy groups worked with already existing institutional forms such as the law and NGOs registered with the state, but their advocacy efforts included member groups that operated at the state's margins. Reports served to make the nonprofit sector legible to the state in a process that may have had political aims but did not represent a particular political party or a singular manifesto. Nonprofits embodied a creative space, a hybrid and flexible site where social concerns could be addressed through democratic processes.

Report writing was institutional in its orientation. The successes of this strategy must be addressed in terms of increasing recognition by other institutional actors. Through reports, the nonprofit sector became legible to the state because it was speaking the bureaucratic language of the state. Report writing, as a social practice, was one way that civil society groups attempted to respond to rapid regulatory reform that directly affected their ability to continue. These tactics aimed to address revisions to the cluster of laws affecting the nonprofit sector, including tax laws, registration requirements, regulations on philanthropy, and new initiatives regarding corporate-sponsored social welfare. The voluntary sector became coherent when represented as a collective group akin to an industrial lobby. Report writing achieved precisely this: the constitution, however fleeting, of a group identity and a collective agenda. Report writing was a dynamic conversation, pursued in the medium of the written form. Reports could be used as assessment tools as well as vehicles for the state to target NGOs. They were also mobilizing strategies for NPOs to set the record straight with the state. If NPOs were in conversation with the state through reports, then report writing was a language of power in the key of bureaucracy, where who wrote and spoke for whom became a political act. Report writing manifested an ongoing dialogue, a strategic back-and-forth between civil society groups and state agencies.

SEVEN

The Responsibility to Act

The Government of India's revised Companies Act (2013) provided a radical new framework for governing civil society, corporations, and social welfare. It levied a social responsibility tax on corporations,[1] offered NGOs registration as charitable companies, streamlined reporting requirements for nonprofit and for-profit institutions, and encouraged a structural collaboration between the voluntary and business sectors. The revised law challenged NGOs to behave like businesses and corporations to be prosocial. With this Act, India became the first nation to integrate corporate social responsibility (CSR) programs into law for all publicly traded companies. CSR funds were to be applied in specific national arenas, such as eradicating poverty, promoting education, combating HIV, ensuring environmental sustainability, enhancing vocational skills, supporting social business projects, and contributing to the Prime Minister's National Relief Fund.[2] Funds could be given to an existing NGO, with preference given to local areas of company operations.

The CSR provision was aspirational; it was a "comply or explain" clause in the law, which regulated reporting but not actual spending. If a corporation didn't spend on CSR, it was not liable. Responsibility resided in reporting CSR expenditures to its board of directors, with companies and their officers accruing steep fines by failing to report. In addition to encouraging businesses-directed social welfare, the Companies Act provided its own category of incorporation: the Section 8 charitable company, which encouraged institutional collaboration between the voluntary and business sectors, and shepherded NGOs and corporations into a single regulatory domain. The revised Companies Act was heralded as progressive regulation. In addition to its social responsibility tax, it mandated that at least one woman sit on a company's board of directors. The Companies Act's mandatory 2 percent provision demanded that large corporations contribute these funds to CSR activities or explain why they were unable to do so. As a comply and explain reporting mechanism, it provided a regulatory framework for prosocial corporate behavior that promised a new arena of funding for the beleaguered nonprofit sector. Accessing the utopia of CSR funds, which lay in sight yet on a distant horizon, became a quest for many nonprofits.

At first, the business community was not unilaterally supportive of the CSR provisions in the Companies Act (Deo 2024; Krichewsky 2019). Some saw it an attempt by the government to shift its development failure to corporations. Some called it the "2 percent solution." For civil society organizations, however, the CSR provision initially generated anticipation and excitement. After the global recession, it became increasingly difficult to garner foreign donations, and with tightening restrictions on foreign philanthropy through the FCRA, the difficulty of navigating state reporting requirements increased exponentially. Some Indian NPO directors, with whom I met, were supportive of the governmental nod to corporations to support social responsibility; they hoped corporations might become more public-minded. Others critiqued it, stating that corporations shouldn't have to be mandated to be good citizens; eliminating corporate tax havens could fund India's development. Corporate philanthropy in India was not new. Many Indian family businesses and corporate groups, like the Birlas and Tatas, had been doing CSR for years (Sundar 1997; 2000). However, with the new regulations, Indian corporations whose shares were more than 50 percent foreign controlled faced more onerous reporting requirements for their charitable work through the FCRA. Together, the 2010 FCRA and the 2013 Companies Act nudged Indian businesses to support social welfare for Indians in India. The language of corporate responsibility, which dominated the landscape of nonprofit legal reform in New Delhi in 2017, inspired a realignment of social welfare practice.

This chapter explores the concept of responsibility in CSR provision. In 2017, five years after the revised Companies Act (2013) was passed, I returned to New Delhi to see how nonprofit advocacy groups had navigated the newly constructed terrain. I also met with corporate actors in a mid-sized north Indian city, and its surrounding rural areas, who had worked in CSR before the CSR mandate, to explore whether—and how—the law had altered their approach. I found that CSR had become an impossible requirement, a contradictory discursive statement that was at once a call to action and a forum for debate. It was a space of contested meaning, a new horizon line of policy, and an impossible dialogue between actors who faced structurally irresolvable aims of profit making and social welfare.

Rule Making

Two countries, India and China, have instituted mandatory CSR provisions (Afsharipour and Rana 2014; also see Van Zile 2012, for India only). Unlike voluntary CSR, India's and China's CSR mandates emerged as the two nations shifted to more market-based economies (Afsharipour and Rana 2014; Huang 2013). I am less concerned here with CSR efficacy—whether it works or not or even the social costs of its deployment—and more focused on how state-legislated and mandatory CSR programs build legitimacy for governments and corporations. In the Indian case, I center the development and early implementation of the revised Companies Act, which was passed at a time of growing inequality and increased public attention to corporate and government corruption. At first, the CSR provision had potential as a governmental attempt to hold firms accountable to society instead of to shareholders. It initially seemed a gesture toward the common good and to righting the ethics of late capitalism. It portended the addressing of a period of rapid and uneven development and growth that had enhanced corporate profits and left much of the population in extreme poverty (Afsharipour and Rana 2014, 178). Was CSR the answer to growing inequality? It seemed a possible response.

Comparatively, in China, mandatory CSR emerged as the nation shifted from a state-run economy to a more privatized one, in which social welfare that had earlier been provided by the state shifted to the private sector and/or individuals. In the process of privatization, the income gap in China grew as did public dissent over government policies. Mandatory CSR in China may have been a governmental attempt to pacify dissent and publicly address growing income inequality. The Chinese mandatory CSR provision had first emerged in China's 1994 Company Law, which stated that "companies must comply with the law, conform to business ethics, strengthen the construction of the socialist civilization, and subject themselves to the government and public supervision in the course of business" (ibid., 199). In China's subsequent shift to promoting a harmonious society, the Communist Party adopted CSR as a policy mandate. The relationship of CSR to control became evident in disaster response settings, and was later codified in the Charity Law (2016) that provided more specific oversight of NPOs (International Center for Not-for-Profit Law 2022). This law sought to challenge Western norms with Chinese ones, asserting that "Chinese legal and business practices can serve as potential models that the United States should look to as it emerges from financial crisis and corporate scandals" (Afsharipour and Rana 2014, 201). China's 2006 Company Law stated: "In the course of doing business, a company must comply with laws and administrative regulations, conform to social morality and business ethics, act in good faith, subject itself to the government and the public supervision, and undertake social responsibility" (ibid., 202). The enforceability of the law, however, was unclear, and much like the Indian CSR mandate, it was largely an aspirational attempt to quelch dissent and enhance the international reputation of Chinese businesses.

In India, the Companies Bill (2012) emerged at a time of growing dissatisfaction regarding the lack of contribution to society by the expanding corporate elite. In addition to an aspirational middle class, there was a growing frustration that opportunities lay out of reach for many, especially the masses. The CSR provision in the Companies Bill addressed a contradictory context: an economic environment of rapid economic liberalization, which included privatization and deregulation, and a constitutional environment that promoted legal and economic equality and articulated distributive rights (De 2014; 2018). At independence (1947), corporate governance was structured by a socialist system, with many industries controlled by the state. State-run industries were governed via central planning and the development of five year plans, and NGOs were part of the socialist planning process through the Planning Commission. In 1991, India experienced a financial crisis, and the IMF agreed to loans on conditions of structural adjustment, including the provisions that India liberalize its economy and privatize sectors. Through economic liberalization, India's economy grew and efforts were made to encourage foreign direct investment. Private-sector entrepreneurship was encouraged and increased, and licensing restrictions were removed to inspire investment (see Van Zile 2012 for details, esp. 286; also see Deo 2024 and Krichewsky 2019).[3]

Despite these liberal economic reforms, the BJP lost elections in 2004, and in 2005 the Congress Party created an alliance with the Communist party, and passed a budget that "greatly increased spending on social welfare and aid to the poor" (Van Zile 2012, 288). including proposed spending on education, infrastructure, housing, and rural development. In the public's memory were corporate disasters and collapses, involving Union Carbide in Bhopal in 1984 and Enron in many countries in 1993, and questions emerged from the public regarding the need to keep corporations accountable. Protests regarding the handling of foreign companies resulted in bad publicity for large corporations in India, which were the very ones targeted for the 2 percent provision in the CSR Bill. In 2011, when the Companies Bill was being debated, the governmental logic became clear—wooing foreign direct investment while using CSR as global public relations to enhance the legitimacy of both the corporate sector and the government in the court of public opinion. Legitimacy in this case entailed publicly taking responsibility for the regulation of corporations vis-à-vis public interests. The Bill was considered pro-business, and the 2 percent clause was considered a concession to pro-development interests, a highly contested political issue (Van Zile 2012, 293; Deo 2024).[4]

Initially, there was corporate backlash against the Bill in formation with its mandatory CSR provision, even though CEOs supported voluntary philanthropy. After back-and-forth with the business industry a compromise emerged such that disclosure was mandatory, but the 2 percent spending provision remained aspirational. The lead-up to the passage of the Companies Act was filled with dialogue and debate between the corporate sector and the government, much like that occurring between the government and the voluntary sector. The revised Companies Act was a retro-fix to appease the public in the face of rapid liberalization without systemic infrastructure investment and development. The shift from a socialist, development-planning oriented government to one that wooed foreign direct investment and expected corporations to solve social ills is the story of late capitalism, and one that affected the nonprofit sector as well. As much as nonprofits swept in to rescue the wreckage of global capitalism by filling the gaps left by the absence of state welfare due to liberalization, they faced a new era in India with the emergence of the CSR provision.

The original Companies Act (1956) did not include a mandatory CSR provision, but Section 166 of the 2013 Act stated boards of directors must "act in good faith in order to promote the objects of the company for the benefits of its members as a whole, and in the best interests of the company, its employees, the shareholders, the community and for the protection of the environment" (Afsharipour and Rana 2014, 209–10). The 2013 revision extended beyond the management of shareholder profits to encompass public arenas of "the community" and "the environment." The law grew out of earlier governmental attempts to hold corporations accountable. In 2009, the Ministry of Corporate Affairs (MCA) had introduced voluntary guidelines for CSR and instituted a requirement for Central Public Sector Enterprises to create a CSR budget designed to "undertake at least one major project of a backward district" in order to contribute "significantly in the long run to socioeconomic growth in all the backward regions of the country." The CSR provision was initially only a symbolic regulatory gesture; however, in 2010, efforts to revise the Companies Act shifted toward the inclusion of a mandatory CSR provision. Review by the Standing Committee of Parliament on Finance included discussion of the need for a more comprehensive CSR policy. The MCA "fluctuated between imposing mandatory CSR requirements by adding them to the Companies Bill and adopting the CSR recommendations with a "'comply or explain' approach, eventually settling on a compromise approach" (ibid., 216). Critics from the business community were opposed to the provision. And the nonprofit sector critiqued it for being a difficult to enforce aspirational exercise. On December 18, 2012, the Lok Sabha (lower house of Parliament) passed the Companies Bill (2012), and it was approved by the Rajya Sabha (upper house of Parliament) on August 8, 2013. It quickly received presidential approval and became law. Its rules were passed, with an effective implementation date of April 1, 2014, in the 2014–15 fiscal year.

This particular CSR provision is found in Section 135 of the revised Companies Act (2013). The provision was structured as a board-level activity addressing governance issues. Companies with a net worth of 500 crore rupees or more (approximately US$81 million at the time), or a turnover of 1,000 crore rupees (approximately $162 million), or a net profit of five crore rupees (approximately $811,400) in any financial year, were required to constitute a CSR committee of the board that consisted of three or more directors. One of the directors was required to be an "independent director." The revised Act empowered the CSR committee with "(i) formulating and recommending to the Board, a CSR Policy which must indicate the activities to be undertaken by the company; (ii) recommending the amount of CSR expenditure to be incurred on such activities; and (iii) regularly monitoring the CSR initiatives of the company" (Afsharipour and Rana 2014, 218). The board was required to take into account the recommendations made by the CSR Committee and approve the company's CSR policy. The revised Companies Act, in effect, gave a company's board power over its CSR programs. It was to develop the policy and govern the programs, including the spending, which had governmental targets. The board was required to "ensure that the company spends, in each financial year, at least two per cent of the average net profits of the company made during the three immediately preceding financial years, in pursuance of its Corporate Social Responsibility Policy" (ibid.). The government had shifted responsibility for CSR to corporate boards. There were no penalties for failing to spend the required 2 percent, but penalties were steep for failing to report, including a fine on the company, and up to three years of prison and a fine for board officers who failed to report to the government. In the final rules of the Companies Act (2013), the CSR mandate included the directive that CSR monies were to be spent in the local areas where companies operated, and a specific list of permissible CSR activities (see Box 7.1).

BOX 7.1. Schedule of Permissible CSR Activities

- Eradicating extreme hunger and poverty;

- Promotion of education;

- Promoting gender equality and empowering women;

- Reducing child mortality and improving maternal health;

- Combating human immunodeficiency virus, acquired immune deficiency syndrome, malaria, and other diseases;

- Ensuring environmental sustainability;

- Employment enhancing vocational skills;

- Social business projects;

- Contribution to the Prime Minister's National Relief Fund or any other fund set up by the Central Government or the State Governments for socioeconomic development and relief, and funds for the welfare of the Scheduled Castes, the Scheduled Tribes, other backward classes, minorities, and women; and

- Such other matters as may be prescribed.

Source: GOI Companies Act (2013), as cited in Afsharipour and Rana (2014, 219).

The draft rules provided that excess CSR funds would be reinvested into CSR programs, that CSR activities must be undertaken in India, and that activities meant for employees were ineligible for consideration as CSR activities. Companies could implement their CSR programs through "(i) the company directly on its own; (ii) the company's own non-profit foundation operating within India and set up so as to facilitate this initiative; or through (iii) independently registered non-profit organizations operating in India that have a record of at least three years in similar such related activities; and (iv) collaborating or pooling their resources with other companies" (Afsharipour and Rana 2014, 220–21).

IN THE RULES: A POSITIVE LIST AND DELEGATED LEGISLATION

The rules were released for feedback and then revised. The final rules also applied to foreign companies with branch offices in India. All companies were required to attend to the CSR mandate, and the final rules expanded the list of permissible activities to include recommendations by the CSR committee (see Box 7.2).

BOX 7.2. Additional Permissible CSR Activities

- Providing safe drinking water;
- Protection of national heritage, art, and culture;
- Rural development projects;
- Measures to benefit armed forces veterans and war widows;
- Promoting rural sports, nationally recognized sports, and paralympic sports;
- Setting up homes and hostels for women, orphans, and senior citizens;
- Reducing inequalities in socially and economically backward groups; and
- Supporting technology incubators in government-approved academic institutions.

Source: CSR Rule Amendments (2014), as cited in Afsharipour and Rana (2014, 222).

The revised list covered government services and left out rights-based advocacy, and any type of advocacy for the marginalized, including that which might threaten the legitimacy of the government. Unlike the "negative list," described in chapter 5, of activities ineligible for tax exemption, this law had a positive list of activities supported by CSR. The CSR provision, though likely well-intentioned, was a governmental legitimacy exercise initiated by the Congress Party that would later be inherited by the BJP in 2014. Advocates for civil society were involved in the debates over the Companies Bill, the draft rules, and in the eventual final provisions, though many criticized the government for privatizing the state's role. An Indian philanthropist called the provision an "outsourcing of governance" that was "taking the failure of the state and the corporates and trying to create a model out of it." The law was toothless because it covered neither enforcement nor compliance.

I met with a civil servant who worked in the Rajya Sabha in 2017, five years after the Companies Act revision was implemented, and we spoke of Parliamentary approaches to civil society governance. Not tied to a political party and having a long view, he was eager to talk about his current responsibilities managing civil society oversight committees. Law had to be futuristic, he said. Legislation was not a product of what he called "short-term reason." Instead, it had to anticipate the future, and it had to be dynamic, and it had to regulate in a futuristic manner. He urged me to understand that only major policy was addressed by Parliament, though "parent legislation," matters of detail were provided by the rules. He considered U.S. legislation to be bulky in comparison to Indian legislation. In India's system of delegated legislation, inherited and adapted from the UK, actual laws were short, developed at the Center and implemented by states. Subordinate legislation could be in the thousands of pages, and included the rules. Policy was determined by parent legislation, developed in Parliament, but the rules were the delegated legislation, written by civil servants like himself. And civil servants wrote the rules in negotiation with specific constituencies.

He explained how. When the government decided to bring up an issue, it circulated a concept paper. He described the process chain as follows: ministry—to cabinet—to administrative ministry—to consultation—to legislative format. Legislation was a long process; that took a minimum of one year. Laws were introduced in Parliament, after which they went to a committee and then to consultation with the public and stakeholders.

A report was made to Parliament, and Parliament had the opportunity to pass the law, and this was where nonprofits, as constituencies, entered the process of dialogue with lawmaking. The concept paper was an internal document for the cabinet, and then the consultation was arranged. He saw his role as neither blocking legislation brought by the executive, nor delaying legislation. Civil servants wanted ideally to ensure laws were passed in perfect form: "there should not be any missing link," he said. Once the report went to Parliament, the executive branch of civil servants figured out how to implement it through the rules, the tools of implementation. He wrote reports as part of his job, and he oversaw four parliamentary committees. His reports, on laws in process, were a vital part of the lawmaking process.

Impossible Responsibility: A Call to Action

The CSR legislation was a call—a demand and an opportunity—by the state that required a response in an impossible dialogue. The state called upon corporations to be responsible to society by abiding by the CSR law, and upon NGOs to avail themselves of CSR funds and follow CSR directives. Meanwhile, NGOs called upon the state and corporations to include their work as CSR. Corporate social responsibility was a discursive impossibility, an impossible situation with essential inherent contradictions. And this was precisely what compelled actors such as states, NGOs, and corporations to act, to respond to the call, to be respond-able and responsible. It was a space of possibility, of new forms and change, that produced a new policy horizon line.

I come to the concept of responsibility through Gayatri Spivak, via Jacques Derrida. In Spivak's application of responsibility to a World Bank development conference in Bangladesh, she found development discourse manifested inherent impossibility that silenced subaltern voices (Spivak 1994, 19). CSR as a discourse followed a similar pattern. It silenced institutional forms that did not fit into CSR parameters, remaking social-sector work in the model of corporate design. The contradiction of responsibility is a limit case: a goal, a boundary a hypothetical ideal, and a policy horizon line. Responsibility is an obligation, a promise and a commitment that can't be fulfilled. As the three sites I explore in this chapter demonstrate, the new discourse of CSR in the Companies Act of 2013 became an ideal to which institutions were required, through law, to strive. The law was a "call," and the actions of corporations and nonprofits were the response. The impossibility of the call for responsibility lay in its constantly shifting horizon.[5] In Spivak's case of a World Bank development report, development was staged as a dialogue between the powerful institution of the World Bank and the voices of a developing nation. The theater of responsibility disguised the mechanics of unrestricted capital investment in development, in which the World Bank spoke while others could not respond. In the Indian case, through CSR, capitalism could be harnessed and regulated in the name of responsibility, but nonprofits could not speak. As the CSR law was rolled out and implemented, the question remained: Who was responsible to whom in the CSR provisions? Did the law mandate corporate responsibility, NGO responsibility, or donor responsibility, all of which were responsible to the government? In Spivak's case, the World Bank could not hear Bangladesh's distinctions between two types of floods altering farming practices. Because it could not register the distinction, it ignored and silenced the "other." In the CSR list of acceptable practices (the "positive list"), action was codified as types of recordable activities that eliminated more loose and spontaneous approaches, including rights-based ones lauded by NPOs that reached the last mile of development activity. Everything outside the frame disappeared and was ignored. In the "dialogue" of CSR, challenges, irritations, and alternate ways were foreclosed and ignored.

Responsibility, like freedom (as in Derrida 1995), is indeterminate and open-ended, but responsibility also inspires guilt: "one is never responsible enough" (ibid., 51). The paradox at the heart of responsibility—of a call to action and the inherent impossibility of response—does not stop it from functioning. Quite the contrary, especially in political and legal matters. Derrida remarks that the lexicon of responsibility, which is found in the "exercise of justice" and in "international law" is a lexicon that hovers "vaguely about a concept that is nowhere to be found" (ibid., 84). The discourse of responsibility is at once a legal directive and a vague referent. Responsibility is not a consequence of a subject's action. It is the response to a call to be, and it is a call that requires a response.[6] The hidden resource of responsibility is that to be responsible is to respond.

Responsibility in CSR was a call to social welfare that contradicted the very profit-making nature of corporations. It produced an inherent contradiction in corporate action: a requirement to do something it could not: to be socially responsible at the expense of profit. Raffoul (2004) references

Derrida, while writing of CSR, urging a focus on the paradoxical nature of CSR's limits. "The impossible *is* possible and takes place as such. In fact, it will prove to be the very structure of the event" (54). When one does not know the right rule, ethical questions arise, and one must make an ethical decision, a response to a call. This is responsibility. The response constitutes both the ethical moment and the act. Raffoul writes, "Responsibility is then understood as responsiveness to the opening of the incalculable [. . .], a responsible decision can never be part of a calculable horizon, that it cannot, for instance, consist in the application of a rule, a determinable rule. A leap into the incalculable is necessary for any decision to take place. This leap is the heart of responsibility, and its 'im-possibility'" (ibid., 55). He continues, "Here im-possibility does not mean that which cannot be, but rather that which happens outside of the conditions of possibility outside of the horizons of expectation proposed by the subject, outside of transcendental horizons of calculability. The incalculable happens." (ibid., 55). It happens outside the parameters of what a subject is prepared for, and it includes the alterity of event, an "other," and this is the challenge—the call—of responsibility. When CSR was mandated through legislation, rules became guidance for ethics that should have already been in practice. That responsibility must be ruled and regulated exposed the impossibility of the call. CSR as a call and response was a demand for relational agency that required a singular language be spoken, and corporations dominated the language of CSR (Deo 2024).

The ambiguity of CSR discourse was where its power resided. Scholars such as Damien Krichewsky (2019) call CSR in India an "intermediary institution," offering corporations and CSOs the capacity for improvisation. CSR pushes corporations to attend to collective values, and CSOs to attend to markets. However, a structural imbalance is at play. Corporations have more resources and political power than CSOs, which are donor dependent. Thus, any dialogue or improvisatory relational agency inspired by CSR will ultimately be one-sided. Sabadoz (2011, 77) writes of CSR, "as a discourse that refuses to conclusively resolve the tension between profit-seeking and prosociality, CSR expresses an important critical perspective which demands that firms act responsibly, while retaining the overall corporate frame of shareholder supremacy. CSR does this by ambivalently affirming both profit-seeking and prosociality, a necessary contradiction."

In the inherent contradiction between profit-making and societal well-being, the responsibility to act emerges. Sabadoz (2011) argues CSR has not been well defined, yet its vague definition is its power. The discursive instability of the concept is necessary for its "success as a normative discourse." CSR cannot resolve its own inherent tension. Rather than attempt to resolve the debate of whether corporations can be good, Sabadoz productively suggests that we focus on how CSR functions as a Derridean supplement: "a type of perpetually ambivalent discourse which assists other discourses that seem insufficient and troubled." CSR affirms corporate profit seeking and demands corporations be prosocial (ibid., 78). Derrida uses the term *supplement* to describe how a "confusing (but necessary) concept oscillates between two, internally contradictory, constituent principles" (ibid., 80). Corporate Social Responsibility, as a conceptual referent, is this type of discursive supplement. And responsibility in CSR entails responding with respond-ability: being able to respond to the ethical challenge of "the call."

Critics of CSR have challenged its depiction as an emancipatory project. CSR has been termed a "neo-imperialist enterprise" (Hanlon and Flemming 2009; Bannerjee 2003; 2008). Bannerjee (2008), for example, calls corporate social responsibility a "praxis of evil," arguing there is no reason to expect corporations will act with that responsibility if it threatens profitability. For corporations to do such work, it must fit into their agendas to make profit and "enhance shareholder value." CSR promotes continued engagement with "the "undecidable" question of corporate profit motives, and the tension with prosociality. To speak of CSR is to discursively provide a space where the impossible, corporate prosociality, can be spoken. Sabadoz urges us to resist the impulse to collapse CSR's internal inconsistency, as well as the similar impulse to subordinate CSR to other discourses that have the illusion of greater stability (2011, 81). The power of CSR lies in its conceptual fluidity, much like the "nonprofit" as an institutional form. Its linguistic instability, with no clear signifier, makes it an active discourse. The imperfect relation between signifier and signified motivates and spurs action.

Discursive supplements like CSR are contested (Sabadoz 2011, 83). They carry within a "regulated contradiction," which helps to articulate how members of society expect firms to navigate business-society relations. CSR regulates corporate behavior by affirming both profit seeking and social welfare. As Hanlon and Flemming (2009), and also Sabadoz (2011), point out, CSR is a post-Fordist argument for dealing with the rollback of entitlements from corporations' alliance with the state in neoliberal capitalism, which produces instability for workers. CSR answers neoliberalism's challenges of structural insecurity and the state's desire for public legitimacy; hence the single supplementary signifier of "CSR," and its linguistic work of serving as a shorthand for the contradictions of neoliberal capitalism. CSR organizes itself around these contradictions. It is middle-of-the-road, always insufficiently modifying the signifier and the polarity between profit and prosocial corporate behavior. It offers a vocabulary for discussing societies' struggles.

Once CSR is fixed into a set path (for example, through law), its potential as an emancipatory discourse falls apart. It becomes, in Derridean terms, "logocentric," reverting to the profit-seeking aspect of the oscillating signifier. "Supplements such as CSR are used precisely because they evade precise definition while retaining an internal logic that encapsulates what speakers want to convey, however contradictory that might be" (Sabadoz 2011, 89). For Hanlon and Flemming (2009), CSR is an element of neoliberalism that assists its search for legitimacy and innovation. It shifts the "nature of social regulation" from the collective to individual solutions and alters capitalist regulation more generally from its old way to a new, predatory form. These authors consider CSR a socioeconomic phenomenon and an extension of corporate power under late capitalism that claims to balance profit seeking with the concerns of workers, consumers, and NPOs ("stakeholders"), as well as being an "ideological smoke screen" that softens the public image of corporations involved in crude profit seeking. In late-capitalist accumulation, corporations have taken over some of the functions previously organized by the state. In post-Fordism, with capitalism's spatial expansion, more areas of social life have opened: "e.g. education, health, childcare, care for the elderly, biodiversity, genes, etc." (ibid., 944). These are also arenas where nonprofits did their work while governments were involved in the Fordist era of capitalism.[7] Critics argue CSR functions as a "social parasite" with a "predatory function," a smokescreen for actual environmental destruction, social alienation, and abuses perpetrated by corporate profit-seeking behavior. CSR is a hegemonic force, whether legitimizing or predatory. It is one in which the state casts aside its social welfare functions, creating a requirement for corporations to do social welfare work. As CSR harnessed corporations to do social welfare work, it sidelined NPOs previously enlisted in welfare service provision. CSR uses a "prospecting logic" to open markets.

Anthropologists have studied CSR in extractive industries, such as mining (see Kirsch 2014; Rajak 2011; and Welker 2014), and have analyzed how CSR opens markets for firms, silences dissent, and reduces conflict in areas where corporations are encroaching on lands and livelihoods. In the setting of mining towns, social discomfort with capitalism becomes a market opportunity, protesters become consumers, and unease turns into a new vista. Ethnographic studies of CSR (Dolan and Rajak 2016; Rajak 2011; Welker 2014; Kirsch 2014) identify CSR as a vehicle of pacification, a means for the state to pave its way, as anti-dissent, and as filling a moral void in the wake of neoliberal capitalism. The fundamental contradiction of CSR lies in its discourse, which enables corporations "to simultaneously assert and displace responsibility" for social welfare (Dolan and Rajak 2016, 4), and obligations to the local communities in which corporations are based, as well as to the larger public. Responsibility is displaced through subcontracting CSR programs down the supply chain. CSR mainstreams alternative movements like fair trade and ethical consumption, reframing community/public concerns to fit corporate interests. Through CSR, businesses assert a forward-facing identity as ethical actors while the essential contradiction between profit and public responsibilities cannot be resolved. Many CSR programs take place in communities where extractive industries, such as mining, labor to secure resources. In these contexts, CSR manufactures compliant "stakeholders" through "local partners," some of which are NGOs and nonprofits. CSR is a depoliticizing force; a close cousin to James Ferguson's analysis of development as an "anti-politics machine" (1994; also see Mosse 2013). It is deployed as a set of tools mobilized to respond and absorb opposition, paving the way for corporate takeover. The performance of partnership marginalizes dissent through compliance. As the state pulls back from infrastructure development due to late capitalism, it gives way to corporations. CSR opens markets for corporations to take on the social welfare responsibilities of the state, which has ceded its responsibility for both infrastructure and welfare.

In India, nonprofits were asked to join or disappear in the call for CSR of the revised Companies Act, to confirm to the "perfect partner model" or be x-ed out, and pressured to become like corporations to be recognized as legitimate. In some cases, globally, legal struggles between activists and corporations have produced what Kirsch has called a "politics of resignation." Kirsch's (2014) ethnography of corporations and their critics focuses on a high-profile legal struggle over mining in Papua New Guinea, and how corporations co-opted the resistance (in this case, Indigenous NGOs). This dialectic between corporations and their critics, Kirsch argues, is a permanent feature of neoliberal capitalism (cf. Rajak 2011 for South Africa; Welker 2014 for Indonesia). Nandini Deo's recent work on corporation–civil society CSR partnerships in India concludes that it is through these partnerships that CSOs became corporatized (Deo 2024). She argues CSR "whitewashes" corporate harms, allowing corporations to forge unequal relationships of patronage with CSOs, which she calls a "forced marriage." CSOs engaged in CSR were required to adopt a corporate approach to record keeping, accounting, and assessment, which altered how they worked internally and what they did in the world (ibid.). Because corporations are averse to conflict with the government, CSR partnerships excluded legal advocacy; they focused on "impact," reducing the voluntary sector's capacity for dissent. Krichewsky (2019), in his study of CSR programs in an Indian cement company, argues that CSR functions as a form of risk management for corporations—a way for corporations to address threats to their activities (cf. Sundar 2000). CSR is a "horizon of contested meaning" (Krichewsky 2019, 206), a space of communicative action, and a zone of potential meaning construction.

Corporate Social Responsibility in Three Sites

Responsibility orients and motivates actors, including institutions to behave in certain ways. We might think of responsibility as an idealized discourse, one that is a form of norm setting, often followed in shadow form with the threat of state coercion or punishment. In the three cases that follow, the CSR provision in the Companies Act reoriented the institutional practice of corporations. While in earlier chapters I discussed how civil society actors addressed regulatory reform and attempted to effect its transformation, here I examine three corporate sites of social reform via CSR in 2017: a national body tasked with coordinating CSR reform, and two large corporations that had been doing CSR for decades before the CSR provision was passed: a large IT company in a midsized northern Indian city and a large fertilizer company in a rural area of Uttar Pradesh. Both companies had established CSR programs and practices. I focus on how their work changed after the passage of the 2013 CSR provision in the Companies Act, which, as we have seen in earlier chapters, also engaged NPOs.

CSR GOES NATIONAL

The Confederation of Indian Industry (CII) was the national organization tasked with organizing CSR development in the country. In addition to developing programs and educating the corporate sector on the how-tos of doing CSR, the director focused on matters of national scale. He described his job of world making, of developing CSR training for the corporate sector. CII worked with business schools (Indian Institutes of Management, or IIMs), training them in CSR, and creating a new world in which corporations were socially responsible. This was a new horizon line. A call that required a response. The law's rules and regulations in the revised Companies Act were written to inspire compliance. CSR must be project based, he explained, with clear outcomes and start and end dates. If corporations worked with nonprofit organizations, the credibility of those NPOs must be confirmed. CSR was to be integrated by corporate boards—leadership was to be involved in the process as CSR heads and corporate leaders; it was these leaders who became responsible. This world making, an institutional design of sorts, was a CSR utopia and a developmental shift, where—as he described—"shopkeepers will be integrated into the law." The CSR provision restricted funding to certain activities and inspired funding to others, and in this manner, it defined action. It was changing the direction of development. The CSR provision introduced a new set of moral directives, with a threat of punishment.

As an organizational body, CII took on the overarching role of coordinating national CSR practices, and training corporations to do this work. The director was interested in creating an "investment friendly ecosystem" through CSR. The goal was to make India a manufacturing base, and there was no other choice to do this but to open the country to foreign investment; it was a matter of scale. CSR activities, given the new Companies Act regulations, had to be project based (earlier CSR was activity based). The onus of development, oversight, and implementation "has conquered boardrooms" and had "moved to the mission of the organization," he said. The aim was to get more top leadership involved. Earlier, corporations had CSR funds, but mechanisms for implementation were abstract. An HR head could do CSR as part of their HR role, but with the new CSR provision all companies had to have a CSR head in place. The Act was reporting-based so projects had to be focused on outcomes with clear end dates, start dates, and specified objectives. There were distinctions to be made: for instance, what corporations did for their employees was not considered part of CSR. An independent director was responsible for leading interventions strategically linked to a company's mission, and an independent CSR director was to be part of the board. Before the new CSR provisions, corporations could contact NPOs without considering qualifications. Now, the selection of NGOs was an issue of credibility. Corporations partnered with NPOs in a patronage relationship, and the corporate board was responsible for NGO activities. To compete in this environment, NGOs had to "show their strengths." NPOs had to show accountability and prove their programs were effective. They were encouraged to be results oriented, with formal reporting structures. If one aimed to "impart literary skills to 100 students" after the new law, monitoring and progress were evaluated, and one had to prove funds were well spent. Reporting, as a form of responsibility to the state, was built into the CSR provision. CII worked with IIMs across the country, thorough workshops, to train entrepreneurs in business skills. It connected small businesses with larger ones to enable small groups to "get into the supply chain of big guys." Large organizations mentored smaller ones. "Members are more than willing to mentor entrepreneurs," he said, "Progress has to be fast. It is gradual but the scale is large." The sea change was structured, and it would affect not only corporations that were beginning to engage in CSR but also those which had been doing CSR for decades, and the nonprofit sector as well.

CSR IS BUSINESS ORIENTED

One large IT company was invested in the business and development of CSR. In this sense, it considered itself a leader in the corporate sector, contributing value-added skills to corporations in terms of CSR training and education. Its CSR was oriented toward the corporate sector through its CSR projects. For example, it ran a literacy program, developing a type of software that could be used in prisons to educate people and reduce the hours it took to become literate. Its CSR programs were aligned with its business objectives of IT and data processing. It nurtured engineering students, creating cultural capital in those without, to develop the business sector. It worked with nonprofits as partners, vetting proposals and using field visits as credibility checks to verify good practices. As a corporation, its approach to development was hierarchically structured and results oriented. CSR, for this company, was a profession; dedicated people organized the company's CSR programs. This had been going on long before the CSR provision became law. The CSR manager described challenges of working with NPOs, which included the necessity of teaching them how to behave properly. It was a slow process to bring NPOs on board, and he used the marriage metaphor of making a good match between corporates and nonprofits in order to do the CSR work. The company's CSR work was, at the end of the day, focused on its own self-interest. Being business-oriented, the company was responsible to the market: making products and focused on market expansion for its goods and services. However, as another senior CSR manager from its head office pointed out to me, before the law, CSR was tied to revenue. After the law it was tied to profit: a small recalculation in the rules that reoriented CSR.

National CSR initiatives were part of the professionalization of social welfare, which included the incorporation of the business sector, as an industry, and the industry of CSR, into the practice of welfare provision. In 2017, I met with the supervisor of this large data processing company's affirmative action programs in a medium-sized northern Indian city. The organization had two types of initiatives: one from its head office and a regional one, which deployed their CSR model of adult literacy and IT employability programs. These were considered an integral part of their business, and a dedicated CSR staff member existed at the regional level. The company developed software to assist its literacy initiatives. The manager explained that it took 200 hours to make someone literate, but the company found it could be done in 50 hours. One arena for their CSR work was district prisons, which had illiterate populations and infrastructure. The company provided software and training, and it also worked with NGO partners, funding their proposals. A third component of the company's CSR work was what it called "IT employability," which involved its employees in CSR and went beyond funding NGOs. As soon as an employee joined the company, they were sensitized to social work. CSR was part of the corporate socialization process. CSR strengthened the company's commitment toward the people with which they worked to "be a part of that change" and they enhanced employee contentment by giving employees a "chance to give back to society." In terms of the discursive theories discussed earlier, CSR developed responsibility toward the corporation and responsibility toward society.

One of these programs nurtured students at rural engineering colleges, addressing class-based distinctions within the corporate sector. The company sought to help students "come at par with contemporaries of metro cities." These students didn't have access to the corporate world, and the CSR program was a form of affirmative action. Employee volunteers were deployed over weekends, traveling to distant locations. According to the manager, it was enjoyable because it helped employees "to re-live college memories, contribute to society, and empower someone." The program presented CSR as an employee socialization benefit. Another program enabled marginalized youths and digital entrepreneurs. The "stakeholders" were the NGO it funded and its technical aid partner. The NGO suggested where to provide the program and specified needs for technical support. Marginalized youths were given a laptop and a stipend for two years, as well as training on computer software. The program was implemented in primary and secondary schools, and had been in operation for one and a half years. The NGO, which was expected to become self-sustaining after two years, was also tasked with finding areas to use laptops to facilitate business and make villages literate. CSR attempted to reach the margins of society via computer literacy. All of the projects were focused on IT, as the NGO was an IT company. "CSR is aligned with business at the end of the day," the manager exclaimed. "It helps add value to programs." The act of volunteering was a moral value-added for the company in its expansion of technological literacy into India's rural areas. These skills were sought after by many. With core competency in computer literacy, those in the rural areas could potentially find employment in the IT sector.

Corporations are hierarchically structured, unlike some NGOs. "Our way of working is entirely different as per NGOs," the manager explained. "We have timelines and goals and have to achieve these goals. In many ways this is good. It helps us achieve results. Sometimes it becomes difficult. We learn from each other." Artifacts mattered when it came to CSR, and NGOs had to share artifacts and testimonials with the company in their partnership. He said, "we don't force but it's in our model. Should have tangible results and artifacts." CSR was a profession in itself, and for a manger in this large corporation who spent much of his time in the city office, there was limited access to "the ground." It was a challenge to find the right partners. To do so, he made field visits to verify information, and to see whether or not their partners were "doing things in letter and spirit." The field visit was a type of credibility check, and in this manner the business aspect of CSR limited the scope of possibility of what CSR could be. This young manager had his own critiques of CSR. He saw the focus on what he called FMGS (Fast Manufacturing Consumer Goals) to be a limitation. Corporations focused on making products, such as soap, for example, were involved with initiatives aligned with health, which inevitably promoted their products. In this case, CSR became a branding program with a very narrow focus on contemporary issues. Corporate interests drove their CSR initiatives, regardless of actual social need. The advantage of following a corporate focus in CSR was that when an organization utilized core competencies in which it was highly skilled, it could add value to a CSR program. The scope of what was to be done was defined by its corporate expertise, including its capacity for execution and deployment. This was an extremely instrumental model—one very different from the more organic, listening and people-focused one popularized by Indian civil society groups and movements.

The NGO sector in India was aging, and many younger professionals sought the security and upward mobility of a position in the corporate sector. A company with a CSR program could, ideally, offer the best of both worlds to employees—a secure job and a focus on social betterment. "In my opinion, to join an NGO at a young age and working solely for the NGO takes a lot of courage," he said. It was a risk. Young professionals wanted both the income and security of a corporate job and did not opt for NGO work. The CSR work with a company was not a requirement, he clarified, "CSR is not a requirement; it is a commitment. We do not force anyone to volunteer. It should be done wholeheartedly."

The 2013 Companies Act changed the work of this company which had previously been involved in social programs. Post-law, there was more focus to their activities, and "Now there is a number" (referring to the 2 percent of the average of the previous three years' profits). Previously, social welfare initiatives were tied to revenue, not profits. Shifting to profits as the indicator brought new initiatives, including trainings with the Confederation of Indian Industry (CII), which was trying to equip companies with the skills to do CSR. This company, due to its long history, was involved with CSR trainings. The CSR landscape was quickly becoming an industry unto itself. Challenges included what exactly was to be classified as CSR, and project proposal plans had to make sense in light of the interests of the company.

The director used the adult literacy program to explain how corporate ideas could be useful for CSR, for example, by proposing "performance linked incentives." The top 20 percent of the field could receive more funds as an "element of appreciation," and this could be linked to compensation initiatives. For example, how did one teach NPOs to behave properly? How do you do the minutes of a meeting? One way is to bring on board technical people from the corporation to help an NGO. "IT guys understanding [their] need to do their bit in this marriage. Both have to take steps to meet common ground." This was a marriage theme, between NGOs and companies. The director described it as a slow process. It took a long time to bring NGOs on board, and it sometimes involved years of grooming. In this example, we see, from a company that had experience in CSR, that the Companies Act CSR provision restructured their efforts: it professionalized CSR and demanded responsibility—on behalf of the corporation—for the work of NPO partners. This in turn required training NPOs to be responsible, and to behave in a manner that was legible to both the corporation, and the government, to which the corporation had to report. The shift from tallying CSR in terms of corporate profits (instead of revenue) added another layer to the new program of responsibilities and obligations in CSR.

CSR IS POLITICAL

A rural fertilizer company experienced a shift in its CSR orientation due to the new law, from being focused on responsibility to the local community and local politics to being focused on responsibility to the central government, reporting, and markets. It found itself pulled in many directions, to competing demands, calls and responses. Like the IT company, it was a corporation that had been doing CSR for a long time. The CSR manager saw CSR as changing in India, becoming a growth sector, merging business and social work. He spoke of something called "business link CSR." The company's work was quite extensive. But in the end, it was a fertilizer company in a rural part of northern India, and its work in what it had called social development—now called CSR—focused on the needs of the community. This was the old type of CSR, where the company responded to community needs in the absence of state provision of goods, services, and infrastructure. The company provided skills training with a vocational school; it helped local communities build productive kitchen gardens; and it built a local hospital that serviced the community and employees of the company and also provided employment. If the company did not respond to these needs and requests, it encountered resistance, so in this manner

CSR work was in its own interest, to keep the locals from potentially interfering with industrial production. Yet this local response to community needs in the form of responsibility to the community also served another purpose: it protected against political blackmail and interference in the work of the company. There was a shift underway, where local politicians also had CSR targets and asked the company to work on specific programs with which the politicians had been tasked. These demands from local politicians did not always get met.

Since the 2013 law was passed, new responsibilities to the central government had emerged regarding meeting governmental development priorities. This was the new type of CSR—a new partnership—whereby corporations partnered with the government to enact development programs. The government, which had depended previously on NPOs to implement development agendas, had turned to the corporate sector, and as described earlier, required that 2 percent of their profits be allocated toward CSR. The company found itself negotiating with the government regarding adding these priorities and schemes to its already existing CSR agendas, like the hospital and the vocational training centers. This shift in responsibility to the central government inspired risk aversion. Corporations veered away from controversy in spending CSR funds. There was more scrutiny into how CSR funds were spent than into how the companies made their profits. There was also a new responsibility that emerged to reporting, because the CSR provision was a reporting law, and some companies found it easier to give directly to the government rather than to go through the process of setting up CSR programs or working with NGO partners. The governmental regulation was bureaucratic, and its instrumental rationality directed social action. As with the urban IT company, all CSR programs for the fertilizer company had to be identified and quantified.

When the factory had moved into the district, it was not well-developed and few industries existed in the area. The factory was an initiative of the Congress Party, and the local area was the administrative assembly seat of the political party. The CSR director explained that, historically, the Congress Party had always won the locality's Member of Parliament seat, and people had high expectations when the fertilizer industry started that jobs would be created. Job creation translated into a constituency, a voter bank, and political support. The company started a vocational training center, so in addition to providing jobs, they trained the local community in electrical work, garment design, auto mechanics, and the electronics trades. The area had health problems, especially when the factory was being set up, so the factory started social initiatives and built a hospital.

Changes he had noticed since the law was passed reflected new reporting and compliance structures and new rules. "Now, government is also asking for a certain set of reports, which we need to give to them so that they are also aware that we are complying with the law," he said. A shift in project orientation took place as well. After talking for some time, he noted: "our Prime Minister [Narendra Modi] has taken a very huge target of making India open defecation free (ODF) by 2019."

> What happens is the district administration approaches us saying that we have to make this district open defecation free. To make a toilet, what happens is . . . To make a toilet, you need at least 15,000 rupees. Government provides about 12,000 rupees for one toilet. This is the subsidy provided by the government to make one toilet. Now, this remaining 3,000, many of the regions in India are still not that capable of putting in that amount, 3,000 rupees for a toilet. That is number one. That is financial crisis. Second is, they are also in the habit of going for open defecation, since they are just there doing that, so they are not used to closed space. They're not being comfortable. Apart from financial support, you also need to create awareness and tell them why open defecation is bad and you have to use toilet for defecation. Health-related aspect also needs to be told to them. What is happening, this remaining 3,000 amount, what the government is saying that the corporates under their CSR budget can support the villages or the government to make them using this toilet, also, simultaneously, organize training or sanitation awareness camps in villages, so that villages are aware that open defecation is not good for their health, and they should take government program and make toilets for this closed defecation.

The company's partnership with the government had increased through CSR as a new responsibility—a call that demanded a response:

> The district administration minister approached, asking for a certain amount of budget to be supported through our CSR initiative. What happens is that during the beginning of the year itself, we plan our activities as to where our funds will be utilized in different activities. For us now, I suppose if the government asked us that you have to invest rupees on toilet project, right, but we have not kept that much an amount. Say, we have kept only ten lakh, or 15 lakh, or 20 lakh, like that. It becomes very difficult for us to reallocate that money and listen to government

and fulfill their demands. Somehow, we try to manage, by doing some kind of again, say, just to . . . Other activities also, we have to tell them that we are doing such activities and because of it you won't be able to do, but yes, we are now getting into some kind of partnership with them.

This partnership involved negotiation. At stake was who decided upon the priorities for social development initiatives, and what social welfare was to be done. Before the new CSR law was passed, the decision was based on corporate philanthropic largess, and interests. After the law was passed, it was being directed by the government, through the new law.

> It also depends on the type of person who is holding the office, because sometimes they become very rigid. It is our target given by the chief minister, so we have to do it. You should check down other activities and you should contribute the majority of your funds to this activity, because it has to be done by 2018. For this district, I mean [x] district, the target is October 2018. There are about two lakh toilets, which needs to be built only in this district. Two lakh into 12,000, it's a very huge amount.

If the government said toilets, and the chief minister was behind the directive, well, then it had to be done. This was how the government was guiding development through the new law. He was not sure the target could be met, but the company was moving 10 percent in this direction and still doing 90 percent of its previously organized CSR/social development work. "Coming back to the main point that, yes, our activities, little bit we are now adhering to the [directives], which the government is putting to us, but mostly 90 percent we are doing ourselves, 10 percent we are listening to as per their demands; we are shifting." Part of the reason for this was that the company had built the hospital with a large staff, which it had to continue. Companies that were less experienced at CSR were giving directly to the government. In these cases, it was easy for corporations to attend to governmental development demands, and to give the 2 percent to the government instead of developing, monitoring, and reporting their own programs. The government could source funds for social development directly from corporations who were just starting their programs and did not know how to proceed.

Before the CSR provision, the government was not involved in CSR. It was involved in development through NGOs and local district councils. The CSR change in the Companies Act was governmental involvement in guiding corporate-sponsored community development: "After this Act, it was mandated do not spend all your activities in certain areas, specific areas. All those things need to be communicated to the government; then how much you have to spend out of what you have planned. Those things changed." It had become more bureaucratic and one needed institutional or bureaucratic literacy to understand how to report to the government, and to comply with the regulations in the CSR provision. The reporting requirement changed the type of work that could be done, toward work that was reportable and quantifiable and away from more amorphous and open-ended aims such as "women's empowerment," which may have been hard to quantify in the short term. Latrines were easy to count; one could report having built five in a particular district. This small governmental regulation directed social action, or attempted to, and reframed the work of corporate and nonprofit sectors. The new regulations redefined what was possible through social action. For companies new to CSR, it was easier to give to the Prime Minister's National Relief Fund than to start their own CSR program.

The director showed me a brochure depicting a small farmer with a family of thirteen, with his primary income coming from agriculture. He was given twenty-six varieties of seeds from the kitchen garden program, and he was able to enhance the nutritional value of his agricultural production for his family and also gain an income of 8000 to 10,000 rupees from selling his vegetables in the market. Whereas he previously grew three to four types of vegetables on his land, he could subsequently grow twenty-six varieties. I wondered why the company would want to stop this program in favor of building toilets. Toilets were a huge governmental initiative, with aims of social transformation bleeding into popular culture (as in the 2017 film *Toilet: A Love Story*). It was a huge social transformational push, but this company had been working in development, already.

The company's sixty-five-bed hospital was run as a charitable trust. "We have a fixed budget every year that we are spending on this hospital for our CSR and with our CSR activities. We have a small leprosy hospital also for the cure of leprosy patients." The company had been running a vocational training center for thirty years, and they had other centers like this, where women were trained in tailoring. These were permanent activities that could not be stopped. The company had an obligation to the local community to continue them. "Even though we are in loss, even though there is no such obligation of us spending 2 percent, even then we have to spend on the activities." These developmental activities involved relationships and commitments with the local community that could not be abruptly halted. The company gave money to the trust it had established, and the trust was endowed to spend funds on CSR activities. The new law created an operational tension between existing development responsibilities to the local community through long-term programs and new governmental initiatives. The CSR director also had to address state governmental tree-planting targets:

> I'll tell you, this year the state government has taken a target of a 6.5 kilos sapling plantation, or you can say a 650 million sapling plantation. This year itself, the state government has taken this target. These trees, or saplings, what they are doing is now they are giving this target not only to the government departments, but also to the companies under CSR initiatives. What they are telling us that you have to plant at least, let's say, one million trees. [. . .] It's a huge job, because you have to dig the pit, you have to [provide] the labor, you have to buy the saplings. A lot of amount is . . .— Again, that sort of demand is also coming to us.

The governmental development targets were passed on to corporations, which could address a portion of a target such as working in "health infrastructure, infrastructure, education, social cause, livelihood promotion." The company was already working in all of these sectors and it had a fixed budget that was allocated and couldn't be reallocated. The one-size-fits-all approach being promoted by the government wasn't appropriate for this company, even though it may have been fine for corporations not already doing CSR in their local communities. This company was already spending above the 2 percent guideline. For example, if they did 10 percent of their CSR work on the designated governmental CSR categories, it would likely meet the 2 percent threshold. In the past two years, the company had won five awards, including a global CSR award. The director showed me a brochure for the tailoring training center for women.

The company also worked with CII. In their vocational training center, the company had signed memorandum of understanding (MOU) with CII, which would provide the technical support for training and certification. Previously, they had run the center independently, but, "now, there is a government recognized body . . . NSDC, National Skilled Development Corporation." He wanted me to understand the difference between the kind of CSR conducted by a manufacturing unit located in a remote place, like his company, versus CSR work done by a corporate house or industry in a metropolitan city. He thought the distinction was due to obligations: "We are bound by our local community expectation, which they are not bound [by]. We have to spend in our local community. For us, as per this Act, there is no such stipulation, that we have to spend our money in this location itself." He described the developmental landscape:

> In this area itself, you see this township. The moment you go out from this township, there is a huge difference, heaven and hell kind of difference. Here, you'll find all the facilities. There is 24-hour electricity, water supply, club facilities, everything. The moment you go out and visit a village nearby, you will find that there is hardly houses having a toilet. There is no toilet. They are struggling to get good drinking water. There is no roads. The schools which the government has built has no good teachers, no good infrastructure. There is a huge difference.

Corporations developed local communities in order to survive, and to support their labor pools. Once a corporation moved into an area, the community began to make demands on the company. "Either they will ask for a job, which the company cannot provide to everyone, or they will ask for their basic needs, which the company somehow will have to do it." If CSR had historically been a tool to keep the peace with laborers and the surrounding area, now, too, it was to keep the peace with the local government officials, and good relationships with the local community helped this too.

> You need to keep yourself in a comfortable position that the local community is supporting you. Also, what happens is that the local administration, they are also wanting such kind of complaints from the community of any kind. If the community is towards in your favor, and the district administration actually tries to blackmail you, that we have got such complaints from the community. Why don't you do this for us, so we will see that. That also we need to manage. If the community is on our side, then even the government would not be able to blackmail us like that.

Some companies were involved in what the director called "strategy CSR or business link CSR": CSR that made it possible for communities to buy products and create markets. It paved the way for capitalism in the "unincorporated areas," expanding markets and the reach of the state through corporations. During election times, this aspect of CSR became more of an issue. In the case of this rural fertilizer company, which had built strong, local community and political ties through its historical CSR programs, the new CSR provision in the 2013 Companies Act added obligations to the central government via targets and programs. It could not abandon its previous CSR commitments even though the new language of responsibility redirected its focus toward central governmental initiatives.

Nonprofit Responses

In 2017, many NPOs were shifting their regulatory identity: moving away from being societies and trusts to being Section 8 companies. In effect, they were becoming nonprofit corporations governed centrally under the Companies Act (2013). Meanwhile, new foundations were being formed, often by corporations seeking to spend their required CSR using the same incorporation strategy. There were risks in supporting external NGOs with increased governmental oversight. One NPO director spoke with me about Public Service Undertakings (PSUs). These were organizations like ONGC (Oil and Natural Gas Corporation), a public sector undertaking owned by the government that was also responsible for contributing to CSR due to its partnership with private corporations. Through CSR, these groups could support government-driven development programs, investing in sanitation and toilet construction in schools and villages. It sounded good on paper. Corporations, in partnership with the government, were funding governmental programs, and some of this was taking place through NGOs. The NPO director used the example of the sanitation campaign: the government wanted every household and schools to have toilets. Much of the CSR work was focused on this too.

The structure of the Companies Act was adjusting the practice of NPOs on the ground. CSR funds were flowing through NPOs, but the director said the data were not that clear. He thought most corporations were doing their CSR on their own and not going through existing NGOs. The government had bypassed the nonprofit sector. He thought that once they realized they couldn't do it themselves, they would come to the nonprofit sector, but for NPOs the regulatory reform was a roller coaster. Initially, the voluntary sector thought that with CSR "Big money has come," but "now every day everyone is saying 'where is the money?'" The Confederation of Indian Industry was involved in helping to develop a database to help match corporations and NGO projects for CSR work. The new arena, like the FCRA shift, spawned its own web-world of broker portals that had proliferated. Capitalism and its relationship with nonprofits created new arenas for ingenuity and business, including donation portals.[8] Before the CSR provision, the GiveIndia portal was an industry stalwart in the business–social welfare matchmaking project. After the CSR provision in the Companies Act was implemented, portal worlds sprouted up everywhere, in the same manner that NGOs had "mushroomed" in the 1990s.

A few corporations had in the past worked in a "social orientation," as one Professional Critic described it, pushing for social change. Many organizations functioned as umbrella groups, funding other groups. This was one way in which foundations sought to reach "the last mile" and "the grassroots." Some of the larger NGOs funding smaller ones were focused on capacity building, and this was necessary for accessing the new world of CSR. Larger NGOs, meanwhile, had much less problems accessing CSR. The Professional Critic explained a fear to me, that the NPO sector would lose its diversity. NPOs were eager to avail themselves of CSR funds, given existing funding restrictions via the FCRA. If nonprofits were an institutional species, they were experiencing a risk of dying off due to climate change. There was a threat of a serious loss of diversity in the sector due to the new regulatory-legal framework shaping funding flows in certain ways. This NGO director was concerned with nurturing and sustaining the existing nonprofit sector, especially small nonprofits. "How do we actually nurture, sustain, and build the capacities of these grassroots groups? . . . We used to have a lot of these tall leaders who created that kind of social activists at the grassroot level also. They were like a role model and so inspirational. These days you don't find those kind of leaders; you find good managers." These new managers had proper degrees. They wanted good jobs and CSR was a good job. As they did their projects, they made enterprises and considered themselves social entrepreneurs.

He considered it an effect of professionalism. Conventional social activism was being replaced with a professional framework. He explained, "Unless you do that community mobilization, mass mobilization around the issues, you can't see the impact. You can't see the changes in the behavior or communities and all that. It has been much more focused on tangible issues." "Impact orientation," along with "outcome mapping," and identifying "externalities," were buzzwords in the industry at the time, global development trends, which had replaced earlier ones, like Participatory Rural Appraisal, as flawed as it was in its own era. Impact orientation, with its outcome mapping and tracking of externalities, demonstrated instrumentalism, not idealism. In this new climate, many international donors had shifted away from funding Indian NGOs. While there was initially an anticipation of a utopia of resources from CSR and the corporate sector, and a moment of hope in the face of great anxiety about sector transformation, increasingly restrictive regulations, and governmental targeting of rights-based social change initiatives, had changed the landscape of social welfare provision.

Conclusion

The imposition of the CSR provision in the Companies Act had a number of effects on civil society in the first five years of its implementation. The reporting requirement changed how existing corporations addressed the government regarding development. It shifted how governmental development targets were oriented in terms of responsibility, moving from one oriented toward communities to one oriented toward the government and corporate sectors (or the "market"). It formalized a partnership model between corporations and NGOs which had existed between government and NGOs in earlier development eras. This changed the type of work that could be done in the name of development. CSR had designated areas of engagement and measured parameters outlined in the law. It also added a dimension of verification and suspicion of NGOs as potential partners, as corporations were on the line for the work of the NGOs, which were increasingly scrutinized and vetted, and it shifted the CSR from being based on corporate revenue to being based on profit.

The call that demanded a response by the government through the CSR provision was a technical requirement that structurally shifted the landscape for NGOs in social welfare work. With new limits on foreign funding through the passage of the revised FCRA, the CSR provision in the Companies Act promised to fill the void. However, it also eliminated dissent with its compliance requirements. This was antithetical to the nature of Indian civil society groups, which had for decades called the state to account for its failures and infiltrated the state in developmental programs in the early phase of economic liberalization. The call for CSR, which was an impossible dialogue, foreclosed certain forms of responses and encouraged others. Although it aimed to inspire domestic contributions to national development, it did so on the state's terms. The new horizon line of CSR privileged corporate actors and the institutional structures of reporting and accountability that corporations were well-suited to reinforce. It added a positive list of acceptable activities, as a counterpart to the negative list of charitable purpose analyzed in chapter 5, and reoriented corporations, nonprofits, and government in relation to social welfare.

CONCLUSION

Becoming Legible

This book has focused on the unsung heroes of policy creation for the nonprofit sector in India: accountants, nonprofit staff, and activist philanthropists. It has not focused on the loud and usual suspects: politicians or parliamentarians. Alongside focusing on local donors and nonprofit leaders with long histories in the sector, I animated nonhuman actors—laws, nonprofits, Workshops, and Reports—and argued that to understand nonprofits we have to look to their regulation, specifically, the regulation of philanthropy. Nonprofits are donor dependent and shifts in the laws and rules governing their life source, philanthropy, alter the nature of nonprofit work. I framed the social worlds of nonprofit legal reform by collapsing diverse sets of actors into analytical types—Accountability Guides, Professional Critics, and Activist Donors—partly to protect the anonymity of those striving to make social change. The people engaged in the type of work about which I write have historically worked quietly behind the scenes, with the state in order to reform the state. They have organized collectivities and convened forums for democratic discussions about the horizon line of nonprofit policy. But the state does not always like to be reformed, and current conditions suggest that to become visible in this endeavor may pose a risk and a threat.

Policymaking is a process of negotiation essential to democracy, and CSOs and NPOs in India are key players. They represent multiple publics, negotiate with the state regarding laws governing the nonprofit sector—such as the FCRA, tax laws, and the Companies Act—and they use techniques such as report making and workshops to consolidate multiple perspectives to become legible, first to themselves as a group, and then to the state. This negotiation involves articulating demands for regulatory reform that facilitates nonprofit work. In India, which has one of the most vibrant civil societies in the world, regulatory reform negotiations are part of democratic practice. Yet, much this key labor of democracy exists in the background and on the margins in the middle zone. The heroes of my narrative are accountants educating the sector about regulatory reform in real time; the Accountability Guides who created educational clinics, wrote norms brochures, led workshops, and wrote reports with NPO leaders; and the Professional Critics, who communicated with the government, by organizing petitions, leading nonprofit advocacy initiatives, and negotiating with civil servants on behalf of the nonprofit sector. And we must not forget the role of philanthropists, the Activist Donors, who sought to reform the philanthropic ecosystem itself in support of civil society work, in collaboration with Accountability Guides and Professional Critics.

Institutions like nonprofits must bend to customary forms and social norms to be recognized as legitimate. No wonder nonprofits are seen as inefficient by corporate regulatory structures; they are failing to be profitable and thus are unrecognizable and considered illegitimate. This became apparent in the revisions to the Companies Act that added a 2 percent corporate responsibility tax to large corporations' obligations and shepherded corporations and nonprofits into the same regulatory terrain. To become recognized by a corporatizing state, an institution must fit a corporate frame, and must efficiently strive to make profit. Nonprofits that organized workshops and conventions, and wrote reports read by few, challenged assumptions of the corporate form. So much of what the actors in this book have sought to do, as persons and institutions, has emphasized legibility in relation to the state. Legibility, for nonprofits, has entailed entitlements and freedoms: to receive funds across borders, to do social work, to work on behalf of a public, and to receive tax exemption subsidies. Yet, the cost of illegibility has remained an ever-present threat, of sanctions or, worse, of frozen funds. When regulatory reform redirected institutional practice, nonprofits turned to domestic resources and morphed into charitable companies. But the threat, and pressure, of legibility remained. When activists and change makers were branded "urban Naxals" by governmental officials (Baviskar 2023; Human Rights Watch 2023), it marked them as illegitimate actors working against the state. Reformers have historically been celebrated in India's past, yet in the decade of legal reform about which I write they became a threat.

I have highlighted unlikely change makers, those behind the scenes negotiating the rules of law as they were being made and then being re-formed. The laws covered registration, taxation, foreign donation, and corporate governance, all through the regulation of charitable groups and the legal category of charitable purpose. Nonprofit labor exists in all of these laws and appears in all arms of the state. Nonprofit accountants and law-yers, NPO leaders and philanthropists worked alongside NPO staff and volunteers to write reports, organize meetings, parse through the thicket of an ever-changing revolution of rules to communicate. Their efforts ad-dressed their constituencies, of small NPOs working with even smaller and more remote communities, of civil servants writing the rules for the government, and of senior nonprofit philanthropists and NPO leaders. This communication involved translation: across governmental, corporate, and nonprofit sectors. Not all of their efforts were successful. For example, the National Policy on the Nonprofit Sector never came to be.

We must recognize processes of negotiation in processes of legal reform as valid arenas of socio-legal process, and democracy itself. The debates occurring in the workshops, conventions, and conferences were not of a single mind. The nonprofit sector in India is one of the largest and most active in the world. It is also one that has witnessed a decade of rapid regulatory reform that has effectively silenced dissent. This has occurred through the revolution of rules and the implementation of laws. It is not the law itself, but how the law is used that matters for a sector as diverse as the Indian nonprofit sector. What we can learn is how the nonprofit sector is shaped by its regulation. The registration laws regarding societies, trusts, and charitable companies, along with regulations regarding foreign philanthropy in the FCRA, taxes in the Income Tax Act, and corporate social responsibility in the Companies Act, contributed to the shaping of what it meant to inhabit the category of a nonprofit in late-liberalizing India. This itself was a radical transformation. From the social reform-ers of the colonial era that influenced national independence movements, through Nehruvian nation building deploying Gandhian ideas of trustee-ship and collectivism, to the restrictive statecraft of the Emergency, the human rights agendas of good governance during globalization, and in late liberal India where corporations entered the social welfare landscape, nonprofits have been central to India's developmental story. They have led reform, and reformers have created and inhabited many of the institutional categories that fall under the nonprofit rubric of societies, trusts, and charitable companies.

Democracy and fascism both begin with the rule of law. Hannah Arendt has written about the banality of evil and how fascism can occur through the most regular of activities of institutional life. Controlling dissent does not always involve exceptional acts. Often, the most ordinary, bureaucratic acts have the most power to change society, for better or worse. Nonprofit advocates in India have used the techniques of bureaucracy to speak with the state, to contest and reform it. Many have worked from within, though law, to change society—through the language of rights in a global frame, focusing on women and children's rights, environmental and economic justice, and religious rights for minority populations in India. The gains of these efforts have been tremendous, and they include the work of historic reformers as well as those working today.

I have tried to shine a light on a community of reformers that may not want so much attention. They are reformers in the background, fighting an institutional system that seems to be closing down on dissent, certainly targeting NPOs. Because NPOs are donor dependent they have become spaces of negotiation, and they have become tightly regulated. They can be used to fight political battles for the Right and the Left, and the state can also harness their efforts for purposes of political legitimacy. NPOs work in public arenas: they are media oriented and can quickly become a platform for either agonistic or antagonistic politics. The small acts of negotiation conducted by those of whom I write in this book, in the past and over a decade of legal reform, are efforts to keep democracy alive. Perhaps they are examples of the banality of benevolence, that works with institutional structures to speak "for the public," to use the majesty of law to support social change and preserve a space for democratic negotiation.

What is democracy but an institutional structure for producing tolerance of radical differences among peoples, ideas, and ways of life. NPOs are critical instruments of democracy. They facilitate multiple voices and create institutional, governmentally recognized arenas for the negotiation of different publics. Of course, not all NPOs are focused on the promotion of democratic dialogue, as are the ones about which I write. Laws can be created to control dissent and promote majoritarian views also through the nonprofit form. Thus, we must attend to the rules of laws, and observe how they are implemented by political groups. In political battles, NPOs can become sites of contestation, platforms for critique, and voices of the weak or the powerful. There is nothing inherent in the category of the nonprofit that makes an NPO belong to a particular political side or adopt a specific social orientation. It is the multiplicity of potential allegiances that lends the nonprofit form to the political imagination. I have made NPOs, laws, workshops, and reports actants in my book because the nonprofit form makes worlds, and by becoming legible, to governments and publics, it embodies the potential to negotiate for, and effect, social change. I aim to elevate an analytical focus on the nonprofit form, which has public and symbolic power. It is the Accountability Guides, Professional Critics, and Activist Donors who strove to keep the democratic potential of the nonprofit form alive, through their ongoing negotiations over the rules of nonprofit law, in their petitions, workshops, reports, conventions, and advocacy. However hard I have tried to animate the social drama of policy in formation, legal reform is a slow process that occurs behind the scenes, often at a glacial pace. Revisions to laws can take years. Though policy reform may seem lifeless to read for some, it has dramatic impacts on people's lives and those working in this sector realize the importance of what they do. I hope readers of this book will as well. While this book has an end, I can only hope the space of negotiation is nurtured, allowing spokespersons of the nonprofit sector to speak collectively and diversely and to continue to advocate for democratic dialogue in nonprofit policy via struggles over the nonprofit form and its regulation.

NOTES

Introduction: Nonprofits Make Worlds

1. See Graan (2022) on institutional forms generally, and Bernal and Grewal (2014) on the nonprofit form.

2. See United Nations, G.A. Res/ 2200A (XXI), International Covenant on Civil and Political Rights (Dec. 16, 1966), regarding the right to peaceful assembly (Article 21) and association (Article 22[2]). https://www.ohchr.org/en/instruments-mechanisms/instruments/international-covenant-civil-and-political-rights.

3. Bloodgood et al. (2014) address both faciliatory and restraining national approaches to nonprofit regulation. Concerned that NPOs may upset political order, some states place barriers to entry and limit NPO political activities and tax status.

4. Comparing NPO regulation in India and in China is a fertile site for research: for example, China's Company Law of 1994 and of 2006 in comparison to India's CSR programs in its Companies Act of 2013.

5. Also see UN Special Rapporteur (2013) and Sidel (2010) on global regulatory restrictions, and Agarwal (2012) on the Financial Action Task Force. In February 2001, the Financial Action Task Force (FATF) on Money Laundering issued an alert on the misuse of charities for funding terrorism. In 2001, the U.S. government passed the Patriot Act and scrutinized international grants. The FATF issued another report on trusts used for terror funding. India, in response to global pressure, passed the Prevention of Money Laundering Act in 2002 (implemented in 2005). The FCRA 2006 rules included greater scrutiny of charitable organizations.

6. See Salamon (2015, 2149) on "the nonprofitization of the welfare state," a service-provision model altering relationships between nonprofits and the state, which moves their work away from dissent. As the state becomes the primary donor base for nonprofits, the capacity of nonprofits to critique the state shifts, and collaboration quiets nonprofits in line with state agendas.

7. Islamic charities in the United States faced increasing scrutiny (ACLU 2009; Niumai 2011).

8. See Hull (2012a, 2012b); Riles (2001); and Hoag (2011) for precedents for the anthropological study of bureaucratic forms; also see Feldman (2008); Bear and Mathur (2015); Baxi (2019); Soules (2018).

9. Bureaucrats such as the state workers described in Gupta (2012); the street bureaucrats/social workers found in Brodwin (2013); the report makers and record keepers in Hull (2008, 2012a, and 2012b); and the activist networks preparing for conferences found in Riles (2001); as well as the organizational ethnographers in Pedersen and Humle (2016).

Chapter 1: Writing the Horizon Line

1. Wikipedia, https://en.wikipedia.org/wiki/Horizon (accessed 1/26/23).

2. Wikipedia, "Russian Foreign Agent Law," https://en.wikipedia.org/wiki/Russian_foreign_agent_law (accessed 6/21/22).

3. Human Rights Watch, "Hong Kong One Year after the National Security Law," https://www.hrw.org/feature/2021/06/25/dismantling-free-society/hong-kong-one-year-after-national-security-law (accessed 6/21/22).

4. Or "colonial," as in in the North American context. See Simpson (2014, 2016) on working from without to avoid co-optation.

5. Cf. Richland (2021) and the concept of "cooperation without submission."

6. As in Mouffe's work (2013), religious identities may become an alternative to Left-Right distinctions; though they may also be taken up by political parties. Distinctions between Left and Right are replaced with right and wrong in adversarial politics, and in the case of religious identities, the politics of opposition play out on a moral register, of good and evil in the moralization of politics. Also see Escobar (2018) for the concept of the "pluriverse," which takes a perspective from the Global South to argue for relational autonomy where difference can prevail in solidarity.

7. See Nader (2018) on harmony ideology, and for alternate dispute resolution (ADR), where disputes become problems of communication instead of power and inequality. ADR eliminates dissent through law. It privatizes mediation, conflict, and justice, and encourages people to avoid legal action and seek mediation instead.

8. The harmony law model "encapsulates coercive compromise and consensus as a form of behavior modification" (Nader 2108, 270).

9. Shree Narayan Singh, dir., *Toilet: Ek Prem Katha*, https://www.imdb.com/title/tt5785170/.

10. R Balki, dir., *Pad Man*, https://www.imdb.com/title/tt7218518/.

11. The informant, an educated intellectual, was obliquely quoting Partha Chatterjee.

12. Two reporting agencies that arranged annual reports on philanthropy in India were Bain and Guidestar; see, for example, https://www.bain.com/insights/india-philanthropy-report-2017/.

13. The first draft of the Direct Taxes Code (DTC) was in 2009. A revised

DTC was introduced in Parliament, and the GOI formed a Standing Committee to discuss it with stakeholders. The committee submitted its report to Parliament in 2012. A revised version of the DTC was released in 2014. It lapsed when the new government came to power in 2014. In 2017, Prime Minister Modi began drafting a new DTC (*Business Standard* 2023).

Chapter 2: Charitable Purpose as a Political, Regulatory Frame

1. NPO Report on National Policy on the Voluntary Sector. I have kept NPO reports anonymous to protect informants.

2. Deo and McDuie-Ra (2011) analyze the birth and success of these two movements, including their growth in relation to institutional strategies and philanthropic initiatives.

3. See Deo and McDuie-Ra (2011). Formally funded organizations have access to transnational networks but are vulnerable to being led by donor agendas, which these authors call "agendas from elsewhere." In contrast, local civic actors with limited access to international funds and partnerships may be more deeply involved in local communities, and consequently more influential in local political activism.

4. Property held as corporation, in trust. Mortmain law is trust law.

5. For historical data on trusts as constituted in India, see Birla (2009). For F. W. Maitland's political philosophy of trusts, corporations, and the state in Britain, see MacFarlane (2002) and Maitland (2003).

6. Notions of charitable purpose are found in the Indian Trusts Act; the Societies Registration Act (1860), which governs literary, scientific, and charitable societies; and the Religious Endowments Act (1863), which resulted from disputes surrounding temple complexes and which governs public Hindu and Muslim religious institutions.

7. See Williams (2010) for gender as a site of national reform in debates over the Hindu Code Bill.

8. Some scholars have critiqued Indian secularism on the grounds that it has reinforced the ability of the Hindu Right to assert its power through majority religious politics; see Chaterjee (1998), Madan (1998), also see Williams (2010) on nation building and Hindu Code Bill debates.

9. As of the time of this writing as well, the possibility of a uniform civil code instead of Personal Laws was a politically contested national, social reform arena.

10. Andersen and Damle (2019, 77–91) note the difficulty of defining *Hindutva*, though it may loosely be defined as Hindu nationalist ideology.

11. This argument is drawn from a collaborative article; see Bornstein and Sharma (2016). Khagram (2002) discusses how the social movement Narmada Bachao Andolan used Indian laws as well as global human rights and indigenous rights instruments to challenge a large dam-building project opposed by many groups in the area.

12. Deo and McDuie-Ra (2011) compared the Indian Women's Movement and the Sangh Parivar, and found these two large civil society movements—one Left and one Right leaning—developed different funding strategies. The progressive

women's movement was largely funded by international donors, which controlled NGO agendas in line with international priorities and limited the autonomy of social reform. In contrast, the Sangh Parivar cultivated small donors in its diaspora, manifesting an alternate form of collective advocacy that increased its political legitimacy: donations had no bearing on institutional agendas, which were run by localized networks.

13. In terms of formation costs, in 2014, trusts ran about Rs 1,000–5,000; societies, Rs 3,000–10,000; and Section 8 companies Rs 30,000–75,000. The cost would weed out smaller, less well-funded organizations from choosing to become Section 8 companies instead of societies or trusts. Annual costs ran about Rs 5,000 for trusts, 10,000 for societies, and 30,000 for Section 8 companies, which were much more expensive. In terms of control, trusts and Section 8 companies were easy to control, societies were difficult. Regarding public transparency, trusts had low demands (no reporting requirements to the public), while societies had moderate demands, and Section 8 companies had high demands. Trusts have little regulation, societies have a moderate amount, and Section 8 companies have a high amount. Trusts required little paperwork, societies a moderate amount, and Section 8's a high amount. Overall, trusts were the least regulated and least controlled institutional form, and Section 8's were the most regulated, most expensive, and incurred the most penalties under governing laws. Societies were in the middle, but the defining difference was that the area of operation for registered societies was usually restricted to their state boundaries. Trusts could operate in most of India, and Section 8's could operate in all of India. This made a difference for organizations that wanted to operate in more than one state; Section 8 companies had more leeway and a wider reach. But they were also more controlled by the central government and more costly to operate.

14. The Income Tax Act specified that donations to benefit religious communities or castes were not tax deductible. A NPO created exclusively for the benefit of a religious community or caste could create a separate fund for the benefit of "scheduled castes, backward classes, scheduled tribes, or women and children." Donations to these funds could qualify for deduction under Section 80(g). The organization must maintain a separate account of these funds.

15. Many activities that NGOs engaged in, such as strengthening local *panchayats* would no longer be applicable. Additional changes included: 100% of income during a year had to be used for permitted welfare activities. If an NGO spent 85 percent of the funds it receives in a year, the remaining 15 percent would be taxed. A trust could no longer be created from business assets. All receipts of an NGO except loans and advances would be treated as "income" (including grants). Restricted funds—grants given by donors for specific funds—would be treated as income.

16. NPO circular, on the Direct Taxes Code Bill, 2010.

17. Significant issues for NPOs included consideration of gross receipts; expending 100 percent of funds; no international activities; and taxable net worth.

Chapter 3: Regulating Philanthropic Corridors

1. Pushpa Sundar (2010) traces the inception of the FCRA to the 1950s, and argues it was codified during the Emergency when Congress used it as a tool during a witch hunt, first for supporters of the opposition party Jay Prakash Narayan, and later during the period of the Kudal Commission in the early 1980s.

2. The Estimates Committee suggested the FCRA be revised again in 1986, and in 1988 a governmental committee was tasked with refining the law, although no changes resulted.

3. Centre for Social Impact and Philanthropy, n.d.

4. All of these are forms of political protest: *hartals* are strikes and *raasta roko* are road blocks; *jail bharo* is a protest tactic of intentionally getting arrested to fill jails.

5. Even NGOs with FCRA accounts, and those receiving funds from donors who were not on the watchlist had difficulty accessing their funds. "Banks feel like they should hold on to these funds and don't release them to the local branch unless they have seen the grant agreement and all sorts of other paperwork." (Centre for Social Impact and Philanthropy, n.d., 19–24).

6. Major donors and receivers of FCRA funds were Christian mission organizations. FCRA funds were utilized for establishment expenses, rural development, welfare of children, construction and maintenance of schools and colleges, and grant of stipend/scholarship/assistance in cash and kind to poor/deserving children.

7. In 2012, only 39,236 organizations had valid FCRA registrations with another 631 having received prior permission to receive funds. The majority of these organizations were focused on "social objectives" (Agarwal 2012, 25).

8. In 2012, the top donor countries in terms of FCRA contributions to India were the United States, United Kingdom, and Italy (Agarwal 2012, 31). Top donor organizations giving FCRA funds were religious organizations. The FCRA in this iteration could be considered an attempt by the government to control religious activities in India, including proselytization and conversion. While the original FCRA, in 1976, did not have specific clauses regarding religion, the 2010 Act did, and they were oriented toward regulating missionary influence along with foreign contributions.

9. Section 25 charitable companies, revised in the 2013 Companies Act to be Section 8, http://mha1.nic.in/pdfs/ForeigD-ForeigD-FCRA_FAQs.pdf (accessed 10/14/16).

10. The Congress Party was in power, and secularism raised issues regarding politics and diaspora philanthropy.

11. It had registered under the Foreign Exchange Regulation Act of 1973 instead.

12. Greenpeace claimed contributions from nearly 75,000 Indians had been rejected by banks where it had its accounts. The Ministry of Home Affairs revealed domestic donations to Greenpeace India were also under investigation since the NGO had not revealed the names and identities of donors. "Even domestic donations need to be transparent. Even the Aam Aadmi Party [a compet-

ing political party to the BJP] put out all its donations on the website," claimed a senior official" (Aurora 2015).

13. Sabrang was the local NGO to which Indian Greenpeace gave funds. Accounts of the trusts were frozen as well as personal accounts. Ford also funded Sabrang and was put on a security watch list, with its funding to Sabrang under investigation.

14. Framing is an activist tactic used to generate support for advocacy campaigns (Benford and Snow 2000). Here the government was using this tactic.

15. "Greenpeace India Executive Director Samit Aich told staff there are only enough funds to support operations for a month. If it's unable to raise enough money from public donations and frozen accounts aren't unblocked soon, Greenpeace India would have to close all of its offices in the country—leaving about 340 people without a job." (Bhalla 2015).

16. A U.S. nonprofit that had its funding blocked said, "civil society was waking up to the fact the FCRA rules can straitjacket organizations, especially those asking tough questions of the Indian government and its development plans." NPO circular, 2015.

17. The 2015 FCRA rules amendment stipulated changes in administration and regulation of foreign contributions, including submitting forms online and posting receipt of contributions on websites, reporting to the central government within 48 hours for FCRA transactions, using new form numbers for filings, and using a new list of approved FCRA categories of activity (Manku 2015b).

18. Sastry (2015) argues there was a lack of trust between the people and the people's organizations on the one hand and the government on the other. FCRA represented a small amount of funds compared to foreign direct investment. Because the FCRA funds were comparatively so tiny, why the fuss? Many FCRA were religious organizations, and religion was a tender area of governmental concern in the amended FCRA.

19. NPO circular regarding GOI Amendment to FCRA rules (2015).

20. A 2013 Foundation Center report, "Advancing Human Rights—The State of Global Human Rights Grantmaking," documented how this trend focused on funding human rights, social justice, and social change.

21. The NPO circular responding to the IB report noted: "Voluntary organizations have been systematically attacked by the government through legal measures such as FCRA and Income Tax Laws amounting to restriction in their activities or at most facing judicial enquiries for speaking on behalf of the poor and marginalized. The regulatory environment for the sector in India has not been conducive for organizations, as repeated instances of punitive measures slapped on the sector have raised questions on its future."

22. The circular noted that in 2009, Indian NGOs had questioned promises made by the government.

23. The circular also referenced the example of INSAF, which had its FCRA registration revoked after the agitation surrounding the Kudankulam Nuclear Power Plant. Although the MHA said it would complete its investigation in 90 days, years passed, and no one had been found guilty. Eventually, INSAF sued

the government, using public interest litigation to argue that FCRA was unconstitutional, and won the case; its funds were released.

24. The circular noted NGOs were supposed to bid on fixed projects without asking questions. The sector, which was known for its innovations, had become a tool for delivering projects.

25. Issues mentioned in the circular: the need to create a mechanism for regulating and promoting NGOs; a centralized law for NGO registration; the need for a separate ministry for NGO governance; and the need for taxation reform.

26. Educational and legal activist workshops were funded by six organizations, including a coalition of more than 140 churches and affiliated groups. Although FCRA funds were a small percentage of foreign funds entering India, most of the funding through FCRA went to religious groups; religion had become a particular target area for scrutiny.

27. It detailed the following FCRA registration cancellation history: July 1996, 203 cancelled; September 1997, 497; November 2005, 8,673; mid-2012, 4,122; March 2015, 1,142; April 2015, 8,975.

Chapter 4: Navigating the Rules

1. Cf. Judith Butler's ideas on gender and the concept of improvisation within a scene of constraint, as in McMullen (2016).

2. Quikr in India is like Craigslist in the United States and Europe. See https://www.quikr.com/delhi (accessed January 26, 2022).

3. I use a gender-neutral pronoun for some informants to maintain their anonymity.

4. The technical term was "compounding." Penalties were steep and increased exponentially for not following the rules. One accountant recounted an instance where an NPO paid 7.5 lakh in penalty for accepting a check without registration or prior permission.

5. In the mid-1990s, one NPO and its member organizations sought to develop consensus on the issue by developing guidelines through regional workshops and discussions and by producing handbooks on "good governance." It produced a report outlining three models of self-certification: accreditation by an independent third party with a proof or seal of approval; peer-certification; and self-certification.

6. Small NGOs, with budgets under 25 lakhs, incurred a fee of Rs 10,400; a budget of 25 lakhs (1 crore) constituted a medium-sized NGO, with a fee of Rs 15,400; and large nonprofits, with a budget of over 1 crore, were charged a fee of Rs 24,800.

Chapter 5: The Power of Association

1. United Nations, G.A. Res/ 2200A (XXI), International Covenant on Civil and Political Rights (Dec. 16, 1966), Art. 22. https://www.ohchr.org/en/instruments-mechanisms/instruments/international-covenant-civil-and-political-rights.

2. "Action Plan to Bring About a Collaborative Relationship Between Volun-

tary Organisations and Government: A Basic Policy That Would Govern Government-Voluntary Organisations Relationships in India" (1994). Republished (2000) by the Planning Commission, Perspective Planning Division, GOI.

3. A workshop was convened by one NPO in response to draft changes to the Income Tax Act, and a report was produced, arguing for the need to institute reforms in the Income Tax Act. The workshop was attended by representatives of twenty-five organizations and chartered accountants. Decisions taken by the group included five proposed actions in response to the draft legislative reform, including preparation of a memorandum to the Finance Minister with suggested revisions to specific provisions for charitable tax exemptions, and a request to the taxation department on tax law affecting NGOs.

4. NPO report on registration policy, 2016.

Chapter 6: Reports as Mobilizing Technologies

1. Prime Minister Narendra Modi dismantled the Planning Commission in 2014, and reconfigured it as Niti Ayog, signaling the end of India's centralized, socialist-era developmental government (Joseph 2014).

2. Government of India. Planning Commission. Voluntary Action Cell. *Approaching Equity.* http://www.undp.org/content/dam/india/docs/approaching_equity_civil_society_inputs_for_the_approach_paper_12th_five-year_plan.pdf (accessed 6/9/16, document no longer available).

3. Court-appointed commissions are not without controversy and have been contested, as they structurally allow evidence to be collected without cross-examination (Bhuwania 2014). Structural innovation produced by the Indian judiciary affects civil society groups working to secure entitlements for marginalized groups in the name of rights.

4. PIL has limitations as well: it encourages judge-shopping by litigants, issue-shopping by judges, and raises issues of political bias. Due to the flood of cases that PIL encourages, the Indian judiciary has established permanent PIL cells in some courts, which are screened and passed to a Chief Justice for assignment to specific judges for review (Cassels 1989). PIL produces power struggles between the courts (judicial bodies) and the legislature (law-making body) of the Indian government, raising issues of legitimacy that harken back to the writing of the Indian constitution. This crisis of legitimacy is not simply a result of PIL but has deeper historical precedents arising from the Emergency and struggles over public moral authority (Baxi 1985; Bhuwania 2014).

5. The Indian SC is based in New Delhi and is the only all-India appellate forum, though state-based High Courts serve as judiciary heads for each state (as intermediate appellate courts) and also have jurisdiction to hear writ petitions on constitutional issues via PIL. In India, there is no bifurcation between court tiers: they form a single hierarchy to administer state and federal laws.

6. Bhuwania (2014) notes that the history of PIL is the history of the Emergency in India, specifically a constitutional conflict (1950–77) that evolved over land reform.

7. Baxi (1985) makes the comparative distinction that in the United States,

public interest litigation is espoused by public interest law firms representing interests without social groups: for example, in cases of consumption or the environment. Because of this structural component, and in contrast to India, in the United States, public interest litigation has been unable to address structural issues of inequality and problems of resource distribution.

8. In February 2016, one NPO proposed recommendations for the Union Budget that included changing the definition of "charitable purpose" in the revised Income Tax Act to distinguish development organizations from other nonprofits; redefining activities undertaken through a new governmental initiative on corporate social responsibility as non-business activities; establishing mechanisms for dialogue between NGOs, Finance Ministers, and banks; and requesting that Indian NGOs be allowed to work outside India, currently prohibited as exempt in the Income Tax Act (Manku 2016).

9. The report included citizen's reports from: "Chhattisgarh, Gujarat, Jharkhand, Maharashtra, Northeast Region, Orissa, UP, Uttarakhand, West Bengal, Bihar, and Andra Pradesh."

10. Dropped from Rs 17,773 crore in 2015–16 to Rs 6,499 crore in 2016–17. https://counterview.org/2018/05/23/voluntary-organisations-shrinking-space-amidst-adverse-impact-on-their-financial-sustainability/ (accessed 6/22/22).

11. Centre for Social Impact and Philanthropy (n.d.).

12. Foreign funding had been growing in India but then had declined significantly. The Centre for Social Impact and Philanthropy report argued this was the result of changing legal restrictions toward foreign funding in India.

13. Centre for Social Impact and Philanthropy (2019), citing a 2017 Bain-Dasra report "individual philanthropic contributions grew six-fold between 2011 and 2016, and private donations made up 32% of total contributions to the development sector in 2016, up from a mere 15% in 2011."

14. (1) Develop mechanisms to better measure rights-based work; (2) Build capacities of social organizations; (3) Develop a media strategy to emphasize the value of civil society; (4) Fund advocacy with the government to make giving more attractive in India; (5) Build the civil society ecosystem; (6) Add rights-based approaches to grant portfolios; (7) Fund research and advocacy for an improved FCRA. It focused on capacity building for NGOs, support for government-NGO relations, and change to law itself.

15. Needed services included assistance with capacity building, fundraising, and financial, tax, and auditing responsibilities, among others (Centre for Social Impact and Philanthropy 2019, 27).

Chapter 7: The Responsibility to Act

1. Companies must establish a Corporate Social Responsibility Committee, reporting to the board of directors, and the board reports the activities to the state.

2. Some feared the new initiative would merely channel corporate money into the government via the Prime Minister's National Relief Fund, affording donors a double whammy of governmental gold stars and a 100 percent tax rebate.

3. De (2018) argues that though the nation had become functionally capitalist, the constitution remained socialist.

4. Referencing Lok Sabha's legislative brief for the Companies Bill.

5. Spivak notes (1994, 22) that responsibility is a response to a call that cannot be grasped; at once a response, and an answering to others.

6. Heidegger, discussed in Derrida 1995. All these authors, including Derrida, argue with the shadow of fascism in Heidegger.

7. See Hanlon and Flemming 2009 for an analysis of the corporate take-over of state responsibilities in post-Fordist society, such as environmental protection, employee welfare, and regional development. Meanwhile corporations downsize and produce job insecurity and inequality.

8. For example: Samhita Social Venture, and Good Era Now, also Danamojo, and Impact Guru.

BIBLIOGRAPHY

ACLU (American Civil Liberties Union). 2009. *Blocking Faith, Freezing Charity: Chilling Muslim Charitable Giving in the "War on Terror Financing."*

Afsharipour, Afra, and Shruti Rana. 2014. "The Emergence of New Corporate Social Responsibility Regimes in China and India." UC Davis Legal Studies Research Paper, No. 386. *UC Davis Business Law Journal* 14.

Agarwal, Sanjay. 2012. *Accountable Handbook FCRA 2010: Theory and Practice.* 2nd ed. New Delhi: Accountaid India.

Agarwal, Sanjay, and Noshir Dadrawala. 2004. "Philanthropy and Law in India." In *Philanthropy and Law in South Asia*, edited by M. Sidel and I. Zaman. Manila: Asia Pacific Philanthropy Consortium.

Andersen, Walter, and Shridhar D. Damle. 2019. *Messengers of Hindu Nationalism: How the RSS Reshaped India.* Hurst.

Appadurai, Arjun. 2006. *Fear of Small Numbers: An Essay on the Geography of Anger.* Public Planet Books, Duke University Press.

Ashok, Sowmiya. 2015, June 15. "NGO License in Limbo? Move Court." *Mint.* https://www.livemint.com/Politics/n6kWS9YLwE5u3ucycqqIcK/NGO-licence-in-limbo-Move-court.html.

Aurora, Bhavna Vij. 2015, May. "Delhi HC Allows Greenpeace to Use Two Accounts to Get Domestic Donations." *The Economic Times.* https://economictimes.indiatimes.com/news/politics-and-nation/delhi-hc-allows-greenpeace-to-use-two-accounts-to-get-domestic-donations/articleshow/47442750.cms?from=mdr.

Aurora, Bhavna Vij, and Aman Sharma. 2015, June 3. "Foreign Funding for NGOs: After Inputs from IB, PMO Tells Home Ministry to Tighten FCRA Regulations." *The Economic Times.* https://economictimes.indiatimes.com/news/economy/finance/foreign-funding-for-ngos-after-inputs-from-ib-pmo-tells-home-ministry-to-tighten-fcra-regulations/articleshow/47521262.cms?utm_source=contentofinterest&utm_medium=text&utm_campaign=cppst.

Bannerjee, Subhabrata Bobby. 2003. "The Practice of Stakeholder Colonialism: National Interest and Colonial Discourses in the Management of Indigenous Stakeholders." In *Postcolonial Theory and Organizational Analysis: A Critical Engagement*, edited by A. Prasad. Palgrave MacMillan.

———. 2008. "Corporate Responsibility: The Good, the Bad and the Ugly." *Critical Sociology* 34 (1): 51–79.

Barry, Ellen, and Suhasini Raj. 2017, March 7. "Major Christian Charity Is Closing India Operations Amid a Crackdown." *The New York Times*.

Baviskar, Amita. 2023. "Decolonizing a Discipline in Distress: Anthropology's Pasts, Present, and Futures in India." *American Ethnologist* 50: 387–95.

Baxi, Pratiksha. 2019. "Introduction: Picturing Sociological Scenes—Social Life of Law in India." *Contributions to Indian Sociology* 53 (1): 1–18.

Baxi, Upendra. 1980. *The Indian Supreme Court and Politics*. Lucknow: Eastern Book Company.

———. 1985. "Taking Suffering Seriously: Social Action Litigation in the Supreme Court of India." *Third World Legal Studies* 4 (Art. 6): 107–32.

Bear, Laura, and Nayanika Mathur. 2015, Spring. "Introduction: Remaking the Public Good: A New Anthropology of Bureaucracy." *The Cambridge Journal of Anthropology* 33 (1): 18–34.

Benford, Robert D., and David A. Snow. 2000. "Framing Processes and Social Movements: An Overview and Assessment." *Annual Review of Sociology* 26: 611–39.

Benthall, Jonathan. 2011. "Islamic Humanitarianism in Adversarial Context." In *Forces of Compassion: Humanitarianism Between Ethics and Politics*, edited by E. Bornstein and P. Redfield. School for Advanced Research Press.

Bernal, Victoria, and Inderpal Grewal. 2014. "The NGO Form: Feminist Struggles, States, and Neoliberalism." In *Theorizing NGOs: States, Feminisms, and Neoliberalism*, edited by V. Bernal and I. Grewal. Duke University Press.

Bhalla, Nita. 2015, May 5. "Greenpeace Faces Shutdown After India Freezes Funds in Charity Crackdown." Reuters. https://www.reuters.com/article/id USKBN0NQ25C/.

———. 2017, March 14. "India's NGO Crackdown Forces U.S. Christian Charity Out After Half a Century." Reuters. https://www.reuters.com/article/india-us -charity/indias-ngo-crackdown-forces-u-s-christian-charity-out-after-half-a -century-idINKBN16MoJE.

Bharat. 2009. *Bharat's Understanding Direct Taxes Code with Discussion Paper*. New Delhi: Bharat Law House Pvt. Ltd.

———. 2013. *Bharat's Companies Bill, 2012 with Comments*. New Delhi: Bharat Law House Pvt. Ltd.

Bhatt, Abhinav. 2012, September 10. "Protests Against Kudankulam Nuclear Plant Intensify, One Killed in Police Firing in Tuticorin: Latest Developments." NDTV.com. https://www.ndtv.com/cheat-sheet/protests-against-kudankulam -nuclear-plant-intensify-one-killed-in-police-firing-in-tuticorin-latest--498957.

Bhatt, Chetan. 2001. *Hindu Nationalism: Origins, Ideologies and Modern Myths*. Berg.

Bhatt, Chetan, and Parita Mukta. 2000. "Hindutva in the West: Mapping the Antinomies of Diaspora Nationalism." *Ethnic and Racial Studies* 23 (3): 407–41.

Bhattacharjee, Malini. 2016. "Seva, Hindutva, and the Politics of Post-Earthquake Relief and Reconstruction in Rural Kutch." *Asian Ethnology* 75 (1): 75–104.

Bhuwania, Anuj. 2014. "Courting the People: The Rise of Public Interest Litigation in Post-Emergency India." *Comparative Studies of South Asia, Africa, and the Middle East* 34 (2): 314–35.

Birla, Ritu. 2009. *Stages of Capital: Law, Culture, and Market Governance in Late Colonial India*. Duke University Press.

Bloodgood, Elizabeth A., Jonnie Tremblay-Boire, and Aseem Prakash. 2014. "National Styles of NGO Regulation." *Nonprofit and Voluntary Sector Quarterly* 43 (4): 716–36.

Bornstein, Erica. 2012a. *Disquieting Gifts: Humanitarianism in New Delhi*. Stanford University Press.

———. 2012b. "Religious Giving Outside the Law in New Delhi." In *Sacred Aid: Faith and Humanitarianism*, edited by M. Barnett and J. G. Stein. Oxford University Press.

———. 2019, Spring. "The Report: A Strategy and Nonprofit Public Good." *Humanity* 10 (1): 109–31.

Bornstein, Erica, and Aradhana Sharma. 2016. "The Righteous and the Rightful: The Technomoral Politics of NGOs, Social Movements, and the State in India" *American Ethnologist* 43 (1): 76–90.

Brodwin, Paul. 2013. *Everyday Ethics: Voices from the Front Line of Community Psychiatry*. University of California Press.

Business Standard. 2023. "Direct Taxes Code: What Is Direct Taxes Code?" Accessed September 12, 2023. https://www.business-standard.com/about/what-is-direct-taxes-code/.

Cassels, Jamie. 1989. "Judicial Activism and Public Interest Litigation in India: Attempting the Impossible?" *American Journal of Comparative Law* 37 (3): 495–519.

Centre for Social Impact and Philanthropy (CSIP). 2019. "Enabling Philanthropy and Social Impact in India: State of the Support Ecosystem." Accessed June 28, 2022. https://wings.issuelab.org/resources/34092/34092.pdf.

———. n.d., *Advocacy, Rights & Civil Society: The Opportunity for Indian Philanthropy*. Accessed June 28, 2022. https://wordpress.caps.org/wp-content/uploads/2019/01/Advocacy-Rights-and-Civil-Society.pdf.

Centre for Advancement of Philanthropy (CAP India). 2023, February 9. "How Does the Finance Bill 2023 Impact NGOs in India?" *IDR Online*. https://idronline.org/article/board-governance/how-does-the-finance-bill-2023-impact-ngos-in-india/.

Chatterjee, Partha. 2014. "Introduction: Postcolonial Legalism." *Comparative Studies of South Asia, Africa and the Middle East* 34 (2): 224–27.

Chimiak, Galia, Zhanna Kravchenko, and Ulla Pape. 2024. "Editorial: Civil Society and the Spread of Authoritarianism: Institutional Pressures and CSO Responses." *Voluntas* 35 (2): 221–25.

Choudry, Aziz. 2013. "Saving Biodiversity, for Whom and for What? Conservation NGOs, Complicity, Colonialism and Conquest in an Era of Capitalist Globalization." In *NGOization: Complicity, Contradictions and Prospects*, edited by A. Choudry and D. Kapoor. Zed Books.

Choudry, Aziz, and Dip Kapoor. 2013. "NGOization, Complicity, Contradictions and Prospects." In *NGOization: Complicity, Contradictions and Prospects*, edited by A. Choudry and D. Kapoor. Zed Books.

Comaroff, John L., and Jean Comaroff. 2006. "Law and Disorder in the Postcolony: An Introduction." In *Law and Disorder in the Postcolony*, edited by J. Comaroff and J. Comaroff. University of Chicago Press.

Dadrawala, Noshir. 2003. "The Legal and Fiscal Framework." In *Working with the Non-profit Sector in India*, edited by C. India. New Delhi: Charities Aid Foundation, India.

———. 2023, May 11. *"Impact of Finance Act 2023 on Grant-Making."* Centre for Advancement of Philanthropy (CAP India). Accessed August 28, 2023. https//capindia.in/impact-of-finance-act-2023-on-grant-making/.

De, Rohit. 2014. "Rebellion, Dacoity, and Equality: The Emergence of the Constitutional Field in Postcolonial India." *Comparative Studies of South Asia, Africa and the Middle East* 34 (2): 260–78.

———. 2018. *A People's Constitution: The Everyday Life of Law in the Indian Republic.* Princeton University Press.

Deo, Nandini. 2024. *Corporate Social Responsibility and Civil Society in India.* Anthem Press.

Deo, Nandini, and Duncan McDuie-Ra. 2011. *The Politics of Collective Advocacy in India: Tools and Traps.* Kumarian Press.

Derrida, Jacques. 1995. *The Gift of Death.* Translated by D. Wills. University of Chicago Press.

DeVault, Marjorie. 2006, August. "What Is Institutional Ethnography?" *Social Problems* 53 (3): 294–98.

———. 2013. "Institutional Ethnography: A Feminist Sociology of Institutional Power." *Contemporary Sociology* 42 (3): 332–40.

Dolan, Catherine, and Dinah Rajak. 2016. "Introduction: Toward the Anthropology of Corporate Social Responsibility. In *The Anthropology of Corporate Social Responsibility*, edited by C. and D. Rajak. Berghan Books.

Dupuy, Kendra, James Ron, and Aseem Prakash. 2015. "Who Survived? Ethiopia's Regulatory Crackdown on Foreign-funded NGOs." *Review of International Political Economy* 22 (2): 419–56.

———. 2016. "Hands Off My Regime! Governments' Restrictions on Foreign Aid to Non-Governmental Organizations in Poor and Middle-Income Countries." *World Development* 84: 299–311.

Dusenbery, Verne A., Darshan Singh Tatla, and Satnam Chana. 2009. *Sikh Diaspora Philanthropy in Punjab: Global Giving for Local Good.* Oxford University Press.

Escobar, Arturo. 1994. *Encountering Development: The Making and Unmaking of the Third World.* Princeton University Press.

———. 2018. *Designs for the Pluriverse: Radical Interdependence, Autonomy, and the Making of Worlds*. Duke University Press.

Feldman, Ilana. 2008. *Governing Gaza: Bureaucracy, Authority, and the Work of Rule, 1917–1967*. Duke University Press.

Ferguson, James. 1994. *The Anti-politics Machine: "Development," Depoliticization and Bureaucratic Power in Lesotho*. University of Minnesota Press.

Financial Management Service Foundation (FMSF). 2023. *"Budget 2023: Summary of Major Amendments for NPOs."* In *Standards and Norms*: Resource Support on NGO Governance, Accounting, and Regulations. Legal Series 15: 10.

Fisher, William. 1997. "DOING GOOD? The Politics and Antipolitics of NGO Practices." *Annual Review of Anthropology* 26: 439–64.

Fortun, Kim. 2001. *Advocacy After Bhopal: Environmentalism, Disaster, New Global Orders*. University of Chicago Press.

Francis, Alys. 2015, May 6. "What Future for India's Environmental and Rights Groups?" *Devex*. https://www.devex.com/news/what-future-for-india-s-environmental-and-rights-groups-86066.

Friedman, Lawrence. 2003. "Philanthropy in America: Historicism and Its Discontents." In *Charity, Philanthropy, and American Civility in American History*, edited by L. Friedman and M. D. McGarvie. Cambridge University Press.

Geithner, Peter, Paula D. Johnson, and Lincoln C. Chen. 2004. "Overview." In *Diaspora Philanthropy and Equitable Development in China and India*, edited by P. Geithner, P. D. Johnson, and L. C. Chen. Harvard University Press.

Government of India (GOI). 2007. *National Policy on the Voluntary Sector*. Accessed June 9, 2016. http://planningcommission.nic.in/data/ngo/npvol07.pdf (site discontinued).

———. 2010. The Foreign Contribution (Regulation) Act. *The Gazette of India*, New Delhi. Accessed August 7, 2014. http://www.mha.nic.in/sites/upload_files/mha/files/FC-RegulationAct-2010-C.pdf (site discontinued).

———. 2011. Report on the Steering Committee on Voluntary Sector for the Twelfth Five Year Plan 2012–17. Planning Commission, New Delhi. Accessed August 2, 2014. http://planningcommission.gov.in/aboutus/committee/strgrp12/str_voluntary.pdf (site discontinued).

———. 2013. The Companies Act. Ministry of Corporate Affairs. Accessed March 4, 2015. http://www.mca.gov.in/Ministry/pdf/CompaniesAct2013.pdf.

Government of India, Planning Commission, Voluntary Action Cell. *Approaching Equity*. Accessed June 9, 2016. http://www.undp.org/content/dam/india/docs/approaching_equity_civil_society_inputs_for_the_approach_paper_12th_five-year_plan.pdf. (Site discontinued.)

Graan, Andrew. 2022. "What Was the Project? Thoughts on Genre and the Project Form." *Journal of Cultural Economy* 15 (6): 735–52.

Graeber, David. 2016. *The Utopia of Rules: On Technology, Stupidity, and the Secret Joys of Bureaucracy*. Melville House.

Gramsci, Antonio. 1971. *Selections from the Prison Notebooks*. Translated by Quintin Hoare and Geoffrey Nowell Smith. International Publishers.

Greenough, Paul R. 1982. *Prosperity and Misery in Modern Bengal: The Famine of 1943–1944*. Oxford University Press.

Gross, Robert A. 2003. "Giving in America: From Charity to Philanthropy." In *Charity, Philanthropy, and Civility in American History*, edited by L. Friedman and M. D. McGarvie. Cambridge.

The Guardian. 2015, September 3. "Greenpeace in India Barred from Receiving Foreign Funding." http://www.theguardian.com/environment/2015/sep/04/greenpeace-in-india-barred-from-receiving-foreign-funding.

Gupta, Akhil. 1995. "Blurred Boundaries: The Discourse of Corruption, the Culture of Politics, and the Imagined State." *American Ethnologist* 22 (2): 375–402.

———. 2012. *Red Tape: Bureaucracy, Structural Violence, and Poverty in India.* Duke University Press.

Gupta, Akhil, and Aradhana Sharma. 2006. "Globalization and Postcolonial States." *Current Anthropology* 47 (2): 277–307.

Gusterson, Hugh. 1997. "Studying Up Revisited." *Political and Legal Anthropology Review* 20 (1): 114–19.

Hanlon, Gerard, and Peter Flemming. 2009. "Updating the Critical Perspective on Corporate Social Responsibility." *Sociology Compass* 3 (6): 937–48.

Hansen, Thomas Blom, and Christophe Jaffrelot, eds. 1998. *The BJP and the Compulsions of Politics in India*. Oxford University Press.

Haraway, Donna. 1988. "Situated Knowledges: The Science Question in Feminism and the Privilege of Partial Perspective." *Feminist Studies* 14 (3): 575–99.

Hardiman, David. 2003. *Gandhi in His Time and Ours: The Global Legacy of His Ideas*. Columbia University Press.

Hetherington, Kregg. 2020. *The Government of Beans: Regulating Life in the Age of Monocrops*. Duke University Press.

Hirschl, Ron. 2006. "The New Constitution and Judicialization of Pure Politics Worldwide." *Fordham Law Review* 75 (2): 721–53.

Hoag, Collin. 2011. "Assembling Partial Perspectives: Thoughts on the Anthropology of Bureaucracy." *Political and Legal Anthropology Review* 34 (1): 81–94.

Holladay, Zachary. 2012. "Public Interest Litigation in India as a Paradigm for Developing Nations." *Indiana Journal of Global Legal Studies* 19 (2): 555–73.

Hsu, Carolyn, and Jessica Teets. 2016. "Is China's New Overseas NGO Management Law Sounding the Death Knell for Civil Society? Maybe Not." *The Asia-Pacific Journal: Japan Focus* 14 (4), No. 3, 1–16.

Huang, Shu-min. 2013. "Building China's Nascent Civil Society: The Roles of Nongovernmental Organizations." *American Anthropologist* 115 (3): 499–501.

Hull, Matthew. 2008. "Ruled by Records: The Expropriation of Land and the Misappropriation of Lists in Islamabad." *American Ethnologist* 35 (4): 501–18.

———. 2012a. "Documents and Bureaucracy." *Annual Review of Anthropology* 41: 251–67.

———. 2012b. *Government of Paper: The Materiality of Bureaucracy in Urban Pakistan*. University of California Press.

Human Rights Watch. 2023, July 18. "World Report 2023: India | Human Rights Watch." https://www.hrw.org/world-report/2023/country-chapters/india.

INCITE! Women of Color Against Violence. 2007. *The Revolution Will Not Be Funded: Beyond the Non-Profit Industrial Complex*. South End Press.

International Center for Not-for-Profit Law. 2022. "China's 2016 Charity Law." Accessed June 28, 2022. https://www.icnl.org/wp-content/uploads/China-FAQ -Charity-Law.pdf.

Jad, Islah. 2010. "NGOs: Between Buzzwords and Social Movements." In *Deconstructing Development Discourse: Buzzwords and Fuzzwords*, edited by A. Cornwall and D. Eade. Warwickshire: Practical Action.

Jaffrelot, Christophe, ed. 2007. *Hindu Nationalism: A Reader*. Princeton University Press.

Jagtiani, Tanaya. 2020. "The Laws That Govern India's Nonprofits." *IDR Online*. Accessed September 11, 2023. https://idronline.org/the-laws-that-govern-in dias-nonprofits/.

Jain, Bharti. 2015, June 26. "Govt Asks Ford Foundation to Register Under FEMA." *Times of India*. https://timesofindia.indiatimes.com/india/govt-asks -ford-foundation-to-register-under-fema/articleshow/47822863.cms.

Jain, Bharti, and Vishwa Mohan. 2015, April 10. "Foreign Funding for Greenpeace Frozen." *Times of India*. http://timesofindia.indiatimes.com/india/For eign-funding-for-Greenpeace-frozen/articleshow/46869420.cms.

Jakimow, Tanya. 2010. "Negotiating the Boundaries of Voluntarism: Values in the Indian NGO Sector." *Voluntas* 21: 546–68.

———. 2012. *Peddlers of Information: Indian Nongovernmental Organizations in the Information Age*. Kumarian Press.

Jenkins, Rob. 2010. "NGOs and Indian Politics." In *The Oxford Companion to Politics in India*, edited by N. G. Jayal and P. B. Mehta. Oxford University Press.

Johansen, Mette Brehm, and Discussant Anne Reff Pedersen. 2016. "Contexting the Patient: A Meeting Ethnography of Patient Involvement in Quality Development." In *Doing Organizational Ethnography*, edited by A. R. Pedersen and D. M. Humle. Routledge.

Joseph, Manu. 2014, August 20. "An Experiment with Socialism Finally Ends: Narendra Modi to Replace India's Planning Commission." *The New York Times*.

Kamat. Sangeeta. 2002. *Development Hegemony: NGOs and the State in India*. Oxford University Press.

———. 2004. "The Privatization of Public Interest: Theorizing NGO Discourse in a Neoliberal Era." *Review of International Political Economy* 11 (1): 155–76.

———. 2013. "Preface." In *NGOization: Complicity, Contradictions and Prospects*, edited by A. Choudry and D. Kapoor. Zed Books.

Kapoor, Dip. 2013. "Social Action and NGOization in Contexts of Development Dispossession in Rural India: Explorations into the Un-civility of Civil Society." In *NGOization: Complicity, Contradictions and Prospects*, edited by A. Choudry and D. Kapoor. Zed Books.

Kapur, Devesh, Ajay S. Mehta, and R. Moon Dutt. 2004. "Indian Diaspora Philanthropy." In *Diaspora Philanthropy and Equitable Development in China and India*, edited by P. Geithner, P. D. Johnson, and L. C. Chen. Harvard University Press.

Karat, Prakash. 1984. "Action Groups/Voluntary Organisation: A Factor in Imperialist Strategy." *The Marxist* 2 (2). Accessed June 26, 2014. https://hindi.cpim.org/marxist/1984-voluntary-groups-prakash.pdf.

Kassam, Meenaz, Femida Handy, and Emily Jansons. 2016. *Philanthropy in India: Promise to Practice.* Sage Publications India.

Kaviraj, Sudipta. 2011. *The Enchantment of Democracy and India: Politics and Ideas.* Permanent Black.

Keck, Margaret, and Kathryn Sikkink. 1998. *Activists Beyond Borders: Advocacy Networks in International Politics.* Cornell University Press.

Khagram, Sanjeev. 2002. "Restructuring the Global Politics of Development: The Case of India's Narmada Valley Dams." In *Restructuring World Politics: Transnational Social Movements, Networks, and Norms*, edited by S. Khagram, J. V. Riker, and K. Sikkink. University of Minnesota Press.

Khilnani, Sunil. 2007. "Nehru's Faith." In *The Crisis of Secularism in India*, edited by A. D. Needham and R. S. Rajan. Duke University Press.

Kingma, Bruce. 1997, June. "Public Good Theories of the Non-Profit Sector: Weisbrod Revisited." *Voluntas* 8 (2): 135–48.

Kirsch, Stuart. 2014. *Mining Capitalism: The Relationship Between Corporations and Their Critics.* University of California Press.

Kirschke, Joseph. 2013, October. "Vedanta Resources, CSR and the Struggle for India's Soul." *Engineering and Mining Journal.* https://www.e-mj.com/features/vedanta-resources-csr-and-the-struggle-for-india-s-soul/.

Kothari, Rajni. 1984. "The Non-Party Political Process." *Economic and Political Weekly* 19 (5): 216–24.

———. 1986. "NGOs, the State and World Capitalism." *Economic and Political Weekly* 21 (50): 2177–82.

Krichewsky, Damien. 2019. *Corporate Social Responsibility and Economic Responsiveness in India.* Cambridge University Press.

Landau, David. 2012. "The Reality of Social Rights Enforcement." *Harvard International Law Journal* 53 (1): 190–247.

Latour, Bruno. 2004. "Scientific Objects and Legal Objectivity." In *Law, Anthropology and the Constitution of the Social: Making Persons and Things*, edited by A. Pottage and M. Mondy. Cambridge University Press.

Latour, Bruno, and Steve Woolgar. 1986. *Laboratory Life: The Construction of Scientific Facts.* Princeton University Press.

Lea, Tess. 2020. *Wild Policy: Indigeneity and the Unruly Logics of Intervention.* Stanford University Press.

Lewis, David. 2001. *The Management of Non-Governmental Development Organizations: An Introduction.* Routledge.

Lewis, David, and Mark Schuller. 2017. "Engagements with a Productively Unstable Category: Anthropologists and Nongovernmental Organizations." *Current Anthropology* 58 (5): 634–51.

Macfarlane, Alan. 2002. "Fellowship and Trust." In *The Making of the Modern World: Visions from the West and East.* Palgrave.

Madhok, Diksha. 2022. December 1. "India on Track for Record $100 Billion in

Remittances, Says World Bank." *CNN Business.* https://www.cnn.com/2022
/12/01/business/india-remittances-record-2022-world-bank-intl-hnk/index
.html#:~:text=The%20extensive%20Indian%20diaspora%20will,World%20
Bank%20report%20published%20Wednesday.

Mahapatra, Dhananjay. 2014, February 23. "India Witnessing NGO Boom—
There Is 1 for Every 600 People." *The Times of India.* http://timesofindia.india
times.com/india/India-witnessing-NGO-boom-there-is-1-for-every-600-peo
ple/articleshow/30871406.cms.

Maitland, F. W. 2003. *State, Trust and Corporation,* edited by D. Runciman and
M. Ryan. Cambridge University Press.

Manku, Moyna. 2015a, June 15. "Should the Social Sector Get Its Own Set of
Laws?" *Mint.* https://www.livemint.com/Politics/PErGloD5uTdDcKHfXgW
wdM/Should-the-social-sector-get-its-own-set-of-laws.html.

———. 2015b, July 1. "NPOs Urge Government to Clarify 'Against National Interest' Phrase." *Mint.* https://www.livemint.com/Politics/ZZ5drO2nlvaf6xI5
QoBo5H/NPOs-urge-government-to-clarify-against-national-interest.html.

———. 2016, February 25. "Budget 2016: NGOs Want an Enabling Environment." *Mint.* https://www.livemint.com/Politics/fjUWOO5smzA58mzHhJp
RPM/Budget-2016-NGOs-want-an-enabling-environment.html.

Mansfield, John H. 2001. "Religious and Charitable Endowments and a Uniform
Civil Code." In *Religion and Personal Law in Secular India: A Call to Judgment,*
edited by G. J. Larson. Indiana University Press.

Mathiesen, Marie, and Discussant Chahrazad Abdallah. 2016. "Doing Strategy:
A Performative Organizational Ethnography." In *Doing Organizational Ethnography,* edited by A. R. Pedersen and D. M. Humle. Routledge.

Mathew, Biju, and Vijay Prashad. 2000. "The Protean Forms of Yankee Hindutva." *Ethnic and Racial Studies,* 23 (3): 516–34.

Mathur, Nayanika. 2015. *Paper Tiger: Bureaucracy and the Developmental State in
Himalayan India.* Cambridge University Press.

McMullen, Terry. 2016. "Improvisation Within a Scene of Constraint: An Interview with Judith Butler." In *Negotiated Moments: Improvisation, Sound, and
Subjectivity,* edited by G. Siddall and E. Waterman. Duke University Press.

Menon, Nivedita. 2013, March 23. "New Social Movements, New Perspectives."
33rd J. P. Memorial Lecture, Gandhi Peace Foundation, New Delhi. http://
www.pucl.org/jp/nivedita_menon_2013.html (page discontinued).

Merry, Sally Engle. 2006. *Human Rights and Gender Violence: Translating International Law into Local Justice.* University of Chicago Press.

———. 2016. *The Seductions of Quantification: Measuring Human Rights, Gender
Violence, and Sex Trafficking.* University of Chicago Press.

Mikkelsen, Elisabeth Naima, and Discussant Barbara Gray. 2016. "Everyday
Conflict at Work: An Organizational Sensemaking Ethnography." In *Doing
Organizational Ethnography,* edited by A. R. Pedersen and D. M. Humle.
Routledge.

Mohan, Rohini. 2015, July 2. "Government Versus NGOs: FCRA to Protect
Transparency and Prevent Misuse of Foreign Funds." *The Economic Times.* http:

//articles.economictimes.indiatimes.com/2015-07-02/news/64039137_1_ngos
-foreign-donations-voluntary-action-network-india.

Moore, David, and Douglas Rutzen. 2011. "Legal Framework for Global Philanthropy: Barriers and Opportunities." *International Journal of Not-for-Profit Law* 13 (5).

Mosse. David. 2013. "The Anthropology of International Development." *Annual Review of Anthropology* 42: 227–46.

Mouffe, Chantal. 2013. *Agonistics: Thinking the World Politically*. Verso.

Mustafa, Tamir. 2018. "The Judicialization of Religion." *Law and Society Review* 52 (3): 685–708.

Nader, Laura. 1972. "Up the Anthropologist: Perspectives Gained from Studying Up." In *Reinventing Anthropology*, edited by D. H. Hymes. Pantheon Books.

———. 2018. "The ADR Explosion: Implications of Rhetoric in Legal Reform." In *Contrarian Anthropology: The Unwritten Rules of Academia*. Berghan Books.

New Indian Express. 2023, March 1. "Surveillance & Clampdown: 'NGOs to Be Linked to Central Data Hub with Unique ID.'" Accessed April 3, 2023. https: //www.newindianexpress.com/nation/2023/Mar/01/surveillance--clampdown -ngos-to-be-linked-to-central-data-hub-with-unique-id-2552166.html.

The New York Times Editorial Board. 2015, May 7. "India's Chilling Crackdown." http://www.nytimes.com/2015/05/08/opinion/indias-chilling-crackdown .html?_r=0.

Nilekani, Rohini. 2019, January 25. "The Social Sector Must Recognise and Talk About Failure." *IDR Online*. https://idronline.org/the-social-sector-must-re cognise-and-talk-about-failure/.

Niumai, Ajailiu. 2011. "Indian Diaspora Philanthropy: A Sociological Perspective." *Man in India* 91 (1): 93–113.

Nyquist, Anette. 2013. "Access to All Stages? Studying Through Policy in a Culture of Accessibility." In *Organisational Anthropology: Doing Ethnography in and Among Complex Organisations*, edited by C. Garsten and A. Nyquist. Pluto Press.

Pande, Suchi, and Shekhar Singh. 2007. *Right to Information Act 2005: A Primer*. National Campaign for People's Right to Information. National Book Trust.

Parry, Jonathan. 2000. "The 'Crisis of Corruption' and 'The Idea of India': A Worm's Eye View." In *Morals of Legitimacy: Between Agency and System*, edited by I. Pardo. Berghan Books.

Pedersen, Anne Reff, and Didde Maria Humle. 2016. "Doing Organizational Ethnography," In *Doing Organizational Ethnography*, edited by A. R. Pedersen and D. M. Humle. Routledge.

Petras, James. 1999. "NGOs: In the Service of Imperialism." *Journal of Contemporary Asia* 29 (4): 429–40.

Power, Michael. 1999. *The Audit Society: Rituals of Verification*. Oxford University Press.

Powers, David S. 1989, July. "Orientalism, Colonialism, and Legal History: The Attack on Muslim Family Endowments in Algeria and India." *Comparative Studies in Society and History* 31 (3), 535–71.

Raffoul, François. 2004, Spring. "The Possibility of the Im-possible: Heidegger and Derrida on Responsibility." *Bulletin de la Société Américaine de Philosophie de Langue Française* 14 (1): 43–60.

Rajak. Dinah. 2011. *In Good Company: An Anatomy of Corporate Social Responsibility*. Stanford University Press.

Rajaratnam, S., M. Natarajan, and C. P. Thangaraj. 2009. *Law and Procedure on Charitable Trusts and Religious Institutions*. Mumbai: Snow White Publications.

Randeria, Shalini. 2007. "The State of Globalization: Legal Plurality, Overlapping Sovereignties and Ambiguous Alliances Between Civil Society and the Cunning State in India." *Theory, Culture, and Society* 24 (1): 1–33.

Randeria, Shalini, and Ciara Grunder. 2011. "The (Un)Making of Policy in the Shadow of the World Bank: Infrastructure Development, Urban Resettlement and the Cunning State in India." In *Policy Worlds: Anthropology and the Analysis of Contemporary Power*, edited by C. Shore, S. Wright, and D. Pero. Berghan Books.

Rautray, Samanwaya. 2017, January 10. "Supreme Court Pulls Up Centre for No Mechanism to Monitor Funds." *The Economic Times*. https://economictimes .indiatimes.com/news/politics-and-nation/supreme-court-pulls-up-centre-for -no-mechanism-to-monitor-ngo-funds/articleshow/56439451.cms?from=mdr.

Richland, Justin. 2021. *Cooperation Without Submission: Indigenous Jurisdictions in Native Nation–US Engagements*. University of Chicago Press.

Riles, Annelise. 2001. *The Network Inside Out*. University of Michigan Press.

Roy, Arundhati. 2011, April 30. "When Corruption Is Viewed Fuzzily." *Indian Express*. https://indianexpress.com/article/opinion/columns/when-corruption -is-viewed-fuzzily/

Rutzen, Douglas. 2015a. "Aid Barriers and the Rise of Philanthropic Protectionism." *International Journal of Not-for-Profit Law* 17 (1): 5.

———. 2015b. "Civil Society Under Assault." *Journal of Democracy* 26(4): 28–36.

Rutzen, Douglas, and Catherine Shea. 2006, September 1. "The Associational Counter-Revolution." *Alliance Magazine*. https://www.alliancemagazine.org/ analysis/the-associational-counter-revolution/.

Sabadoz, Cameron. 2011. "Between Profit-Seeking and Prosociality: Corporate Social Responsibility as Derridean Supplement." *Journal of Business Ethics* 104: 77–91.

Salamon, Lester, ed. 2014. *New Frontiers of Philanthropy: A Guide to the New Tools and Actors Reshaping Global Philanthropy and Social Investing*. Oxford University Press.

———. 2015. "Introduction: The Nonprofitization of the Welfare State." *Voluntas* 26 (6): 2147–54.

Sarin, Alok, et al. 2023, January. *India's Million Missions: 75 Years of Service Toward Nation-Building: India's Non-Profit Sector Report*. CSO Coalition@75. Accessed August 28, 2023. https://pria-digitallibrary.org/index.php?p=show_detail&id= 10772&keywords=.

Sastry, Trilochan. 2015, June 29. "NGOs' Foreign Funds and a Trust Deficit." *The Hindu*. https://www.thehindu.com/opinion/op-ed/ngos-foreign-funds-and -a-trust-deficit/article7364282.ece.

Schwartzman, Helen B. 1989. *The Meeting: Gatherings in Organizations and Communities.* Plenum Press.

———. 1993. *Ethnography in Organizations.* Qualitative Research Methods Series, 27. Sage.

Seider, Rachel. 2020. "The Juridification of Politics." In *The Oxford Handbook of Law and Anthropology,* edited by M. Claire-Foblets, M. Goodale, and M. Sapignoli. Oxford University Press.

Sen, Siddhartha. 1992. "Non-Profit Organizations in India: Historical Development and Common Patterns." *Voluntas* 3 (2): 175–93.

———. 1993. "Defining the Nonprofit Sector: India." In *Working Papers of the Johns Hopkins Comparative Nonprofit Sector Project, No. 12,* edited by L. M. Salamon and H. K. Anheir. Johns Hopkins Institute for Policy Studies.

———. 1999. "Globalization and the Status of Current Research on the Indian Nonprofit Sector." *Voluntas* 10 (2): 113–30.

Sen, Sreeja. 2014, December 27. "Supreme Court Is Essentially Acting as an Institution of Governance: Upendra Baxi." *Mint.* https://www.livemint.com/Poli tics/5hhv9cYP6x98pK9rTwv2lM/Supreme-Court-is-essentially-acting-as-an -institution-of-gov.html.

Sharma, Aman. 2015a, July 8. "Government Determined to Put NGOs Under Scrutiny Despite Objections." *The Economic Times,* https://economictimes.in diatimes.com/news/politics-and-nation/government-determined-to-put-ngos -under-scrutiny-despite-objections/articleshow/47980105.cms?from=mdr.

———. 2015b, March 18. "MHA Cancels Licenses of 1142 NGOs and Associations Including Osmania University." *The Economic Times.* https://economictimes .indiatimes.com/news/economy/finance/mha-cancels-licenses-of-1142-ngos -and-associations-including-osmania-university/articleshow/46600062.cms? utm_source=contentofinterest&utm_medium=text&utm_campaign=cppst.

Sharma, Aradhana. 2008. *Logics of Empowerment: Development, Gender, and Governance in Neoliberal India.* University of Minnesota Press.

———. 2013. State Transparency After the Neoliberal Turn: The Politics, Limits, and Paradoxes of India's Right to Information Law." *PoLAR: Political and Legal Anthropology Review* 36 (2): 308–25.

———. 2014. "Epic Fasts and Shallow Spectacles: The 'India Against Corruption' Movement, Its Critics, and the Re-Making of 'Gandhi.'" *Journal of South Asian Studies* 37 (3): 365–80.

———. 2024. *A Technomoral Politics: Good Governance, Transparency, and Corruption in India.* University of Minnesota Press.

Sharma, Sanjay. 2001. *Famine, Philanthropy, and the Colonial State: North India in the Early Nineteenth Century.* Oxford University Press.

Sheth, D. L. 1983. Grassroots Stirrings and the Future of Politics. *Alternatives* 9 (1): 1–24.

Sheth, D. L., and Harsh Sethi. 1991. "The NGO Sector in India: Historical Context and Current Discourse." *Voluntas* 2 (2): 49–68.

Shetty, Smarinita, and Rakija Seth. 2023, March 23. *IDR Online.* "Who Loses

When FCRA Licenses Get Cancelled?" https://idronline.org/article/fundrais ing-and-communications/who-loses-when-fcra-licenses-get-cancelled.

Shiveshwarkar, Shyamala. 2004. *Mapping Diaspora Investment in the Social Development Sector in India*, edited by R. Prasad. Charities Aid Foundation.

Shore, Cris, and Susan Wright. 1997. "Introduction: Policy: A New Field of Anthropology." In *Anthropology of Policy: Critical Perspectives on Governance and Power*, edited by C. Shore and S. Wright. Routledge.

———. 2011. "Conceptualizing Policy: Technologies of Governance and the Politics of Visibility." In *Policy Worlds: Anthropology and the Analysis of Contemporary Power*, edited by C. Shore, S. Wright and D. Pero. Berghan Books.

Shukla, Ashutosh M. 2023, February 20. "'Easier to Do Business Than Charity': Experts on Budget 2023." *The Free Press Journal* (Mumbai). https://www.freepress journal.in/business/easier-to-do-business-than-charity-experts-on-budget-2023.

Sidel, Mark. 2004a. "Diaspora Philanthropy to India: A Perspective from the United States." In *Diaspora Philanthropy and Equitable Development in China and India*, edited by P. Geithner, P. D. Johnson, and L. C. Chen. Harvard University Press.

———. 2004b. "States, Markets, and the Nonprofit Sector in South Asia: Judiciaries and the Struggle for Capital in Comparative Perspective." *Tulane Law Review* 78 (5): 1611.

———. 2010. *Regulation of the Voluntary Sector: Freedom and Security in an Era of Uncertainty*. Routledge.

———. 2019a, May. *The Law Affecting Civil Society in Asia: Developments and Challenges for Nonprofit and Civil Society Organizations*. International Center for Not-for-Profit Law (ICNL).

———. 2019b, May. *Nonprofit Legal Reform in India: The Legal Treatment of For-Profit Entities and Other Approaches to the Reform Question*. International Center for Not-for-Profit Law (ICNL).

Simpson, Audra. 2014. *Mohawk Interruptus: Political Life Across the Borders of Settler States*. Duke University Press.

———. 2016. "Consent's Revenge." *Cultural Anthropology* 31 (3): 326–33.

Simpson, Edward. 2014. *The Political Biography of an Earthquake: Aftermath and Amnesia in Gujarat, India*. Oxford University Press.

Singh, Vijaita. 2022, February 8. "Now, Home Ministry Renews FCRA of PHFI." *The Hindu*. https://www.thehindu.com/news/national/now-home-ministry-re news-fcra-of-phfi/article38397498.ece.

Sinha, Ashish. 2013, July 5. "MSSR Bill to Get More Teeth, Regulate Over 1.5m Societies." *Financial Express*. https://www.financialexpress.com/archive/mssr -bill-to-get-more-teeth-regulate-over-15-m-societies/1137778/.

Smith, Dorothy E. 1987. *The Everyday World as Problematic: A Feminist Sociology*. Northeastern University Press.

Souleles, Daniel. 2018. "How to Study People Who Do Not Want to Be Studied: Practical Reflections on Studying Up." *PoLAR: Political and Legal Anthropology Review* 41 (S1): 51–68.

Spivak, Gayatri Chakravorty. 1994. "Responsibility." *boundary 2* 21 Autumn: 19–64.

———. 1988. "Can the Subaltern Speak?" In *Marxism and the Interpretation of Culture*, edited by Cary Nelson and Lawrence Grossberg. Macmillan.

Srinath, Ingrid. 2022, March. "COVID-19, Corporatisation and Closing Space: The Triple Threat to Civil Society in India." *LSE International Working Paper Series*, no. 22–206. London School of Economics, Department of International Development.

———. 2024, June 15. "Adapt or Perish: NGOs Struggle to Survive." *Deccan Herald*. https://www.deccanherald.com/india/adapt-or-perish-ngos-struggle-to -survive-3068451#:~:text=As%20most%20of%20funders%20play%20it,the%20means %20to%20stay%20afloat%3F&text=A%20team%20from%20Wildlife%20SOS% 20releases%20a%20shikra%20into%20the%20wild.

Strathern, Marilyn. 1996/7. "From Improvement to Enhancement: An Anthropological Comment on the Audit Culture." *Cambridge Anthropology* 19 (3): 1–21.

———. 2000. *Audit Cultures: Anthropological Studies in Accountability, Ethics and the Academy*. Routledge.

Sundar, Nandini. 2004, April 17–23. "Teaching to Hate: RSS' Pedagogical Programme." *Economic and Political Weekly* 39 (16): 1605–12.

Sundar, Pushpa 1997. *Charity for Social Change and Development: Essays on Indian Philanthropy*. Occasional Papers. Indian Centre for Philanthropy.

———. 2000. *Beyond Business: From Merchant Charity to Corporate Citizenship: Indian Business Philanthropy Through the Ages*. McGraw Hill.

———. 2010. *Foreign Aid for Indian NGOs: Problem or Solution?* Routledge India.

———. 2018, December 22. "Using CSR for Political Gain." *The Wire*. https:// thewire.in/business/modi-government-csr-political-gain.

Tandon, Rajesh. 1996. "Board Games: Governance and Accountability in NGOs." In *Beyond the Magic Bullet: NGO Performance and Accountability in the Post–Cold War World*, edited by M. Edwards and D. Hulme. Kumarian Press.

———. 2000. *Dimensions of the Voluntary Sector in India: CAF's Validated Database 2000*. Delhi: Charities Aid Foundation.

———. 2002. *Voluntary Action, Civil Society, and the State*. New Delhi: Mosaic.

———. 2003. "Overview of the Non-Governmental Sector in India." In *Working with the Non-Profit Sector in India*, New Delhi: Charities Aid Foundation, India.

———. 2017, January 21. "The Hidden Universe of Non-Profit Organisations in India." *Economic and Political Weekly* 52 (3).

Thachil, Tariq. 2014. *Elite Parties, Poor Voters: How Social Services Win Votes in India*. Cambridge University Press.

Thedvall, Renita. 2013. "Punctuated Entries: Doing Fieldwork in Policy Meetings in the European Union." In *Organisational Anthropology: Doing Ethnography in and Among Complex Organisations*, edited by C. Garsten and A. Nyquist. Pluto Press.

UN Special Rapporteur. 2013. "Discussion: Funding Restrictions for Civil Soci-

ety." Accessed June 20, 2014. http://freeassembly.net/rapdiscussions/discussion
-funding-civil-society/.

UN Special Rapporteur. n.d. "Protecting Civic Space and the Right to Access
Resources." Accessed August 23, 2024. https://www.ohchr.org/sites/default/
files/GeneralPrinciplesProtectingCivicSpace.pdf.

Van Zile, Caroline. 2012, January. "India's Mandatory Corporate Social Responsibility Proposal: Creative Capitalism Meets Creative Regulation in the
Global Market." *Asian Pacific Law and Policy Journal* 13 (2): 269–303.

Vevaina, Leilah. 2023. *Trust Matters: Parsi Endowments in Mumbai and the Horo-
scope of a City.* Duke University Press.

Viswanath, Priya. 2003. *Diaspora Indians—On the Philanthropy Fast-Track.* Centre
for Advancement of Philanthropy (CAP), Mumbai, India.

Viswanath, Priya, and Noshir Dadrawala. 2004. "Philanthropic Investment and
Equitable Development: The Case of India," In *Diaspora Philanthropy and Equitable Development in China and India,* edited by P. Geithner, P. D. Johnson,
and L. C. Chen. Harvard University Press.

Watkins, Susan Cotts, Ann Swidler, and Thomas Hannan. 2012, August. "Outsourcing Social Transformation: Development NGOs as Organizations."
Annual Review of Sociology 38: 285–315.

Weisbrod, Burton. 1992. "Tax Policy Toward Nonprofit Organizations: A Ten-
Country Survey." In *The Nonprofit Sector in the Global Community: Voices from
Many Nations,* edited by V. A. Hodgkinson and K. D. McCarthy. Jossey-Bass.

Weinstein, Jeremy M., and Darin Christensen. 2013. "Defending Dissent: Restrictions on Aid to NGOs." *Journal of Democracy* 24 (2): 77–91.

Welker, Marina. 2014. *Enacting the Corporation: An American Mining Firm in
Post-Authoritarian Indonesia.* University of California Press.

Williams, Rina Verma. 2010. "Hindu Law as Personal Law: State and Identity in
the Hindu Code Bills Debates, 1952–56." In *Hinduism and Law: An Introduction.* edited by T. Lubin et al. Cambridge University Press.

INDEX

Note: page numbers followed by "b" and "n" indicate boxes and endnotes, respectively.

The authorized representative in the EU for product safety and compliance is:
Mare Nostrum Group
B.V Doelen 72
4831 GR Breda
The Netherlands

www.ingramcontent.com/pod-product-compliance
Lightning Source LLC
Chambersburg PA
CBHW020503270326
41926CB00008B/726